Gender and Violence in the Middle East

Gender and Violence in the Middle East

DAVID GHANIM

PRAEGER

Westport, Connecticut
London

Library of Congress Cataloging-in-Publication Data

Ghanim, David.
    Gender and violence in the Middle East / David Ghanim.
        p. cm.
    Includes bibliographical references and index.
    ISBN 978–0–313–35995–8 (alk. paper)
    1. Women—Violence against—Middle East. 2. Sex discrimination against
women—Middle East. 3. Patriarchy—Middle East.   4. Violence—Middle East.
I. Title.
    HV6250.4.W65G528 2009
    362.83—dc22   2008039561

British Library Cataloguing in Publication Data is available.

Library of Congress Catalog Card Number: 2008039561
ISBN: 978–0–313–35995–8
ISBN: 978–1–4408–3614–5 (pbk.)

First published in 2009

Praeger Publishers, 88 Post Road West, Westport, CT 06881
An imprint of Greenwood Publishing Group, Inc.

www.praeger.com

Printed in the United States of America

The paper used in this book complies with the
Permanent Paper Standard issued by the National
Information Standards Organization (Z39.48–1984).

10 9   8   7   6   5   4   3   2   1

For Middle Eastern men and women who
indubitably deserve less violent and more
tolerant and constructive gender relations.

Contents

Nature and Social Existence
The *Self* and the *Other*

PART TWO: POWER, VIOLENCE, AND GENDER

PART THREE: IMPACTS OF FEMALE POWER
AND AGENCY

PART FOUR: PATRIARCHY AND AUTHORITARIANISM

Preface

The most important event that has inspired this work was the Iraq War in 2003. No matter what we think about this controversial war, it represents what would have been a historical opportunity to end the country's long history of violence and dictatorship and to engage in building a more peaceful and tolerant society. Yet the events following the outset of the war took another direction. The capacity of Iraqi society to generate and maintain all of this violence is utterly astonishing. While the Iraqi case is complex, extreme, and continuously changing, violence is a constant feature of life in the Middle East.

A simpler, yet futile and less constructive way of explaining this violence is to externalize it. Rulers in the Middle East are fixated on projecting the ills of society onto imaginary, external enemies. It is no wonder that conspiracy theories have become the most dominant aspect of political and intellectual life in this region.

Internalizing violence is the contrary option that Middle Eastern societies, which are in the midst of a deep multidimensional crisis, seriously need to consider. Violence is a part of the social structure that defines and influences people's lives. By linking violence to the dominant gender structure, this work is an attempt in this direction. Gender violence, particularly in its broadest and most inclusive sense that includes both male and female violence, is a central aspect of the deeply rooted crisis in Middle Eastern societies. This study shows that everyone plays a part in reproducing and sustaining high levels of violence: men, women, society, the political system, patriarchy, religion, and culture.

Contrary to popular opinion and media portrayal, violence in Middle Eastern societies is not predominantly an external phenomenon imposed by faceless forces of foreign aggression and internal repression. Rather, violence in the Middle East is a thoroughly familiar, mostly private fact of daily life, an instinct woven into the very fabric of domestic relations. This pervasive, intimate style of violence takes many forms: physical, psychological, deliberate, unconscious, covert, and public. The contextual role that endemic domestic violence plays with regard to the notorious societal problems of the Middle East, such as the institutionalized violence of terrorist organizations and of repressive autocratic governments, is not widely appreciated. Contextual violence has not received anywhere near the level of empirical study or, even less, the analytical attention that it deserves. While this study focuses on the Middle East, the implications of this study are relevant far beyond this region.

CHAPTER 1

Introduction: Internalizing Middle Eastern Violence

> When violence is understood as fundamental to gender, and power is recognized as adhering to all social relationships, then a different kind of social theory is required.
>
> —*Jeff Hearn*

VIOLENCE

Recent developments in the Middle East indicate that the region is not only failing to progress along the various political, economic, and social fronts associated with an increasingly global and dynamic world, but it is also degenerating back into further violence and marginalization. Never in its modern history has the Middle East been so alienated from the global world as it is today. The survival and perseverance of authoritarianism, the rise of Islamic fundamentalism, the spread of terrorism, the spread of violent and destructive cultures, the revival of conservatism, the continued debasement and re-veiling of women, and failed economic development, despite huge oil revenues, are illustrations of how this region is deteriorating. This deterioration is leaving younger generations with increasingly dismal circumstances, which depreciate the lives of those whom the future of the region is dependent on. The leadership in the region, on the other hand, invests its energies and resources in glorifying its distant past rather than nurturing the human capital available in these societies and fostering a brighter future. In the words of Thomas Friedman: "In the Middle East the past always buries the future, not the other way around."[1]

While these reproachable aspects of life in the Middle East fail to stir the region into action, the fact that the region was moved by a remote and insignificant incident involving caricature drawings of the Prophet Muhammad is a clear illustration of intellectual decline in the region. The popular intellectual world of the Middle East is still dominated by conspiracy theories and rampant blaming of the others for the ills of these societies. Yet increasing degeneration within these societies is a sufficient reason for scholars of this region to initiate a critical analysis of the political, economic, social, and cultural values that dictate life in Middle Eastern societies. A critique of the region is necessary in order to identify the real internal causes of this decline. Acknowledging internal problems is to take a critical first step towards serious and veritable change.

Two of the repugnant aspects of life in Middle Eastern society, I argue, are authoritarianism, including the theocratic version, and the patriarchal structure of gender relations. Together, these two social systems dominate nearly every aspect of citizens' lives in these societies. The question in this regard is whether these two systems work in isolation or if there is a symbiotic relationship of support between the two. Whereas authoritarianism is obviously an institution of violence, the gender structure is not necessarily thought of in the same way, except in its most extreme and violent forms. However, the intersection between authoritarianism and gender, which is violence, is the main focus of this book.

Despite the dominance of violence in the Middle East, little attention is paid to this important subject in the academic world. The little attention that the subject of Middle Eastern violence does receive is confined to civil wars, conflicts between states, or the Israeli-Palestinian issue. This limited attention, at best, spotlights violence coming from the top, the authoritarian state. However, structural violence, which is rarely addressed, is a routine part of life in these societies. In reality, violence is much more integrated into ordinary life than we are willing to acknowledge.

It is not only the Middle East that suffers from an insufficient amount of attention dedicated to the issue of violence and the lack in understanding of the relationship between gender and violence. Other regions and social theories suffer from these shortcomings as well. Green argues: "Violence is portrayed as relatively isolated exceptions to normal life. Violence often does not even figure prominently in debates in social theory on power. In such formulations, violence is not understood as integral or embedded or immanent in social relations, and social relations are not understood as characterized by violence, actual or potential. Violence is incidentalized.

It is understood as occurring as exceptions within non-violent, ordinary normal life."[2]

Violence in the Middle East, as an area of investigation, has been neglected, or the issue has been externalized. The predominance of conspiracy theories that infest many social components within these societies has contributed to the externalization of violence within this region. That is, violence is explained away by assumptions of conspiracies and plots of external forces who intend to harm the region. Thus, violence is reduced to the Arab-Israeli conflict, or to the resistance of foreign attacks or threats against the region. There is a strong link between the dominance of conspiracy theories in intellectual life and the perception of externalized violence. While not denying the role of the external factors and problems, I argue that it is high time to focus on, and invest in, exploring the internal causes, problems, and variables that feed, sustain, and intensify violence in Middle Eastern societies. One can also add that these external factors make more sense only in conjunction with causes that are internal to these societies. Also, in the absence of attention to internal causes of violence, the overemphasis on the external factors might serve as an apologetic function that can lead to more harms than benefits to the societies of the region. By deliberately excluding external factors, this work is an attempt at scrutinizing the domestic structure of violence in Middle Eastern societies.

The dominance of conspiracy theories is, in fact, an expression of the very high and intense level of violence in the region. The spread of conspiracy theories is a compensating mechanism for internal failures in various domains of life in the Middle East. These failures are violent shortcomings with violent consequences. In this sense, conspiracy theory is not only an effect of this failure but also feeds and supports failure. Conspiracy theories offer an easy, simplified, and naïve way of explaining Middle Eastern failures. The fact that conspiracy theories have become the dominant, if not the only, way of explaining the failures of the region is proof of the deep level of violence within these societies. Narrowing down the various possible explanations of certain phenomena to only one "legitimate" and "acceptable" explanation is an exercise of violence. This reduction and social construct of reality tend to increase violence and help prevent these societies from facing their basic problems. It also hampers the use of the region's potential and engages this potential in a futile conflict with the outside world rather than putting potential to good use; this is, in fact, an act of violence. Is this a perpetually vicious cycle in the Middle East, in which violence leads to conspiracy and conspiracy theories, in turn, feed and foster violence in the region?

While violence exists in different forms and in different places in the world, violence is prominent in the Middle East, and the persistent intensity of violence in this region is extraordinary. The Middle East is one of the most militarized and conflict-ridden regions in the world. Is violence, therefore, a Middle Eastern phenomenon? Does the Middle East represent the zenith of violence? Has this region been eternally condemned to harbor violence? The multifaceted failure to develop and implement the potential of this region for constructive purposes merits raising these important questions, in hopes that doing so might lead to a more serious investigation of how violence fits into the overall failures of Middle Eastern societies. Middle Eastern violence is at odds with today's global world and with the heavy investment in globalization and the promotion of mutual interests, all of which depend on the control or elimination of violence. Violence, in this sense, is an obstacle to Middle Eastern integration into the world community.

Nonetheless, Galtung warns against confusing cultural violence with violent cultures: "Entire cultures can hardly be classified as violent. Aspect A of culture C is an example of cultural violence,"[3] which is possible to discuss, however. This distinction is crucial in any analysis of a social structure. However, arguing that the gender structure is an intrinsically violent social system does not necessarily mean that Middle Eastern cultures are violent. I make no such claim that Middle Eastern cultures are violent in the sense that they are different from other cultures. In fact, there are aspects of violence in every culture. The experience of human civilization and development clearly shows that violence has been a part of social development in every culture; and completely violence-free cultures do not exist.

Thus, Middle Eastern culture is no different from any other culture in this regard. Every culture, and every individual for that matter, is both violent and peaceful at the same time. Historical development and the mainstream psychological profile of certain nations may prove to be slightly more violent than others, but this difference, arguably, is minimal or insignificant. What is even more important is that many nations have learned to contain and control the violent side of existence, by burying it beneath the surface. This has only been possible through a complex process that entails agreement on the fundamental principles of peaceful coexistence, increasing opportunities to participate in society, nurturing a respect for the natural existence of every citizen, and diminishing discrimination.

Yet even though violence is a worldwide, non–culture specific phenomenon, it seems that violence in the Middle East is particularly distinct in certain ways. The combination of gender and political violence increases the overall level of violence to the point that it is all-encompassing, total, comprehensive, and extreme. This is partially why certain nations appear to be more violent than others. Nations that have come a long way in respecting basic human rights have been able to neutralize political violence by adopting democratic political systems. However, in the Middle East the lack of democracy and the domination of authoritarianism enable unchecked violence to remain rampant throughout society.

Unlike other regions, the Middle East overlooks violence rather than acknowledging it and acting against it. One way of doing this is by externalizing it and restricting the perception of violence to the role of external forces. Yet admitting violence is the first step in combating and controlling it. This is where societies differ most, in their seriousness about minimizing violence. Furthermore, there is an unjustifiable hesitation, if not opposition, to adopting the latest achievements in human rights for fear that it will antagonize Middle Eastern traditions, religion, and culture. Therefore, opposition to these advancements is steadfast because culture, religion and traditions are part of the structure of violence in society. This failure to incorporate a culture of human rights is another way violence is supported and maintained in Middle Eastern societies. This is particularly true considering that cultures and religions that are perceived to be in conflict with advancements in human rights tend to be both a source and justification for socially legitimate violence.

However, violence must be taken seriously in the Middle East. Violence needs to be internalized by society and treated as a part of the social structure. Rather than stemming from outside sources, violence is rooted in the structures, cultures, perceptions, and social values that dominate society. Yet the process of transforming this popular understanding of violence as an external force into one that recognizes violence as an internalized aspect of societies is a sensitive and challenging task. Addressing the internalization of violence in Middle Eastern society requires an honest, responsible, and investigative approach to the social, cultural, and political values that govern ordinary life in the region. This work is an attempt in this direction.

One way to internalize violence is to link it to the gender structure that underlies society. Gender construction is central to understanding the social and political order. While the gender structure is a major conditioning factor in women's lives in the Middle East, gender does not only affect women. It is a part of the social structure that influences all other aspects of life including the political economy, culture, and intellect. Because of this, gender shares the responsibility for the crisis that is engulfing the region. Therefore, any attempt to address this crisis should call into question the very cultural, religious, and patriarchal social values that dominate gender relations in these societies. Karmi calls attention to the fact that "the profound depth and extent of the patriarchal oppression of women and its crucial role in maintaining a stagnant social and political status quo are widely underestimated or even ignored, by women as well as men."[4]

This book is about the intrinsically violent nature of gender relations in the Middle East and how this manifests within society and the authoritarian political system. However, this book does not claim that gender is the only cause of violence and authoritarianism. In fact, it is better to renounce such unrealistic and futile claims. Social reality is too complex and dynamic to reduce violence to a single aspect, no matter how significant that aspect might be. Gender structure cannot by itself account for the entire process of violence in society. Gender relations are constructed, perceived, enforced, negotiated, made, and remade through a set of interplaying economic, political, religious, cultural, and social factors. The aim of this book, nonetheless, is to assert that there is a strong linkage between the patriarchal construction of gender roles and authoritarianism in the creation of violence in Middle Eastern societies.

WOMEN AND VIOLENCE

The conventional, orientalist view of women portrays them as mostly passive and powerless. Göcek and Balaghi argue: "Women in the Middle East have often been portrayed as mute followers of tradition, bound to a static and powerless existence."[5] While there is some truth to this, this perspective fails to embrace the entire story and the role women play in promoting violence within society. Perceiving women as only victims of gender relations and society is misleading. Women are both victims and abusers at the same time. According to Keddie there is a tendency to

> exaggerate the negative side of gender relations in the Muslim world, and a tendency to present Muslim women primarily as victims. The ideals of women's seclusion and the separation of

genders were misinterpreted to mean that most women lived lives without meaning or satisfactions. Today there is a counter-tendency among many scholars of the Middle East, both Muslim and non-Muslim, to stress the positive aspects of women's lives, which is understandable as a reaction to the predominant highly negative view.[6]

Thus, there is a counter-discourse to portraying the positive sides of this picture as well. There is also a tendency to convolute negative aspects into positives. However, I argue that emphasizing positive aspects is one thing and turning negatives into positives is another. Marcus states: "Seclusion might offer some benefits to women as well as disadvantages."[7] Indeed, there are some benefits to the seclusion of women, yet these benefits make more sense within the patriarchal structure of gender relations. Likewise, one could claim there are advantages to the veiling of women. Yet away from patriarchal structure and the resurgence of conservatism that the rise of political Islam has spawned, the veiling of women becomes an even more controversial issue.

In discussing female gatherings in Yemeni society, Makhlouf argues that it is easier for women to enter the world of men, while the opposite is nearly impossible. Only singers, servants, or inferior men can enter the world of women. This tempts Makhlouf to reach the following conclusion: "One can venture that in fact the men are excluded from the female world as much, if not more, than females are excluded from the world of the men."[8] However, the fact that only inferior men can enter the gatherings of women demonstrates the point that these are the gatherings of an inferior world, one in which only inferior men can freely enter without disturbing. It is curious that this approach considers the exclusion of women from the public world a problem, while the exclusion of men from the domestic world of women is considered desirable and a source of power for women, even. Yet a soundly functioning, inclusive society aspires for the entry of both sexes in both directions. In this sense, men's difficulty in entering the private world of women is neither desirable nor a source of satisfaction or power for women.

As Mir-Hosseini argues: "It is misleading to take Islamic family at face value and evaluate women's position according to what the law entitles them to. Despite the overt inequalities between the rights of men and women within Muslim marriage, there are mechanisms both in Islamic law and in social practice that can balance the situation."[9]

She continues: "The dowry, *mahr*, an inherent element of every Muslim marriage plays an important role as both deterrent and compensator, by providing women with a bargaining position to negotiate the terms of marriages, if not divorces."[10] Thus, one of the main instruments of oppressing women and ensuring their inequality and inferiority in marriage is perceived as a source of power for women. Once again, though, obviously this claimed sense of power that women derive from dowry make more sense within patriarchal societies where inequality between men and women is the norm.

In the same vein, it has also been argued that the family provides protection from state aggression and is not an institution for the oppression of women. One wonders, however, whether these two aspects are truly mutually exclusive. Why could it not be both? Why should a vibrant and intricate social reality be condensed to a simplified either/or kind of analysis? Surely, the family can function as both a site of patriarchal oppression and a site of refuge from the domination and violence of the authoritarian state. While individual scholars are not to be blamed for these kinds of conclusions, these conclusions nonetheless function as apologies for women's plight in the region. The satisfaction and comfort that women may receive from these far-fetched conclusions may very well induce a sense of acceptance and accommodation of their circumstances. Yet one side of this picture, I argue, does not necessarily negate the other.

While the disapproving depiction of powerless Middle Eastern women is misleading, so too is the opposite analysis that portrays women in only the positive sense. Again though, there is some truth in the depiction of women in this region as positive and powerful. Indisputably, these women have great willpower and survival skills, which allow them to endure the harsh conditions females face in Middle Eastern societies. Yet there are at least three risks involved in assessing women in only a positive manner. The first is viewing the positive role of women in society in absolute terms, which is a rather simplified picture of women in these societies and, in a way, is similar to the older approach of viewing women only in a negative light in the region. Women everywhere, and men as well for that matter, posses both positive and negative qualities at any given time.

The second risk is that these assessments are made mostly in reaction to criticism of women's situation in Middle Eastern societies. Viewing women in a positive way is an attempt to negate the conventionally negative picture of women in this region. The aim of this approach is to deny the sense of powerlessness and oppression of women in Middle Eastern societies. Yet this is unsupported by the grim reality that women and, indeed, even men truly live in. Thus, this claim is merely an ideological, defensive exercise against critics of an indefensible and inexcusable situation. In this respect, this approach is an apologetic position and, therefore, is harmful to women's long-term interests in this region. Denying women's miserable existence in the Middle East in this way tends to dissolve the need to address these real and serious issues, even though addressing them could help advance the status of women, who otherwise remain second-class citizens in these societies.

Another risk, which is even more relevant to the discussion of this book, is that the preoccupation with scoring points or victories against critics of the female state downplays one of the gravest realities of gender structure: female violence. This confuses the issue and blinds us from the reality that women, like men, are responsible for feeding and sustaining violence in society. When power and violence are strongly interlinked, acknowledging female power only, and not the violence that is undeniably associated with it, is unfathomable. The approach of this book is not to see women as merely powerless and innocent victims of the patriarchal order, but it is to discuss the role women play in the cycle of social violence, whether it is direct or indirect, conscious or unconscious, overt or hidden. The project is, then, to point out the burden of responsibility that women bear, along with men, with regard to the intensity and dominance of violence in Middle Eastern societies.

Much of the literature specialized in gender issues is focalized around the discussion of male violence against women. However, this is at the expense of a more balanced approach in which men and women commit violence against one another. Therefore, the role that women play in the implementation of violence is often neglected or overlooked. However, it is important to mention that discussing violence on both sides of the gender line does not justify in any way violence from either side. Thus, male violence is not a legitimate source of validation for female violence, nor would the opposite be. Yet patriarchal and authoritarian structures create this cycle of violence and animosity, which is difficult for both men and women to break away from. Violence breeds violence at an increasing rate.

In fact, patriarchal structure creates the necessary conditions for a conflict model of gender relations that comes to govern the lives of men and women in the Middle East. To be sure, there are two different models of relationship between the sexes. The first is the conflict model of gender relations, in which each partner seeks power, domination, and conquest. This model becomes not only the dominant model within the patriarchal system but also is in constant clash with the second model. This second model is the natural, unpatriarchal model of gender relations, in which the *self* is never fully destroyed but retains some autonomy and agency and a capacity for love, tenderness, and affection. So there are within men and women some natural parts and qualities that are not an internalization of the external social system and the patriarchal construct. The conflict between these two models is a conflict between natural existence and social existence. A well-established and internalized patriarchal value system results in the supremacy of the conflict model and thereby explains the inherently violent nature of gender relations between the sexes in Middle Eastern societies. Conversely, gender reconciliation that aims to deemphasize gender violence is strongly linked to the supremacy of the natural model of gender relations that is based on love, understanding, tolerance, and respect.

There are several reasons, I argue, for neglecting the issue of female violence. First is the fact that the widespread dominance of male violence in society leaves little room for attending to female violence. Violence is an aspect of social masculinity construction that tends to naturalize male violence, giving it a sense of normality. The second reason is that the social recognition of female violence is more difficult, because it necessarily implies the victimization of men as well. The highly exaggerated and inflated male ego and the patriarchal construction of masculinity, which is associated with aggressiveness and violence, leave no room for male victims. A male victim is inconceivable or a contradiction in terms in the patriarchal context where men's weaknesses are to be hidden and unspoken of.

The third reason is that perceiving women as weak creatures makes it difficult to recognize or admit female violence. It is easier to establish a connection between toughness and violence than between inferiority, or weakness, and violence. Dispelling the myth, however, that women are inferior and weak would certainly expose the paradox that female violence does, in fact, exist. Would women necessarily be happy about this, though? Could they cope with the consequences?

The fourth reason is the predisposition to only associate women with the dominant male form of violence, thus denying women an independent role and their own agency regarding violence. Ortner argues: "There is a tendency to see women as identified with male games, or as pawns in male games, or as otherwise having no autonomous point of view or intentionality."[11] The fifth reason is that we do not see female violence because we look for power in the wrong places. Singerman explains this myopic position:

> Political science suffers from a classic case of methodological bias: where one looks determines what one finds. For example, when one suffers from this type of myopia, one assumes that if women are rarely visible in the upper echelon of the state bureaucracy, the military, or among the elites, then they must not be engaged in politics. However, if one investigates politics at the level of the household and community, women are obviously engaged in decision-making processes, distributional activities, and in informal institutions.[12]

Rassam concurs: "Ethnographic studies of Middle Eastern societies usually acknowledge the existence of two separate and sharply differentiated social worlds. Implicit in this dichotomy of public/male, private/female is the assumption that power, viewed as belonging to the public-political domain, is a male monopoly and that women, confined to the domestic sphere, are powerless."[13]

Thus, the recognition of female power and violence represents a challenge to the theoretical feminist approach. Lazreg recognizes: "When the power of men over women is reproduced in the power of women over women, feminism as an intellectual movement presents a caricature of the very institutions it was meant to question."[14] Kelly, Burton, and Regan elaborate: "There is no unproblematic relationship for feminists to power. Just as the concept itself is intensely contested, so its use in relationships with others. Moreover, 'using the power one has' for oneself departs markedly from the original ambition of feminism to end the systematic oppression of all women."[15] However, female violence is a neglected subject, not only in gender literature addressing the Middle East but also in gender literature in general. Yet this is an issue essential to understanding the mechanisms of gender violence, as well as understanding the way violence relates to the gender structure and society at large. A more effective theoretical framework for understanding gender issues is one that admits and discusses female violence as well as recognizes that both men and women are responsible for the perpetuation of violence.

Foucault argues that not only do the dominant produce power, but so do the subordinate.[16] This does not mean, however, that the power produced by the subordinate is equal to that of the dominant. Gender

hierarchy manifests in the structure of male and female power. Female power is informal, unassigned, and illegitimate power. Women's informal power does not contradict patriarchy, as it is still achieved *within* the patriarchal structure. Patriarchy tends to tolerate female power as long as the foundation of the patriarchal gender structure remains intact. Within the patriarchal structure, female power can take the form of resistance, subversion, or compliance, without implying that these are mutually exclusive. By cultivating female power, women play an essential role in supporting the endurance of patriarchal social structures. Kousha contends:

> The irony lies in the fact that while it is the patriarchal structure that determines women's status, it is often the mother who carries and passes on to her daughter a devalued view of the feminine and of women's role in society. Socialized according to dominant gender roles, mothers pass on a cycle of powerlessness that becomes instrumental in perpetuating the patriarchal structure where masculinity and its attributes are more valued.[17]

In fact, the role that women play in supporting the patriarchal social system clearly illustrates one of the puzzles that is a bane of the social sciences: victims' compliance with their oppression. Why do women play their gender roles that support the same gender system that oppresses them? Why do women decide to stay in abusive relationships? Yet one could also ask: What other choice do women have within patriarchal and authoritarian social systems? One of the significant approaches to the puzzle of the compliance of women is the process of internalization, a key concept in gender literature. Socialization of women tends to enforce and normalize patriarchal social construct in the lives of women. A particular social construction enters into conflict with reality and natural existence. This social construct becomes the only "reality" that women experience in a patriarchal system. Thus, internalization is the process where the socially constructed appears natural to women. Internalization is a crucial process that can offer an explanation, at least partially, to the endurance and dominance of the patriarchal system and mentality.

However, compliance with the gender order does not negate the fact that women do resist their designed fate in various ways. Keddie and Beck state: "Women have a variety of strategies enabling them to mitigate the effects of male control. To the female belongs the domestic domain, and the tasks she performs there are by right exclusive to her. In controlling much of this domain, she partially controls its inhabitants, including men. Part of his honor is defined by the degree of this control, and a woman by subtle means can undermine it."[18]

As Foucault argues, where there is power there is resistance.[19] Gender relations are the sum, the intersection, and the interplay of power and resistance. Power and resistance are never one-sided or one-dimensional. Power and resistance make and remake gender relations. Patriarchal gender ideology forces female resistance to transpire in mostly destructive and violent ways. Thus, the implementation of power and violence lead to a return of violence in a long-lasting cycle of violence and conflict. The acts of subversion women employ within gender relations, as part of their resistance, tend to not only feed violence but support the patriarchal gender system also.

There is a Middle Eastern tendency to exaggerate and romanticize resistance, which extends into gender issues as well. This romanticization is possible because female resistance is not seen as a form of agency that produces violence in society. One of the reasons women's resistance and subversion is not perceived as violence is closely related to the definition of violence in gender literature. If violence is narrowly understood to be direct and physical only, then violence becomes associated with men and not with women, who are perceived only to be victims. The question is, then: To what extent does this simplified and condensed perception reflect the true, complex, and multidimensional nature of violence in society? In this way, feminist gender literature falls into the same biological trap that it is supposed to combat. This rather biological construction of violence provides a misleading picture of violence by negating the agency of women and their ability to perpetrate violence. Women are, in fact, just as capable of committing violence as men.

One of the main objectives of this book is to discuss women's contribution to violence through the power and agency they access. I argue that women share equal responsibility with men for gender violence. The patriarchal gender structure and the authoritarian order give women and men little option but to exercise their power and agency in a way that leads to an increase in social violence overall. Therefore, the role that women play in the cycle of violence is a natural extension of the agency and power allocated to them under the dominance of the patriarchal gender structure.

Thus, limited notions of violence should be contested. Instead, we should opt for a broader sense of violence that can include not only direct and physical violence, but also subtle, psychological, structural, cultural, verbal, and subversive forms of violence. This broader concept of violence will allow us to accommodate or incorporate the violence committed by women too. Much of the direct and physical violence is a reaction to the other, subtler forms of violence. However, it is important to mention that these different modalities of violence overlap and coexist. One form of violence feeds the other in a vicious and continuous cycle.

To be sure, a more inclusive concept of violence that includes female violence will not negate the harsh reality of male violence towards women. The following four chapters of this work address the various modalities of violence towards women that lead to the degradation, dehumanization, and victimization of women in Middle Eastern societies. The important questions that I attempt to answer in this regard are: Where do the effects of this violence go? Does violence end with the victimization of women, or does it set up a vicious cycle of victimization involving men, women, and society at large? Are women the only ones who pay the high price for patriarchal violence in society? It would be naive to assume that as women face the harsh reality of patriarchy, they would completely resign themselves to the role of mere victims. Complete or final surrender is more theoretical than actual. To be sure, the resistance of women results in violence, which also affects men as well.

In this context, using the terms "male" or "female" violence may actually be misleading or confusing. They could indicate that there is a specific kind of violence perpetrated by men only and, likewise, a specific kind of female violence. In reality, however, there is structural patriarchal violence that accommodates the agency of both men and women. Even though male violence is mostly direct and physical, it is still conditioned by patriarchal and societal structures. Female violence is also tied to these structures in a similar way. One Iranian woman made this clear: "He was not a happy man either. He was not a mean man. They were both victims of their society and the conditions under which they lived . . . I don't believe my mother was not oppressed, but I believe it was not my father's fault that she was oppressed."[20]

However, while both male and female violence are conditioned by social structures, there are several differences between the two. There are differences in the way the patriarchal gender structure positions men and women in their access to structural violence. It is also important to note the differences in the cultural legitimization of different forms of gender violence. There are also possible differences in the impacts and consequences of male and female violence. There is a great disparity in the scale, intensity, and degree of injury between male violence and female violence. The impact of one incident of rape can forever scar a woman, but a comparable lifelong injury for men is limited. Social construction of masculinity tends to minimizes long-term and more profound consequences of gender violence for men. This construct of masculinity can even have a positive outcome to violence perpetrated by men against women. A rapist, for instance, can even get to marry the female victim and thus regain respectability and acceptance of society. This is part of a Middle Eastern tradition where the concept of honor is central to the dominant cultural values. This "traditional" solution to sexual violence tends to further victimize the victim and to reward the abuser. Differences in the forms of gender violence reflect the power structure, or the power relationship, between men and women. It is an expression of the power and status inequalities between men and women that influence the way gender violence manifests. While male violence is more physical and direct, female violence is subtle and subversive. However, due to the structural disadvantages of women, female violence tends to differ depending on the receiving party of this violence.

If the superior and strong cannot be openly challenged, then subverting male power is the only option. Thus, female violence towards men is usually subtle in form. Conversely, female violence against other women is more direct and explicit because it is violence between culturally constructed inferiors. However, in both cases, female violence and the agency of women are evident. While violence towards men is subversive agency, agency garnered through violence against other women is more pronounced, direct, open, and possibly even more damaging. The end result is the indirect victimization of men and the direct victimization of women. This explains the role women play in reinforcing the violent gender structure in society.

One of the deficiencies in gender studies is the restriction of the concept of agency to men only and the consistent relegation of women to the role of victim. Where victimhood may offer women some comfort, material benefits, or an excuse for failing to take control of their own lives, women need to escape the role of the victim. After all, the interpretation that women are only victims is not supported by reality, or in the words of Friedl: "No matter how contradictory the concept of the oppressed-yet-powerful woman might seem, the contradiction is contrived."[21] Like men, women are both victims and victimizers in the patriarchal system. In fact, everyone, regardless of gender, plays the role of abuser and victimizer at the very same time.

Discourse in gender literature that portrays women only in a positive light tends to exclude the social structure from its analysis. Denying any sense of female victimization in this regard is meant to deny any role or influence that the social structure has in the victimization of women. In this sense, acknowledging female agency is perceived to be a negation of the social structure. Thus, within this discourse, female agency and social structure are understood to be completely opposing aspects and mutually exclusive categories. Yet this is a rather simplified and far-fetched assertion. The mutual influence that agency and social structure have on one another makes their relationship complex and dynamic. While one can easily recognize and discuss agency within a well-defined social structure, the existence and the influence of female agency does not allow social structure to reflect or maintain a rigid and static existence.

This discussion also raises the question of whose interest female agency serves. Does female agency help women advance their status and achieve gender equality, or does it support the very same patriarchal gender structure that oppresses women? Without falling into the trap of simplifying agency into a dichotomy by assuming female agency is either positive or negative, we can assert that female agency, like that of men, is both positive and negative at the same time. In other words, one way to achieve a more productive and positive form of female agency is for women to admit the violent and destructive aspects of their agency in the patriarchal gender structure. Thus, gender relations should be discussed within the totality of all the actors involved in these relationships, including women. It is true that this will make gender issues even more complex and contradictory. However, that is what makes gender an even more interesting subject to explore.

STRUCTURE OF THE BOOK

While gender issues in the Middle East have been studied extensively, the distinct approach in this book highlights the violent nature of social gender construction. The central theme of this work is the intrinsically violent structure of gender relations and its impact on men, women, and society. In this project I intend to scrutinize the issues of power, violence, victimization, resistance, and agency against the background of the inherently objective and undiscriminating violent patriarchal structure of gender relations. This work adopts a broad, comprehensive, and inclusive concept of violence to accommodate the agency of both men and women. Both men and women share the roles and responsibilities of initiating, feeding, and sustaining violence in society. All modalities of violence perpetrated by both men and women are related to the intrinsically violent patriarchal gender structure. This work highlights female power and agency at its pinnacle stage in the cycle of violence, the role of the mother-in-law, and how this form of power and agency feeds the cycle of violence and victimization in the Middle Eastern gender structure. This work also attempts to make a connection between the violent structure of patriarchy and the violent nature of authoritarian politics that dominate the Middle East. I argue that violence is the common dominator, and a major point of intersection, between these two social systems.

This book consists of 16 chapters, divided in four parts. Part One, "Modalities of Violence against Women," consists of the first four chapters that provide a picture of violence committed against women from different levels of male authority: individual, political, and societal. Chapter 2, "Violence against Women in the Middle East," provides an outline of the different modalities of violence toward women in the domestic sphere, such as wife battering, physical, and psychological violence as well as rape and sexual violence. It discusses sexual mutilation, known as female circumcision, that is practiced on women in some parts of the Middle East as a modality of extreme violence and discrimination against women. Chapter 3, "Crime and Honor," discusses the extreme modality of physical violence against women, honor killing, how male-centered society and the cult of virginity exemplify the extreme violence committed against women in the name of honor, and how these crimes cultivate a culture of fear among women. It also presents real crime stories from the Middle East that share the common motivation of honor.

Chapter 4, "Islam, Gender, and Violence," explains how Islam, as an agent of patriarchy, offers religious and cultural rationalization and legitimization for violence towards women. The obsession of political Islam with the control and subjugation of women is obvious in all aspects of the militant Islamic groups that have come to power in the Middle East. Chapter 5, "Gender Alienation," discusses how the cultural preference for boys, unequal treatment of boys and girls, gender segregation and discrimination, and social control over women contribute to polarization and the creation of futile dichotomies between: nature and social existence, the *self* and the *other*, femininity and masculinity, and emotionality and rationality. These enforced dichotomies color the background in which violence is initiated and supported at various levels of society.

Part Two, "Power, Violence, and Gender," consists of the following four chapters that focus on the relationship between power and violence and how they intersect with gender relations. Chapter 6, "Gender and Power," discusses the fact that female power in the Middle East is illegitimate and unacknowledged, yet women's surreptitious power is manifested in many ways. While female power is undeniable, it nevertheless needs to be discussed through the lens of socially hierarchicized power and female power in relation to male power in both the domestic and public domains. Chapter 7, "Power and Price," explores how hierarchical gender power leads to a destructive gender game between men and women. Women's power in the Middle East is confined almost exclusively to socially unrecognized power exercised in the private domain and informal networks. Because female power is informal and fragmented, a formidable female power at the national level is still missing in the Middle East.

Chapter 8, "Violence, Victimization, and Conformity," highlights the power-violence nexus and its effects on women in society. It discusses the relationship between agency and victimization and whether or not they are mutually exclusive. It also discusses the pressures on Middle Eastern women to conform to their role of complicity in the gender structure, which actually encourages their own subjugation despite the limited advantages that women can benefit from through compliance. Chapter 9, "Gender, Resistance, and Subversion," analyzes the indispensable relationship between power and resistance that shows how resistance manifests within gender relations as a form of violence. This is reflected in the fact that women's resistance to the oppressive gender structure fosters violence in Middle Eastern society. I argue that instead of helping women advance their status in society, subversion as a form of female power coincides with the patriarchal gender structure that oppresses and degrades women.

Part Three, "Impacts of Female Power and Agency," consists of the next two chapters, which discuss how the manifestation of female power affects men, women, and children. Chapter 10, "Status and Victimization," focuses on the special relationship that exists between mothers and their children and whether or not these special bonds lead to victimization, violence, and exclusion at the domestic level. Women also suffer from a multidimensional situation of dependency that corners them into a precarious position within the family. Within the family structure, the relationship between the mother and her daughter, both victims of the same system, is of special interest. Chapter 11, "Patriarchy and Agency," highlights the role of the mother-in-law, which represents a niche within the patriarchal power structure for women and the climax of female power in society. This role causes further victimization and violence between men and women within the family and sets the grounds for a perpetual cycle of conflict and violence. However, does society reward or punish this form of female power?

Part Four, "Patriarchy and Authoritarianism," contains the next four chapters, which highlight the relationship between patriarchy and authoritarianism and between domestic violence and political violence. Chapter 12, "Authoritarian Family Structure," discusses the notion that the authoritarian structure of the Middle Eastern family is the bedrock of the political authoritarian orders of the Middle East. The gender structure is connected to the political authoritarian order in society. Obedience is the necessary "virtue" that feeds the mechanisms of both patriarchy and authoritarianism. Chapter 13, "Gender and Authoritarian Social Contract," discusses the three levels of the social contract that are prevalent in the Middle East: the religious, sexual, and political levels. This social contract is based on the offering of loyalty and obedience in return for material reward and security, the result of which is a dissipation of society's available human resources.

Chapter 14, "Gender and Authoritarian Politics," discusses how patriarchal and authoritarian systems unite to politically dehumanize both men and women. Politics of exclusion are a common feature of both patriarchy and authoritarianism that tend to polarize society into subsocieties with their own subcultures. This results in a culture of inaccessibility, a culture of passiveness, and a culture of silence and apathy. Chapter 15, "Gender, Authoritarianism, and Violence," discusses how gender relations support authoritarianism by normalizing violence within the family and expanding access to violence to everyone in society. It also addresses how the inflated male ego is constrained by the limitations of the authoritarian state and explains the implications that result from this disharmony. Rather than gaining a sense of pride from legitimate sources, the inflated pride and honor of men, which is encouraged by both patriarchy and authoritarianism, leads to the invention of enemies that the Middle East is notorious for being in constant conflict with.

Chapter 16, "Conclusion: Toward Gender Reconciliation," is a short concluding chapter that argues that gender reconciliation, as a significant part of national reconciliation, should be an indispensable item on the agenda of Middle Eastern societies in order to break the futile and destructive cycle of violence and victimization that dominates gender relations in the region. This process can open new horizons in advancing the Middle East into modernity and tolerance.

PART ONE

MODALITIES OF VIOLENCE AGAINST WOMEN

CHAPTER 2

Violence against Women in the Middle East

You break one rib of a girl, she gets 24 new ribs.

—*Egyptian saying*

DOMESTIC VIOLENCE

Violence toward women is not strictly a Middle Eastern phenomenon but a worldwide problem found in every society. According to the United Nations Development Fund for Women (UNIFEM), "Violence against women and girls is a problem of pandemic proportions. At least one out of every three women around the world has been beaten, coerced into sex, or otherwise abused in her lifetime—with the abuser usually someone known to her."[1] According to Parrot and Cummings it is estimated that between 10 and 50 percent of women worldwide have been beaten by their intimate partners.[2] Even in Scandinavia, where women's position in society has made considerable advancements and where gender equality is highly venerated, violence against women is still a grave, pervasive problem. In Norway, with a population of 4 million people, each year 10,000 women ask for medical treatment because of physical damage due to domestic violence.[3] Research shows that 16 Swedish women are murdered annually by their Swedish male partners in intimate personal violence.[4] In 1999, the United Nations adopted a resolution to tackle the problem, designating November 25 as the International Day for the Elimination of Violence against Women. The resolution broadly defines violence against women as acts capable of causing physical, sexual, or psychological harm, either in the public or private lives of women.

The Middle East is not exempt from this global predicament, despite rhetorical claims that women are dignified and respected in these societies. There is a long, extensive list of various modes of violence found in these societies: physical violence; psychological violence; intimate violence and wife battering; cultural and religious sanctioning of women's obedience; polygamy; sexual violence in the form of rape, including marital rape, gang rape, and incest, both paternal, fraternal, and otherwise; criminalization of pre- or extramarital sexuality; criminalization of homosexuality; sexual harassment in the workplace; female genital mutilation; honor killing; forced, early marriages; trafficking in women; forced pregnancies; divorce threats; suppression of freedom of expression; deprivation of basic rights; segregation and gender-based discrimination; male guardianship; and rigid restrictions on the movement of women.

Even though violence against women is customary and widespread, incidents of violence are rarely documented and draw little attention from the public eye. Statistics of domestic violence in the Middle East are difficult to come by. Most incidences go unreported, and the few that are reported are not taken seriously by authorities. The few cases that are reported are considered to be the private business of the family and are therefore not treated as serious crimes. Dismissed as trivial complainants by authorities, women who report violence risk facing the consequences of reprisal from their abusers. Still, little protection is offered in these cases. The Lebanese Association to Combat Violence against Women, a civil society organization, says that usually women do not tell their stories until they reach an insupportable level, and the law does not help much. If a woman decides to complain, the husband can divorce her and take the children away from their mother. The victim, on the other hand, usually has no economic independence of her own.[5]

According to Parrot and Cummings, 70–90 percent of women in Pakistan experience domestic violence.[6] An official, governmental report states that in Algeria 1 in every 10 women aged 19–64 are battered every day. In these cases, the husband is the most likely abuser of married women; widowed and divorced women are most likely abused by a brother.[7] A 2002 report conducted by the World Organization against Torture (Organisation Mondiale Contra Torture, or OMCT), a nongovernmental organization based in Geneva, revealed that 46.3 percent of women in Yemen had experienced violence from their spouses or other family members at some point in their lives. The report also notes that 50.9 percent of women had been threatened with violence,

54.5 percent had suffered physical abuse, 17.3 percent had been sub-jected to sexual violence, 28.2 percent had their freedom restricted, and 34 percent had property either damaged or stolen, while a sizeable 44.5 percent suffered from three or more modes of violence.[8] Violence towards women in Lebanon occurs in all social classes, regardless of wealth or poverty. About a third of Lebanese women are victims of physical and psychological violence.[9] A study done by UNIFEM in November of 2007 found that at least 122 women have been killed in Jordan between the year 2000 and 2003 as the result of physical abuse from family members.[10] Another study of Jordan found that domes-tic violence is on the rise. A study including 11 of the 62 courts in the country revealed that the number of incidents of marital violence reached 132 cases in the year 2007. In most of these cases, victims re-mained in bed for multiple days because of their injuries.[11]

The Land Center for Human Rights in Egypt issued a report moni-toring violence against women published by all Egyptian newspapers during the second half of 2006, During this period, 261 articles have been published citing crimes that have led to the death of 123 women.[12] Fifty-two percent of the women who participated in the 1995 national census in Egypt had been beaten by their husbands at least once dur-ing the year 1994, and 17 percent had been beaten three to six times or more. Ninety-five percent of the domestic violence cases were per-petrated by men.[13] There is a story of a 21-year-old girl who, after coming home late one night, was insulted and beaten harshly by her father. Her injuries resulted in a broken nose and the need for hospital treatment. In another case, a girl was severely beaten by her father for responding in kind to the swearing of her brother who was eight years younger. She was in such a critical psychological state following the incident that she attempted suicide the following day.[14]

Generally speaking, Middle Eastern governments deal with issues of violence against women by either completely denying their existence or by trivializing these occurrences, dismissing them as isolated incidences perpetrated by psychopathic male individuals. These are the words of the deputy of social affairs in the General People's Congress in Libya re-garding investigations of violence against women, conducted by Human Rights Watch in 2005, "We don't have violence against women . . . if there was violence, we would know . . . we can't deny that previously be-fore the revolution, there were wrongdoings against women."[15] The fact that these comments come from a woman indicates the limitations and ineffectiveness of women's agency in the Middle East and demonstrates that this agency may even cause further harm.

Luckily, things have recently begun to change. After a long period of silence, the first comprehensive field study of violence against women in Syria concluded that nearly one in four married woman have been beaten. The study was done in 2006 under the supervision of the General Union of Women, funded by UNIFEM. It included nearly 1,900 families selected as a random sample from a broad range of income levels from all regions.[16] According to the study, 22 percent of married women were assaulted either verbally or physically, with 50 percent of respondents citing verbal abuse and 48 percent admitting they had been beaten. The study describes 19 different types of domestic violence, revealing that women are beaten for reasons ranging from the neglect of household duties to "bombarding husbands with too many questions."[17] Another study cited physical violence as the cause of 90 percent of divorce cases raised by women.[18] A woman who works at the only shelter for abused women in Syria observed: "Violence is in every home in the Arab world. Women start to feel like abuse is a normal part of life. They no longer believe it is violence."[19]

A study conducted by the Supreme Council for Women in Bahrain indicates that 95 percent of the respondents admitted women in Bahrain are exposed to violence at home and at work. The study found the husband was the main abuser and that women's education and employment did not decrease women's chances of being a victim of violence. Eighty percent of respondents believe that sexual problems and unsound sexual relations between married couples are the main reasons for physical and psychological violence against women.[20] Violence against women exists within all social classes; however, it is more widespread among the poor. The lower the family income, the more violence is likely to occur. Families with higher incomes experience less violence against women, and this violence is likely to be a form of psychological or verbal violence.

A study conducted by the Supreme Council for Family Affairs in Qatar involved 2,778 female Qatar University students aged 17–25 disclosed many interesting facts. Sixty-three percent of those surveyed had been beaten, usually by male relatives. Forty-five percent of victims had been subjected to violence since childhood, 34 percent since adolescence. Forty-seven percent said they had suffered from various disorders including depression, as a result of the abuse. Two percent said they had attempted suicide.[21] A 2006 report by the Palestinian Central Bureau of Statistics states that of the 4,000-plus households surveyed, 23 percent of women reported they had experienced domestic violence, but only 1 percent had filed a complaint. Two-thirds of these women also said they were subjected to psychological abuse at home.[22]

According to a 2003 report by OMCT, domestic violence is a pervasive problem in Turkey. As many as 97 percent of women experience both physical and psychological forms of abuse from their partners and relatives. Another study found that more than 88 percent of the women surveyed were living in violent situations and 68 percent had been beaten by their husbands. A study conducted in 2003 by the Istanbul Bilgi University found that more than 32 percent of women were beaten by their husbands and 22 percent had been beaten by their fathers.[23] Domestic abuse, which is generally treated as a private matter, is a problem exacerbated by traditional attitudes and concepts of family honor in Middle Eastern societies.

In a study regarding domestic violence in low-income families in Lebanon, Keenan, el-Haddad, and Balian point out: "Traditional Middle Eastern social and family structure is patriarchal and characterized by male dominance and authority. . . . Clearly defined gender and marital role expectations prevail within the family." In this study, the researchers concluded the factors that trigger abuse fall under three main categories: unmet marital role expectations, conflicts with in-laws, and alcohol abuse.[24] One Lebanese woman recalls: "He came home after work and the meal was not ready, and he beat me. He has become very nervous since the [civil] war. My children are not doing well in school. He holds me responsible, so he beats me." Another woman mentioned: "The baby was crying at night and I couldn't stop him. My husband got upset and hit me." Another story reveals that men's suspicion of women and male jealousy can also trigger violence, "I was wearing shorts in the presence of one of his friends, so he beat me hard. He is the jealous type."[25]

Even in a country like Tunisia, where women's social status within the Arab world has been most drastically improved, violence against women is still a neglected problem. Regarding their 2002 report of violence against women in Tunisia, the OMCT "is concerned by the fact that the government reports appear to minimize the problem of domestic violence while simultaneously promoting a conciliatory approach that would leave the regulation of domestic violence largely in the hands of the victim's extended family," and that "the reasons that many women decide not to pursue criminal complaints in relation to domestic violence are not related to the absence of this violence but rather to its consequences which include an ingrained sense of dependence and lack of self-esteem as well as the serious social and familial pressures that are brought to bear on women who publicly denounce acts of domestic violence."[26]

As many young girls are forced into marriage and sexual relations, early marriage is a common form of sexual violence in the Middle East. Early, forced marriage is a phenomenon that is strongly tied to the concept of honor and provides a solution to the fear that a girl will lose her virginity before marriage. In tribal disputes, settlement may also involve giving women away in marriage. A United Nations report estimated that 57 percent of girls in Afghanistan are married before the age of 16. A survey conducted in Yemen in 1997 found that over a quarter of participants felt that 15 years is the ideal age for girls to marry.[27] Even though Yemeni law establishes the age of 15 as the appropriate age of marriage, tribal customs and strict interpretations of Islam often trump the law. A 2006 study conducted by Sana University reported that 52 percent of girls were married by the age of 18, while the average age of marriage in Yemen's rural areas is 12 to 13. According to this study, the most important reasons for marrying children at a young age are poverty, fear of abduction and forced marriage, and the cultural tradition and belief that a young virginal bride is most easily shaped into a dutiful wife.[28]

In the eastern and southeastern regions of Turkey 16.3 percent of women were married before the age of 15. One in every 10 women from these areas lives in polygamous marriages, despite the fact that the practice of polygamy has been banned in Turkey under the Civil Code of 1926. Fifty-one percent of women were married without their consent, despite the fact that under Turkish law the consent of both parties is a necessary precondition for marriage.[29] It is difficult for girls who are forced into early marriage to take care of their own children in a proper, healthy way considering *they are merely children themselves.* Because of the drastic age difference between husband and wife, the prospect of creating a successful marriage is, sadly, a remote possibility. A study shows that the age difference between spouses in 25 percent of marriages in Yemen exceeds 14 years.[30]

Early child marriage is widespread in Yemen. The rise of political Islam helped the Islamist conservatives to defend this practice of the marriage of minors by referring to the example of the Prophet Muhammad's marriage to a nine-year-old girl. Also, early childhood marriage is deeply rooted in the local customs of Yemen and is even enshrined in the old tribal expression "Give me a girl of eight, and I can give you a guarantee" of a good marriage.[31] Sally was a Yemeni child who, at the age of 11, was forced to marry a 25-year-old man.

Amina was a Yemeni girl accused of killing her husband and was subsequently sentenced to death even though she was only 15 years old at the time.[32] There is another story of a man in Yemen who was so poor that the only dowry he could offer his bride's family was his 10-year-old sister's hand in marriage to the 40-year-old brother of his bride. The girl was beaten by her husband and by her brother, who was mostly interested in preserving his own marriage. As a result, she suffered from deep depression.[33]

Nujood Ali is a little Yemeni girl who, at the age of 10, was forced by her impoverished and unemployed father, a father of 16 children with two women, to marry a 30-year-old man who abused her sexually and beat her regularly. She recalls: "Whenever I wanted to play in the yard he beat me and asked me to the bedroom with him." A lawyer commented: "Nujood did not get married, but she was raped by a 30-year-old man." Her husband, on the other hand, defended himself: "Yes, I was intimate with her, but I have done nothing wrong, as she is my wife and I have the right and no one can stop me." When she complained to her parents, they refused to help her, for they feared breaking the marriage would expose the family to shame. Her father told her, "My cousins would have killed me if I dishonored the family by asking for a divorce." Despite this, on April 2, 2008, Nujood mustered the courage to go to court on her own and request a divorce. She was freed from her marriage in June 2008. The husband agreed to divorce her under the condition of paying him $250, the equivalent of four months' salary for a poor Yemeni. As for Nujood, following the ordeal, she said: "All I want now is to finish my education. I want to be a human rights lawyer. I want to defend oppressed people. I want to be an example for all the other girls."[34] This case has sparked a public discussion regarding child brides and the appropriate age of marriage in Yemen. Only one month after Nujood's landmark legal case, another girl, Arwa Abdu Muhammad Ali, aged nine, demanded a legal divorce in the Yemeni town of Jibla. The case revealed her husband had beaten and sexually abused her during the entire period of eight months of her arranged marriage. Her case is still awaiting resolution.

Another story that illustrates women's hardships is that of a 16-year-old Iranian girl named Mariam whose father gave his word of "honor" to marry her to a relative. After discovering the relative was a drug addict, she protested the forced marriage and her father reacted violently. He told her "even if I have to kill you you're going to marry him." She said: "He beat me till I was black and blue . . . eventually, he kicked us all out, my mother and her seven children." Mariam was taken out of school and therefore was denied her high school diploma.[35]

Sexual violence is a sobering problem in the Middle East. Ninety-eight percent of rape cases in Egypt go unreported because of the social consequences associated with these reports. Incest is also common, despite the widely held belief that these are rare occurrences. Sixty-four percent of women and 68 percent of men have heard of incest cases.[36] According to the National Council for Social Research, there are 20,000 cases of rape in Egypt every year; 60 percent of these are cases of incest.[37] Sexual harassment affects 66 percent of Egyptian women at their workplaces. Regardless, their financial situations do not allow them to leave their jobs.[38] A study in Qatar shows that 4.3 percent of women have been sexually harassed and 2 percent have experienced "strong violence" such as rape.[39]

However, rape cases are extremely difficult if not impossible to report for many reasons including the stipulation that raped victims must be accompanied by a male guardian when reporting a case to the authorities. Ruggi points out that according to Palestinian legislation: "If a woman is raped, she cannot go to court on her own. Her case is only valid if she is accompanied by her father or her brother."[40] The Islamic stipulation that adultery cases can only be accepted if proved by four witnesses also complicates the choice to report cases of rape. What is worse, if a rape case is reported and is not substantiated by four witnesses, which is a difficult condition to achieve, the case may result in accusation of the victim for having committed adultery. This is an accusation that could lead to very harsh sentencing including incarceration, flogging, or death by stoning.

A visit by Human Rights Watch (HRW) to Libya in 2005 revealed serious violations of the most basic principles of human rights in the operation of social rehabilitation facilities. Calling these facilities de facto prisons, the report says: "The government of Libya is arbitrarily detaining women and girls in 'social rehabilitation' facilities for suspected transgressions of moral codes, locking them up indefinitely without due process. . . . Some are there for no other reason than that they were raped, and are now ostracized for staining their family's 'honor.'"[41] In these cases, the victim is blamed for the rape and is held accountable for illicit sexual behavior. This fact is well illustrated in the Yemeni proverb: "A dog won't come unless it is called." Another Yemeni proverb of the same sort states: "Don't put the gas next to the match."[42] However, incidences of rape and sexual violence are used, particularly by religious fundamentalists, as a pretext for reinforcing the segregation of women in society. In this sense, women are doubly victimized.

There is another tradition in the Middle East that worsens female victimization even more. This tradition is to ask the abuser, in cases of rape, to marry the victim. This sort of "compromise" offers the victim the chance to marry, since marrying a victim of rape is unacceptable in these societies, even though it means marrying her rapist. By accepting to marry the victim, the abuser avoids legal prosecution and jail sentencing. Yet it is not uncommon that the abuser will agree to marry the victim in order to avoid jail sentencing, only to divorce her shortly afterward, leaving the victim to face her grim future. The cultural toleration of rape and sexual violence not only fails to combat sexual violence but actually legalizes it.

Violence against women is not the only injurious phenomenon found throughout Middle Eastern society. Condoning of violence by women themselves is also widespread and pervasive. Parrot and Cummings argue: "Due to social or religious beliefs, many cultures do not define battering as a problem. Some countries support wife-beating as an attempt to control women. The women themselves sometimes expect battering as an inevitable part of an intimate relationship."[43] A government study found that 42 percent of young Qatari women condone the use of domestic violence and abuse against them, believing that they deserve the physical abuse.[44] Eighty percent of women surveyed in rural Egypt reported that beatings were commonplace, even justified, particularly if a wife refused sex to her partner.[45] In her study of Persian folktales, Friedl concludes: "When a father marries his daughter off to a most unfitting suitor, none of these acts constitutes a misuse of authority in these folktales."[46] In a critique of human rights organizations' campaigns, a Yemeni writer published an article titled "There Must Be Violence against Women," in which he writes "If a daughter or sister makes a mistake—especially a moral one—that negatively affects the entire family and its reputation, what's the solution by such organizations?"[47]

In summary, violence against women is widespread in the Middle East. Even so, this region is not necessarily exceptional in this regard alone. Violence towards women is a worldwide and cross-cultural phenomenon. However, it is important to emphasize that societies do differ in their level of toleration of violence and what is done about it. One difference is whether the society considers it a societal problem requiring involvement of the state, the law, civil society, or the media, or whether it is merely treated as an individual problem perpetuated by individual abusers. Different societies have different degrees to which culture and religion sanction violence against women.

FEMALE GENITAL MUTILATION

The World Health Organization (WHO) and Amnesty International estimate that there are 130–135 million girls and women who have undergone genital mutilation throughout the world and some 2 million girls who are at risk of undergoing some form of mutilation every year.[48] According to WHO, female genital mutilation (FGM), often referred to as "female circumcision," includes all procedures that involve partial or total removal of the external female genitalia and any other injuries to the female genital organs, whether it be for cultural, religious, or other nontherapeutic reasons. There are several different known types of FGM practiced today. The most common include: Type I: Excision (removal) of the clitoral hood, with or without removal of part or all of the clitoris; Type II: Removal of the clitoris together with part or all of the labia minora; and Type III: Removal of part or all of the external genitalia (clitoris, labia minora and labia majora) and stitching and/or narrowing of the vaginal opening, leaving a small hole for urine and menstrual flow (also referred to as infibulation).[49] The United Nations considers these practices to be violent discrimination against women and has designated February 6, as a day of Zero International Tolerance of FGM.[50]

FGM is mostly practiced in Africa and in some parts of the Middle East, particularly Egypt and the Sudan. In 1995, WHO estimated the rate of FGM among women in Egypt was 97 percent and 89 percent in the Sudan.[51] However, a survey conducted in 2005 by the UN Children's Agency, UNICEF, revealed that the rate of FGM, a figure that includes over 90 percent of women living in Egypt and the Sudan, has remained virtually unchanged for the past decade.[52] In Egypt it is practiced by both Muslims and Coptic Christians alike. Type I FGM, which is called "Sunna circumcision" in its religious reference, is the most common type of FGM practiced in Egypt, while Type III, also called "Sudanese circumcision," is more common in the south.[53] FGM is a deeply rooted tradition in Sudan. Unlike the Christians in the south, FGM is practiced by Muslims only. About 85 percent of FMG practiced in the Sudan is the most severe type, infibulation (also called "Pharonic circumcision" in reference to its historical origins). Usually it is performed on girls between the ages of 4 and 7. It is often performed by traditional practitioners under improvised, unsanitary conditions, causing severe pain, trauma, and risk of infection to the child. No form of FGM is illegal under the criminal code of the Sudan.[54]

Although there is a lack of national reporting in this area, FGM is also believed to be practiced in other parts of the Middle East, such as Yemen, Oman, Bahrain, northern Saudi Arabia, United Arab Emirates, southern Jordan, Syria, and also among the Kurds in Iraq, Turkey, and Iran.[55] It is also practiced within some African and Middle Eastern immigrant communities in the Western world. A survey conducted by a German nongovernmental organization, WADI, involving 40 villages in the region of Iraqi Kurdistan, revealed that about 60–70 percent of the women living in these villages are circumcised. There are other estimates that about 10–20 percent of the women living in Iraqi Kurdistan go through this mutilation.[56] It is estimated that the prevalence of FGM in Yemen is about 20 percent,[57] while UNICEF figures suggest that 23 percent are affected.[58] In some regions of Yemen these figures can even reach 50 percent, particularly in communities trading across the Red Sea.[59]

A UNICEF study reveals that there is little variation, if not a negative correlation, between education level/household wealth and the prevalence of the practice of FGM in the three Middle Eastern countries included in the study: Egypt, the Sudan, and Yemen. The prevalence rate of FGM among illiterates in Egypt in 2000 was 98.8 percent, while the rate among those having secondary education or higher was 94.8 percent. While Egypt shows a modest positive variation, the other countries demonstrate a negative correlation between education and the practice of FGM. In the Sudan the prevalence rate of FGM among illiterates was 85.2 percent while the figure for the educated was 97.6 percent. Likewise, the figures for Yemen were 22.1 percent and 34.1 percent, respectively. With respect to household income, prevalence figures of FGM in Egypt were 98.2 percent among the poorest 20 percent of the population and 92.1 percent among the richest 20 percent. For Yemen, the figures were 30.2 percent and 26.3 percent respectively. No figures were available for the Sudan.[60] The same study found that only Egypt shows some differences in the practice of FGM regarding place of residence (urban versus rural). The prevalence rate for women 15–49 years old having at least one daughter circumcised in Egypt was 52.9 percent for urban women and 39.8 percent for rural women. Yet the figures for the Sudan were almost the same, 58.7 percent and 58.1 percent respectively, and likewise for Yemen, 19.7 percent and 19.6 percent respectively.[61]

Because of the multiple, severe health effects associated with this practice, FGM is clearly a form of violence and gender discrimination against women. These health effects vary according to the type and severity of the procedure performed. According to WHO, FGM can have several short-term as well as long-term health implications: severe pain and shock; uterine, vaginal, and pelvic infections; urine retention; hemorrhaging; damage to the external reproductive system; sexual dysfunction; difficulties in menstruation; complications in pregnancy and child birth that can increase the risk of maternal and child mortality; reproductive morbidity and women's infertility; psychological damage; anxiety; and depression.[62] The psychological impacts these experiences have on women are enormous. These impacts stem not only from physical pain and trauma but from the social messages implied by the ritual.[63]

Furthermore, FGM is not only discrimination and violence against women but also against children and the very concept of childhood as well. FGM destroys an individual's potential to experience a healthy, normal childhood. El-Saadawi recalls the night of her mutilation: "I was six years old that night when I lay in my bed, warm and peaceful in that pleasurable state which lies half way between wakefulness and sleep, with the rosy dreams of childhood flitting by, like gentle fairies in quick succession."[64] The WHO study states: "FGM is usually performed on legal minors with no power or faculties to consent. Consent of parents or guardians is not acceptable when the act performed is damaging rather than beneficial to the child."[65] Rahman and Toubia concur by saying that it is noteworthy that this is a procedure that is performed primarily on children, who have no say in the matter.[66]

FGM is strongly linked to the fear of female sexuality within the patriarchal context. The study of this practice, conducted by WHO in 1995, clearly states that "FGM entails the cutting of healthy functioning body organs to comply with a traditional ritual which has no justification on health grounds. The female genital organ plays a vital role in the sexual response of women, and cutting or removal of even a few millimeters of highly sensitive tissue results in substantial damage."[67] The honor of the community is strongly linked to female sexuality, and FGM is a method to control the sexuality of women. The good woman is the less sexually active and conscious woman, and there is a belief that amputation of the clitoris will reduce female sexual desire and, therefore, make her more likely to be chaste and faithful.

FGM, as the physical expression of fear of female sexuality, is violence against women's sexuality and their healthy sexual enjoyment. It is the violation of a woman's right to own a healthy body and to enjoy the functioning and feeling of a healthy body. When the patriarchal gender structure succeeds in alienating the female body, FGM represents the ultimate, explicitly violent culmination of this alienation. If society can tolerate the alienation of the female body, it can easily tolerate the mutilation of the female body. Reflecting on her own mutilation, el-Saadawi says: "Now we know what it is. Now we know where our tragedy lies. We were born of a special sex, the female sex. We are destined in advance to taste of misery, and to have a part of our body torn away by cold, unfeeling cruel hands."[68]

The fear and pain associated with this practice are enormous and have deeply pervasive psychological effects on girls. The vivid accounts of Nawal el-Saadawi's own experience with FGM leaves no doubt that FGM is nothing but a violent act against women:

> All I remember is that I was frightened and that there were many of them, and that something like an iron grasp caught hold of my hand and my arms and my thighs, so that I became unable to resist or even to move. I also remember the icy touch of the bathroom tiles under my naked body, and unknown voices and humming sounds interrupted now and again by a rasping metallic sound which reminded me of the butcher when he used to sharpen his knife before slaughtering a sheep for the *Eid* [religious festival]. . . . I screamed with pain despite the tight hand held over my mouth, for the pain was not just a pain, it was like a searing flame that went through my whole body. After a few moments, I saw a red pool of blood around my hips.[69]

The impact of society's tolerance of pain and violence in the name of ritual and sexuality can also be understood through men's experiences with circumcision. Even though this practice is perceived to be associated with an increase in masculinity and male potency, pain is the only lens through which men experience it. Dwyer in her study of Morocco remarks: "Most feel that the memory has little social, religious, or psychological meaning; the boy remembers only the gross outlines of pain."[70]

Thus, FGM is clearly experienced as pain and violence by those who are subjected to it. The WHO Technical Working Group on FGM concludes that this practice is "a form of violence against girls and women that has serious physical and psychological consequences which adversely affect heath. Furthermore, it is a reflection of discrimination against women and girls."[71] Rahman and Toubia also assert this fact: "The act itself—the cutting of healthy genital organs for non-medical reasons—is at its essence a basic violation of girls' and women's rights to physical integrity. This is true regardless of the degree of cutting or of the extent of the complications that may or many not ensue."[72] Cases of death resulting from this mutilation occur frequently. In Egypt, this practice has led to the death of an 11-year-old girl, Budour Ahmed Shaker, in June 2007 while undergoing the procedure at a private, illegal medical clinic in the southern province of Minya.[73]

There are studies that also reveal a correlation between supporting FGM and condoning other types of violence against women. A study conducted by UNICEF found evidence of a correlation between views on wife-beating and women's support of FGM. In Egypt, women who support the continuation of FGM are 2.3 times more likely to agree that wife-beating is acceptable than those who do not support the continuation of the practice. Also, women who support FGM are 3.2 times more likely to agree that a husband is justified in beating his wife if she argues with him.[74]

Considering the strong link between FGM and violence, it is natural that the trauma, fear and pain a genitally mutilated woman experiences will gradually nurture her more negative, violent, abusive, and apathetic characteristics. It is a deeply traumatizing experience that leaves severe psychological scars and that will impact the personality of the woman and her relation to the outside word. It is very possible that this experience of violence will spawn a subconscious apathy or violent feelings toward her relationships with her children, husband, and others.

One of the manifestations of this violent act is the feeling of betrayal and indifference, which characterizes the relationship between mother and daughter after this experience. It is no wonder that the mother herself takes active part in the exercise of mutilating her own daughter, considering the impact it has had on her own life. According to UNICEF, 79 percent of women support this practice in the Sudan, 71 percent in Egypt and 21 percent in Yemen.[75] The mother's support of the mutilation of her own daughter clearly shows that women are also capable of perpetrating violence. Having little concern for the pain that the daughter will be subjected to is a form of violence. The story of el-Saadawi illustrates how the mother acts as an accomplice in this form of violence and it highlights the relationship of betrayal and apathy between mother and daughter:

I did not know what they had cut off from my body, and I did not try to find out. I just wept, and called out to my mother for help. But the worst shock of all was when I looked around and found her standing by my side. Yes, it was her, I could not be mistaken, in flesh and blood, right in the midst of these strangers, talking to them and smiling at them, as though they had not participated in slaughtering her daughter just a few moments ago.[76]

Camilia is an Egyptian Copt who remembers this about her experience: "My mother kept reassuring me by telling me: 'Once you have the operation, you will grow taller and prettier and your complexion will be fair and clear.' They deceived us with such remarks. I particularly resented this deception when I learned that my cousin, who was circumcised on the same day in another house, had severe hemorrhaging and was about to die."[77] Alice Walker comments on the seriousness of the implication of this betrayal:

But the mother's betrayal of the child is one of the cruelest aspects of it. Children place all their love and trust in their mothers. When you think of the depth of betrayal of the child's trust, this is an emotional wounding, which will never go away. The sense of betrayal, the sense of not being able to trust anyone, will stay with the child as she grows up. I think that is a reason why in a lot of the cultures that we are talking about, there is so much distrust, so much dissension, and so much silence. There is all this unspoken pain, this unspoken suffering that nobody is really dealing with, nobody is airing, and it goes somewhere, it always does.[78]

It has been argued that there is a strong cultural justification for the practice of FGM. This practice has been associated with the rites of passage for girls to womanhood; sexual maturity and reproduction; purification and cleanliness; preserving virginity and prevention of promiscuity and adultery; better marriage prospects; enhancement of male sexual pleasure; and religious requirement. However, the relationships between FGM, culture, religion, tradition, and modernity are issues too complex to be dealt with within the limited scope of this study. Further research is needed in this area.

CHAPTER 3

Crime and Honor

El-khammeh ma ilha illa el-tammeh (The best way to treat filth is to bury it).

—Palestinian proverb

HONOR KILLING

As in many cultures, taboo subjects are rarely spoken of in the Middle East, and the issue of honor killing is one that remains buried particularly deep underneath the rug of society. Formal information about honor killings is scarce. The scale of honor killings in the Middle East is unknown because few studies have been conducted in this area. The figures that do exist are based on cases that have been reported to authorities or have come to court. The actual number of these cases is much higher, but it is difficult to estimate because these killings are often disguised as accidents and often go unreported. The United Nations estimates that more than 5,000 women worldwide are killed each year in the name of honor.[1] In Pakistan, 600 women were killed in 2003. In Jordan, 18 women between the ages of 18 and 45 were killed in 2006. In the Palestinian territories, 15 women were killed from May, 2004 to March, 2005.[2]

According to the Mediterranean Women Web site, 25 women are killed annually in Jordan in the name of family honor. Honor crimes constitute 25 percent of the annual homicides in Jordan. Official statistics indicate that the majority of women killed in honor crimes are teenagers. Most are buried in unmarked graves and are disgraced even in death.[3] Police records in Amman show that every year some 20–25 unmarried women who have been involved in "honor" issues are held in protective custody. Most of them were killed hours or days after their release from custody. According to police records, every year 20–25 women are killed "in the name of honor." In many cases, autopsies revealed that the victims were virgins. These crimes are handled most discreetly by authorities, and in some cases the offending women were killed and buried without the knowledge of the authorities.[4] A study conducted by the UN Development Fund for Women (UNIFEM) in November of 2007 states that a quarter of all women killed in Jordan under the banner of illicit relationships are put to death because they are merely suspected of being involved in a clandestine relationship. Yet only 15 percent of these women are killed after adultery is actually proven. Figures also show that 45.1 percent of crimes are committed by the victims' brothers, 15 percent by their husbands, and 14 percent by a close relative. According to the study, at least 97 women were killed for so-called reasons of honor between 2000 and 2003.[5]

Even though it is conventionally believed that honor killings are crimes restricted to rural or tribal areas, there are reports of these occurrences in major urban cities across the Middle East. A UN report indicates that this is, in fact, an urban phenomenon, as the majority of honor crimes committed in Jordan were in major cities rather than rural areas normally dominated by conservative tribes. According to the study, between the year 2000 and 2003, there were as many as 36 cases of murder in Amman, 17 in Irbid, 13 in Balqa, and 11 in Zarqa. However, the number of honor crimes committed in the smaller conservative city of Maan, near the Saudi border, was 2, and in Tafelah 3.[6] An alternative explanation for this is that the number of cases that are actually reported is much higher in cities than in more traditional and conservative areas.

According to the statistics of the Ministry of Women's Affairs in the Palestinian territories, in 2004 alone, 20 girls and women were murdered in the name of family honor. Another 15 women were victims of attempted murder, and 50 women committed suicide. The ministry also believes that these numbers do not reflect the full extent of the problem.[7] It is suspected that 70 percent of all murders in Gaza and the West Bank are the result of honor killings.[8] Between January of 2006 and March 7, 2007, 17 women were targeted and killed in Gaza for reasons of honor. This is an increase from an average of 10 honor killings per year that occurred between the years 2000 and 2005, according to the Women's Center for Legal Aid and

Counseling in Gaza, citing statistics from the Palestinian Authority's attorney general. About half of the recent honor killings in Gaza were carried out by armed religious groups rather than family members. According to human rights organizations this is a new and alarming phenomenon.[9]

A Web site devoted to women's rights in Syria states that there are an estimated 200–300 women killed in Syria under the name of honor. Despite the seriousness of these statistics, the minister of social affairs and employment, a female, believes this number is insignificant to represent "a phenomenon worth stopping at," and the Syrian Union for Women denies these crimes exist. Parliament, which is composed of both men and women, has dismissed these claims as incidents merely relating to "customs and traditions."[10] According to the *New York Times*, until recently, the discussion of honor killing was banned from Syrian media. The incidents were allowed to be discussed individually as "accidents," but speaking of honor killing as a phenomenon was forbidden. Now, the media is becoming much more open to exposing these subjects.[11] In Lebanon, an average of one woman per month is killed by a close male relative.[12]

Dozens of young women are murdered in Turkey every year by their elder brothers, younger brothers, male cousins, and fathers. There are no reliable statistics, but it is thought that at least 60 women die in honor killings in Turkey each year. Others believe the true figure is much higher.[13] Honor killings are rampant in the Kurdish areas of Turkey, Iraq, and Iran. Kurdish women are killed almost every day for supposedly dishonoring their families.[14] The UN Assistance Mission for Iraq's (UNAMI) reports on human rights have regularly pinpointed honor killings as one of Iraq's most serious human rights abuses.[15]

However, these statistics do not portray the picture of honor killing in the Middle East and the severity of this problem to its fullest extent. Many honor crimes are disguised as accidents or suicides. A 2003 report by the UN states:

A problem closely related to the maintenance of female virginity and family honor is the high rate of suicide among young girls in Turkey. Girls commit suicide in large numbers because they have lost their virginity or because they have been forced into marriage or sent away to special reeducation establishments. Oftentimes, a woman who has somehow violated the family "honor" is given the choice of committing suicide, rather than being killed by a family member, and usually women choose this option.[16]

Honor killings also occur in immigrant communities in Western countries. On February 3, 2008 a 16-year-old girl died after falling from a fourth-floor balcony in Malmö, in the south of Sweden. Police investigations in Sweden reported that in less than a year, from March 12, 2007 to February 3, 2008, there were seven cases of alleged suicide attempts involving young women with Middle Eastern backgrounds who had jumped from balconies. Three of these cases resulted in death, and four caused severe injuries. The police suspect this to be a new pattern of hiding homicide or forced suicides.[17]

The *Los Angeles Times* reported the story of a 16-year-old Turkish woman who accused her father of ordering her death. He had arranged for her to marry a man she wanted nothing to do with, but she complied long enough to become pregnant by him. She then left her husband, inciting her father to offer her one single option, suicide. She fled to the police and was placed in a shelter where she gave birth to her child. Victims in the same shelter also said they had been ordered by relatives to kill themselves and had been locked in a room with a gun or a rope and were expected to slit their wrists as their relatives watched over.[18] In Shalhoub-Kevorkian's interviews with Palestinian police regarding the incidences of honor killings she mentions the following:

> The interviewed police officers stated that there is an apparent trend in society to cover up the crime expeditiously to reduce the subsequent damage that may be incurred on the family and community. The need to cover up was mentioned by a respondent who explained that a father killed his daughter and reported to the police two hours later that she was missing. One police officer stated, 'They do what they feel they need to do to protect their honor, but then they cover it up with stories such as she fell, was burned, or wanted to commit suicide. We suspect that it was murder rather than suicide, but we also do not want to add pain to the family. The woman is dead, why cause more pain?'[19]

Honor killing is strongly related to the protection of honor in patriarchal societies. Perpetrators of these crimes are loaded with the pressures of a male-centered culture. The honor of men and the community is mostly, if not solely, linked to the restriction of female relatives' sexuality, thereby establishing a cult of virginity within the lives of Middle Eastern families. Forced virginity testing by family members continues to be widespread and according to UN reports is, in fact, endorsed by government officials in Turkey. "Women are frequently taken to the hospital for a virginity test by parents who suspect that the woman has lost her virginity, or by husbands who, on the wedding night, suspect that their new wife is not a virgin. Although the doctors must ask for the woman's consent before performing the exam, women have little choice but to consent given the circumstances and the social pressure to obey their husband and parents."[20]

A man's masculinity is socially constructed through his ability to deny other men sexual access to his female relatives. Therefore, masculinity is also related to punishing transgressions of this moral code. In her study of Palestinian society, Shalhoub-Kevorkian argues: "The concept of 'rujuleh' (manhood) is incorporated in the mental perception of the family. One cannot remain a 'rajul' (man) if he remains silent towards perceived sexual transgressions by his female relatives."[21]

Under the rule of the strictly rigid moral code, there is zero tolerance toward women who violate this moral code to the point that women are expected to defend the code until death. If a woman has not died defending herself in the case of misbehavior, it is the duty of the men in the family to make sure that she does. One Palestinian tribal leader put it this way: "So if they are still alive, which they should not, then they do not deserve to survive the dishonoring and therefore they should die." Another tribal notable stated: "Women in this society know very well that behaving contrary to social norms could very well lead to their death and no one will hold the killer responsible for his act. To the contrary, he will be seen as honorable."[22] The Palestinian press also reported the story of a 4-year-old girl who was raped by a 25-year-old man; her family left her to bleed to death because she had "dishonored" her family. The child survived, but her "honor" was marred for life.[23]

Apart from killing, another way these transgressions are dealt with is to force the girl to marry her abuser, or another much older man, resulting in a very incompatible marriage. Thus, once a woman has been abused, there is no way for her to escape her destiny of victimization and violence. This fact is made clear by the Palestinian tribal notable's recommended courses of action for stopping the killing of women: prohibition of mixing between the sexes; prohibition of women working outside their homes; marrying girls at an early age so that they do not have the opportunity to become "loose"; and encouraging polygamy.[24]

Since the honor of men is linked to female sexuality, condoning honor killing is widespread in the Middle East. Parrot and Cummings contend: "There is a deep rooted cultural acceptance of honor killing in many communities resulting in inaction to stop it. There is little public moral or social outrage about honor killing. It is related to perceptions of worth of women and their role in society."[25] A report by the UN states that many nongovernmental organizations do not consider honor killings to be a human rights concern but rather a "social issue."[26] In fact, in societies in which culture revolves around a strong and central form of the male ego, shaming the honor of men is considered to be the real crime rather than the killing of women. In this twisted moral reality, the offender is not the killer, *but the girl* who has tarnished the family's honor and reputation. In this sense, honor killing *is considered justice.* In her study of honor killing in Palestine, Ruggi comments: "In many communities, this means that murder in the name of honor is family business, not frowned upon by the local community. As a result, the murderer is unlikely to be reprimanded in court."[27] A UN poll conducted in 2006 points out that 17 percent of Turkish men said they approved of honor killings. A much higher percentage approved of lesser punishments.[28] A poll conducted through a Syrian Web site devoted to women's issues, during a period from January 16 to February 16 of 2008, asked participants to respond to the question: "Do you agree that your female relative should marry a man who is convicted of honor killing?" According to the results, 55.6 percent answered "no" and an astonishing 41% answered "yes."[29]

Very few reported cases of honor killings reach the trial stage due to social condoning of these acts. The exceptional cases that do end in conviction receive only token sentences. This leniency renders the law inadequate for the protection of woman's social rights, including the right to live. Most of the penal codes in the Middle East contain conditions of leniency in cases involving men's honor. A few months of incarceration are a common punishment for these crimes. A royal commission on human rights in Jordan has proposed stricter measures of controlling honor killings by introducing a bill outlining stiff penalties for convicted killers. However, the parliament rejected the bill claiming that it would encourage adultery and create new social problems.[30] A law introduced in northern Iraq in 2002, in theory, allowed convicted killers to be sentenced to death; however, in practice this has occurred only rarely.[31]

Honor killing is such a culturally entrenched tradition that few killers ever express remorse. A UN report mentions the story of Mohammad Rai, from Salt, a town about 20 miles west of the capital Amman, Jordan. He killed his cousin to uphold his family's honor. He was

17 years old at the time and said he was pressured to do it by family elders. A few years later he does not regret his actions: "I would do it again if I had to. People here would have stigmatized my entire family if I had not killed her and shame would have followed us wherever we went." He served only six months in prison because the victim's father had dropped the charges. Her only crime was that she had confessed to her strictly conservative father that she was in love with a man from another family who wanted to ask for her hand in marriage.[32]

The other important factor to note regarding to honor killing is the extent to which women themselves are involved. Mothers and sisters help arrange murders or even kill with their own hands. In Jordan, in 2006, a girl was killed by her mother and sister after they discovered she was in love with one of their neighbors.[33] Shalhoub-Kevorkian also tells the following two stories from Palestine: A married woman felt that the presence of her sister-in-law was negatively affecting her relationship with her husband. Consequently, she claimed that her sister-in-law was having an extramarital affair with another man. Her false claim led to the death of her sister-in-law.[34] In the other case, a female had been subjected to incest with her paternal uncle and conceived a child with him. The family attempted to conceal the crime by hastily marrying her to another man. When the husband discovered that his wife was pregnant, he killed her with the help of her mother.[35]

Women's complicity with honor killings and the support they provide is an interesting issue requiring further academic study. While the involvement of women is a form of female agency, the nature and consequences of this agency must be called into question. Patriarchy restricts women's choice of action to only a few destructive and violent options. Female agency is molded by the patriarchal structure into the form of violence against their own sex, thereby forming a linkage between female agency and criminality in the name of honor. From the perspective of women who perpetrate or contribute to honor killings, they have been forced into obedience and oppression their entire lives; why, then, would they choose to take a different course of action, by allowing some women to behave differently? After all, violating the strict and rigid sexual moral code would mean violating a fundamental sense of life women come to know in the patriarchal context. If the "crime" of one woman, or perhaps a few, goes unpunished, what sense would the majority of submissive women make of their obedience and misery? If honor and pride are not forcefully linked to submissiveness, how else would women tolerate their misery? This destructive, patriarchal, female agency, which causes death and misery for many women, also reflects the self-interestedness of some women in this respect. In this situation, it seems as though patriarchy is the antithesis of empathy and solidarity in the female world.

STORIES FROM THE MIDDLE EAST

In 2007, two girls in the town of Edleb, Syria were killed for committing crimes of honor. Jasmine Kefaya's brother murdered her by slicing her throat with a knife. He went straight to the police surrendering himself, and shouting: "I washed away the shame!" Another victim, Eman Watta, had not reached 23 years of age when she was divorced by her husband because he suspected infidelity from her. He sent her to her parents' house knowing fully what her fate would be. It was not long before her brother slew her in the bathroom of their parent's house and then turned himself in to the police.[36]

Omaima was disposed of within minutes of her birth on September 4, 2007 in a rubbish bin in Jordan. This is her story. A young man and woman from the Jordanian middle class fell in love. The girl's family refused to allow them to marry, which led to the couple's clandestine relationship resulting in pregnancy. As abortion was out of the question, the delivery took place in a quiet room in the family house while all the men were away. The mother's mother and her two sisters delivered the baby girl, and were prepared to send her straight from womb to tomb. The baby's life was saved by a care center. The parents are now facing charges of adultery, which carries a minimum sentence of five years in Jordan. Not only that, but the police fear that Omaima's mother could be killed after leaving prison.[37]

Faten Habash is a Palestinian woman who died at the hands of her father after being beaten repeatedly over the head with an iron bar. Her desperate cries drew in people from the street, but they were too late to help and only her lifeless body was found. This happened shortly after she had returned to the family house from the hospital where she had spent time recovering from a broken pelvis and various other injuries that were the result of an earlier beating by her father and other family members. Her crime was her insistence on marrying a man her parents did not approve of.[38] "One day my brother took me to a deserted area and began beating me with a rock," said another girl after her family had suspected she was pregnant out of wedlock and had tried to kill her. The victim's brother severely beat her and slashed her with a knife before leaving her to die in an abandoned area near the Baqaa refugee camp in Jordan.[39]

Sevda Gok was 16 years old in 1996 when she was knifed to death by her 14-year-old cousin, Mehemet, in a village in Turkey. He stabbed her with a knife in the stomach and hip and then slit her throat in a public area so that the killing would "serve as a warning to others." Mehemet said: "She made us suffer, shamed us, and disgraced us. We were insulted by people in our community. I restored our honor." Yet, Sevda was a virgin.[40] Also in Turkey, Recve Aslan was killed in 2002 by her brother, in order to restore the family's honor, because she had been raped at the age of 11 and was therefore no longer a virgin.[41] A UN report tells this story from a village in southeastern Turkey:

> Desperately unhappy, 21-year-old Sahe Fidan left the husband she despised and sought refuge in her parents' home. But they refused to take her in. A married woman can leave her husband only in a coffin, they told her. Fidan returned to the husband, and she left him in a coffin. She was found hanged in the bathroom, her infant son strapped to her back with a sheet. Fidan had committed suicide. Yet, in the village, another version circulated: she may have joined the ranks of Turkish women forced to kill themselves, or whose slayings are disguised to look self-inflicted. Women are compelled to commit suicide in so-called honor killings.[42]

Another report by the UN tells this story of forced suicide in Jordan:

> They put me in the guest room and everybody started suggesting how I should kill myself. Even my aunt said everybody should leave the house to allow me to turn on a gas cylinder and kill myself. My brother suggested I hang myself with a rope. I tried to run away but I could not. They kept me in a cupboard under the stairs and gave me a little food every four to five days. I even called out to neighbors to give me food because it was not enough.[43]

Shalhoub-Kevorkian tells this story of a case in which the Palestine police suspect a murder was committed: "A 23 year-old unmarried woman was burned to death. Her family stated that it was an accidental burn from the stove. Her younger sister, however, began to scream at her funeral '*Kataluha . . . Kataluha*' (They killed her; they killed her). The sister's screams were muted because she was unable to prove her allegations. The family explained the sister's behavior to the police as 'delusions' resulting from the deep loss of her beloved sister."[44]

In Jordan, a 16-year-old female was raped by her brother who also threatened to kill her if she told the family. When it was discovered that the young woman was pregnant, she confided in an older brother. When the perpetrating brother learned of this, he tried to kill his sister by cutting her wrists. Another brother of the victim revealed to the police that his family and relatives had then urged *him* to kill his sister in order to cleanse the family's honor. As urged by his family, he stabbed his sister to death with a kitchen knife. The neighbors reported that the relatives who had gathered to witness the event cheered and praised the young murderer because he had cleansed the family's honor.[45] The following case of rape and incest was also reported in Jordan. A 16-year-old was raped several times by her older brother until she became pregnant. Upon returning to her family, she underwent an abortion and was forced to marry a man 50 years older who divorced her six months later. She was immediately killed by her family, ultimately because her brother had raped her.[46]

This story from Palestine also involves a victim's sister. The family of a young 16-year-old female suspected she had become pregnant. She confessed to her sister that she had been impregnated by her cousin. While the girl was sleeping, the sister put ten bags of detergent into a larger plastic bag and placed it on her sister's face, mouth, and nose, and firmly pressed it against the face. She then went to bed knowing her sister had just died. Although an autopsy revealed suffocation was the cause of death, the accused sister was convicted of involuntary manslaughter and sentenced to a term of imprisonment of only one year.[47]

On January 22, 2007 Zahra Ezo gasped her last breath on an intensive care bed in a hospital in Damascus, Syria after being stabbed in her back four times and once in her neck. The crime was committed by her brother in defense of his "honor." Zahra, who had just turned 16, was kidnapped by a family friend. While the kidnapper went to prison, *she* became the target of her family in order to wash away the shame. Even though she reached the girls' care center in Damascus, she could not be saved. During the nine months of her stay in the center, she had escaped two murder attempts. The first had been an attempt by her brother and the second by her uncle. She was finally killed by her brother on January 21, 2007.[48]

In September 2007, a 90-year-old man from the Abu Nusseir village, 19 miles west of Amman, Jordan, shot and killed his 35-year-old daughter because the neighbors had seen a man leaving her house. The killer confessed to committing the crime in order to cleanse the family's honor. The victim, Khitam, had been divorced and lived with her two daughters and her son near her parent's house.[49]

Kifaya, a Jordanian girl of 12, was intelligent and full of curiosity. But when she returned home one evening from a walk in the neighborhood with some friends, she was confronted by her infuriated father. Amidst his shouting that she has dishonored the entire family, her father proceeded to beat Kifaya with sticks and iron chains until she died. He told the police he killed his only daughter because she went for walks without his permission.[50] Shaaban witnessed an honor killing during her childhood in a Syrian village:

> I had just reached the police station, heading towards the school, when I saw my class-mate Aziz joyfully descending a hill in the centre of the village, waving a dagger dripping with blood and chanting, "I've killed her and saved the family's honor!" He ran up to two policemen who were standing outside the station, handed them the dagger and said in a voice loud enough for everyone around to hear, "I have killed my sister and have come to hand myself over for justice." The three of them strolled slowly into the police station, chatting amicably. Yemen, his sister was only sixteen years old. But what happened to the killer? Aziz was imprisoned for only six months. What is more, he emerged from prison with a mysteriously heroic air. Somehow he became one of the most notable personalities in the village. Shortly afterwards he left for the Gulf States, where he worked to get some money together. When he came back he opened up a bakery in the village and started feeding the village people with bread made with the same hands that had cut his sister's throat and had been dipped in her blood.[51]

In a shelter secretly located near the town of Suleimaniya in the region of Kurdistan, Iraq, 12 women are hiding together for protection. One pretty girl who identified herself only as "H" described how she had fallen in love with a 25-year-old man when she was 18. Her father had ordered her to marry an older business associate instead and was so enraged when she refused that he sent her to live with her grandmother. There, she learned that her boyfriend had been shot dead by her father and brother who had also bragged that she would be next. Another woman there, "J," was forced to marry a much older man when she was only 16 years old. She had bumped into a former sweetheart while shopping and was discovered by her relatives. Assuming

the worst of the situation, her family drove the two of them to a remote area where J's nose was cut off with a knife and her ex-boyfriend
lost an ear.[52]

In the same region, Rustum Mohamed Ali, aged 32, has been unable to provide for his wife and four children, ages 7 to 12, since he has
been jailed two years previously for killing his pregnant, unmarried
niece and her lover. He first shot the lover in the garden of his home
with a Kalashnikov and then went indoors and shot his niece with the
same weapon. He said: "No man can stand for his family's honor to
be defiled."[53] Even Kurdish immigrant communities in the West have
failed to escape this phenomenon. On January 22, 2002 Fadime Sa-
hindal, a Kurdish university student from Turkey, was killed by her
father while living in Sweden because she rejected her arranged marriage and chose to select her own partner instead. Several other cases
of honor killings involving girls from various immigrant communities
have been reported in a number of Western countries.

In 2007 another despicable crime was reported in the Kurdish hill-
side village of Basshiqa in northern Iraq. Du'aa, a 17-year-old girl
from a Yazidi sect, a religious minority living mostly in northern Iraq,
and a 19-year-old Sunni Muslim, Muhannad, fell in love and wanted
to get married. However, their determination to marry outraged
their respective communities. The lovers fled but were soon found
together in an olive grove. They were suspected of illicit sexual behavior and Du'aa told her mother, in what would prove to be a poignant
last meeting, "I promise you I am still a virgin, I did nothing wrong,
Mama." While Muhannad was locked up in prison, Du'aa found herself being dragged to the marketplace to be stoned to death for the
sake of her family's honor. A mob of more than 25 male relatives came
with guns and stones, shouting and screaming in anger, demanding
that she be killed in order to "cleanse the family honor." Neither the
objection of the father, nor his solution that they marry her off to a
cousin and move to Syria could stop the mob. In the marketplace, she
came under a hail of stones and her face and clothes were soon covered
in blood. Finally, one cousin smashed a large piece of concrete over
her head to end the spectacle. The atrocious event was filmed using
a mobile phone and was posted on the internet. Her body was tossed
in a rubbish pit. Afterward, even her grave was attacked. A grenade
was lobbed into the garden of the family's home, shattering windows
and leaving the family in no doubt that the community wanted them
to leave. Every day after sunset the mother would throw herself on
the mud grave and cry in deep bitter grief, howling: "Come to mama,

Du'aa . . . the last thing you told me was that you were hungry. Come home. Let me cook, and feed you . . . You were a good girl, you were honor itself and I miss you, so please come to me in my dreams, I beg you." Du'aa's final words pleading her innocence had been confirmed afterward with an autopsy, Du'aa was a virgin. [54]

Norma Khouri is a woman from Jordan who wrote a book dedicated to her friend and business associate, Dalia, whose life was precipitately ended in a crime of honor. The 25-year-old Dalia, happy and full of life, had defied the strictly rigid moral and religious code on two accounts. The first act of defiance was that she had fallen in love within a culture that criminalizes premarital love; her second indiscretion was that she, a Muslim girl, had fallen in love with a Christian man. Even though the autopsy confirmed that Dalia was still a virgin, the outcome of her dual insolence proved to be the tragic end to her life in the name of family honor.[55]

CHAPTER 4

Islam, Gender, and Violence

In front of me are a thousand and one executioners
Behind me, are a thousand and one butchers
Dear Lord, is there no disgrace but my nakedness?
Dear Lord, does this East have no occupation
But to fuss over my hemline?

—*Nizar Qabbani (1923–1998), poet*

ISLAM AND DOMESTIC VIOLENCE

Islam plays a significant role in defining the terms of social existence in the Middle East, and this influence has increased tremendously with the recent rise of political Islam. Despite Islam's increasing impact on life in the region, Islam's principles are far beyond critical discussion at the societal level. Surely, religion is sacred, but only in so much as it is a private relationship between the individual and God. Once religion has imposed itself on society and politics, there is no doubt that religion *must* be scrutinized in the same way as all other aspects of social existence are. Yet this kind of critical discussion is not the examination of Islam in religious terms but is a discussion of Islam as politics. In this sense, every religion should be open to inquiry, and Islam is no exception.

All monotheistic religions reflect the patriarchal systems they exist in, and they help enforce patriarchal structures on society. Not only did the emergence of Islam indicate a shift in the society where it first developed (Arabia) toward patriarchy, but it served as an agent of this transition. Islam encompasses all the patriarchal values that emphasize gender inequality, male control and domination, and the inferiority of women. Yet Islam is not alone in this regard. Other religions also preach the superiority of men and the debasement of women. For example, a Jewish Orthodox prayer states "I thank thee, lord, that thou has not created me a woman." In fact, in a study of domestic violence in low-income Lebanese families, Keenan, el-Hadad, and Balian find that violence against women is even more prevalent among Christian Armenians.[1]

The Qur'an, which is central to the religious doctrine of Islam, clearly enforces patriarchy and inequality between the sexes:

> If you fear that you cannot treat orphans with fairness, then you may marry other women who seem good to you: two, three, or four of them. But if you fear that you cannot maintain equality among them, marry one only or any slave-girls you may own. This will make it easier for you to avoid injustice. (Q 4:3, Women)
>
> Allah has thus enjoined you concerning your children: A male shall inherit twice as much as a female. (Q 4:11, Women)
>
> You are also forbidden to take in marriage married women, except captives whom you won as slaves. Such is the decree of Allah. (Q 4:24, Women)
>
> Men have authority over women because Allah has made the one superior to the others, and because they spend their wealth to maintain them. Good women are obedient. They guard their unseen parts because Allah has guarded them. As for those from whom you fear disobedience, admonish them and send them to beds apart and beat them. Then if they obey you, take no further action against them. Allah is high, supreme. (Q 4:34, Women)
>
> Women are your fields: go, then, into your fields as you please. (Q 2:223, the Cow)
>
> Divorced women must wait, keeping themselves from men, three menstrual courses. It is unlawful for them, if they believe in Allah and the Last Day, to hide what He has created in their wombs: in which case their husbands would do well to take them back, should they desire reconciliation. Women shall with justice have rights similar to those exercised against them, although men have a status above women. Allah is mighty and wise. (Q 2:228, the Cow)
>
> Call in two male witnesses from among you, but if two men cannot be found, then one man and two women whom you judge fit to act as witnesses. (Q 2:282, the Cow)[2]

In fact, the Qur'an contains many positive references to women. Yet it is clear from the verses above taken from the Qur'an that there is a strong relationship between Islam and the patriarchal notion that men are superior to women. With time, these verses became "legitimate" sources for suppression and debasement of women throughout the Middle East. Several of the Prophet Muhammad's sayings, called *hadith*, also support this linkage, such as "Women are deficient in intellect and religion," or "Women have been omitted by God from his mercy." These sayings, which coexist with several positive sayings of Muhammad about women, are fully embraced in the cultural traditions of the Middle East. However, the controversy over the authenticity and conscious historical manipulation of these sayings makes it difficult to incorporate them into the discussion as a reliable source. Regardless of Muhammad's sayings, it is apparent in many verses of the Qur'an that Islam reflects and enforces patriarchal gender values.

Social inequality and the obedience of women, which are values sanctioned by Islam and enforced by the patriarchal gender structure, encourage violence toward women. The inequality enshrined by Islam leads to the institutionalization of structural violence. Because of Islam's association with patriarchy, religion becomes a "legitimate" source of gender violence found in these societies. Parrot and Cummings assert: "The root cause of violence against women is patriarchy and gender inequality. Evidence suggests that patriarchy holds the most prominent position in supporting and promoting violence against women cross-culturally . . . patriarchy neutralizes women's potential within a culture."[3] They continue: "The more traditional the gender role and male dominance over women, the more likely that violence occurs . . . cultures with more traditional patriarchal attitudes and more extreme condition of subordination, generate more violence."[4]

The Qur'an states that obedient women are good women. Yet a relationship based on obedience is a concrete expression of power and violence. Thus, the Qur'anic injunction that a wife should obey her husband is an unmistakable invitation of domestic violence. Al-Torki stresses: "The Islamic view equates obedience to a husband with obedience to Allah. She must obey her husband and observe his wishes, as a religious duty that is backed by the value system of the community."[5] Thus, religiously and culturally sanctioned obedience of a wife to her husband inevitably increase domestic violence, hidden animosity, and conflict between partners.

Any violent relationship based on domination and obedience generates an opposite reaction or a likewise violent tension of resistance between abuser and abused. It is clearly stated in verse 4:34 of the Qur'an, referenced earlier, that the Qur'an allows a husband to beat a disobedient and resistant wife. There are, however, some translations of the Qur'an that add the word "lightly" after "beat them." However, this is unsupported by the original Arabic text. Likewise, some modern interpretations of this verse actually soften the harshness of this sanction. Nevertheless, this verse clearly bestows religious legitimization on violence against women. Mernissi states: "The duty of the man to command his wife is embodied in his right to correct her by physical beating. The Qur'an itself recommends such a measure, as a last resort."[6] Being the champion of patriarchy, Islam naturally discourages resistance to patriarchal dominance and increases the intensity of domestic violence in society overall. Because open resistance is religiously suppressed, resistance is driven to more covert forms that are not necessarily less violent than overt acts of resistance.

Marriage is the only form of romantic and sexual interaction between the sexes that is tolerated or encouraged by Islam. However, Islam also imposes patriarchal gender values on marriage, which negates any sense of equality between partners. In this sense, Islam is a destabilizing factor in the structure of power between men and women united in marriage. The superiority of men, emphasized in verse 2:228 and the controversial verse 4:34 of the Qur'an, is justified on two grounds: God prefers one sex over the other, without further explanation of why this is so; the second is that men provide for women. The religiously warranted exclusion of women from the financial domain, a defining aspect of the power relationship between partners, tips the balance of power between husband and wife in the man's favor. Yodanis suggests: "A physical violence by intimate partners is better explained by the relative resource distribution between male and female partners, rather than women's overall social standing in educational and occupational institutions."[7] Inevitably, imbalances in any power structure will lead to violence, and this is no exception.

Thus, the kind of marriage Islam encourages is patriarchal marriage in which the superiority of the man and submission of the woman are unquestionable. Joseph argues: "A Muslim marriage left women structurally vulnerable. Due to this structural vulnerability of inequality, submission to the religiously prescribed control of the husband, easy divorce and polygamy, the need for the support, and therefore the control of natal family over the life of women is even felt more. By so doing, Islam is supporting patriarchal gender structure in society."[8] Friedl contends that women refuse to obey their husband's orders as a way of challenging or inconveniencing their husbands. "Yet, for a woman refusing obedience or services to her husband, no matter how extreme the demand, is a sin, and a 'female' sin is sanctioned negatively in the Islamic moral code . . . Women who resort to refusal as a tool of power are told they are courting punishment in the afterlife as well as in this life."[9]

Thus, there is a clear correlation between patriarchal gender inequality and violence against women. Yodanis affirms: "A structure of gender inequality is associated with a culture of violence against women. The more unequal women are compared to men in a society, the more likely men are being violent toward women."[10] Indeed, religiously inscribed male superiority and control, along with female inferiority, submission, and obedience, contribute to daily violence against women in the Middle East. Women who participated in a study conducted in Bahrain in 2006 identified the following reasons for violence committed against women: men's desire to control and dominate women, social upbringing and socialization, and "narrow interpretation" of religious texts that refer to the excellence of men over women and men's right to discipline women, (ta'deeb).[11]

There is a story of a man who divorced his wife in the town of Ta'if, Saudi Arabia. In an act of revenge, the woman's male relatives collectively divorced their own wives—relatives of this man. This act left six wives, with 14 children between them, divorced.[12] This kind of behavior aligns with the religious sanctioning of male domination over women and the unilateral male right to divorce. Divorce threats are, in fact, part of the daily drama caused by male supremacy in many households in the Middle East.

However, in addition to the conservative, orthodox, and explicitly misogynist version of Islam, two tendencies in Middle Eastern society that explain violence against women need to be mentioned in this regard. The first tendency is to claim that originally Islam was an egalitarian and women-friendly religion and it is only later interpretations of the text that have created a misogynistic Islam. The claim is that if it weren't for the male, conservative interpretation of this religion, Islam would have otherwise remained egalitarian and women-friendly. This argument makes a distinction between intent, which is always good and egalitarian, and actual practices that dominate the region that represents a departure from the true intention of original Islam. While it is true that Islam, like any religion, has eventually become more conservative and misogynist, discussing this important debate and the merits and limitations of reforms within the Islamic thinking

goes beyond the limited scope of this book. However, a less controversial issue is the fact that religion, and Islam as it is understood and
practiced by Muslims in the present-day Middle East, supports patriarchy, violence against women, and authoritarian order in society.

The second tendency is to explain away violence against women as
a part of culture or tradition, something separate from religion. Violence against women, honor killing, and female genital mutilation can
be blamed on cultural traditions having nothing to do with religion.
However, this is a simplified solution used to explain away complex
issues like violence, honor, and sexuality. These concepts are, in fact,
strongly related to a set of complex political, economic, social, cultural,
and religious factors. There are two extreme orientations regarding
the relationship between culture and religion. Culture can be understood to encompass religion only, or as being something completely
separate from religion. While culture is not the equivalent of religion,
culture is strongly shaped and influenced by religion. In societies that
still struggle with modernity and its meaning and how it relates to tradition, religion can have a primordial impact. The powerful relationship between religion and culture is not necessarily an illustration of
religious beliefs but is rather a function of the political economy that
is dominant in these societies. More precisely, the influential impact
of religion on culture is an illustration of the failure of the political
economy to advance these societies into a modern, global age.

ISLAMISM AND WOMEN

The rise of political Islam in the Middle East is more an indication
of authoritarianism's failure than it is a revival of religious beliefs in
the region. The failure of the authoritarian regimes to deliver on its
promises and to create a decent and dignified life for citizens has led
to the rise of political Islam in the region. Authoritarian regimes' dis-
enchantment with the nature of secularism has also helped strengthen
political Islam. While Western secularism is based on the separation
between religion and politics, as well as respecting individual rights,
Middle Eastern authoritarian secularism is mostly based on the state's
domination over society and the complete lack of individual freedom
and democracy. The disappointment with authoritarian secularism,
along with economic miseries and the lack of political freedoms, have
made it easier for the rise of militant Islam in the region.

Islamist movements have succeeded in rising to power in several parts
of the Middle East. Nevertheless, Middle Eastern societies' experiences

with political Islam have also been disappointing. Political Islam has not only failed to offer serious, concrete programs to relieve the political-economic crisis in this region, but militant Islam has worsened the calamity through its prioritization of politics of identity, which the Islamists perceive to be in constant conflict with the outside world. For this reason, political Islam is a part of the crisis rather than a solution.

Political Islam's obsession with women and its prioritization of issues regarding women, which constitute a significant part of identity politics, is remarkable. This is not a new trend in Islam, however; it has deep historical roots. From the very early stages of Islam and throughout the long and rich Islamic history, politicization of gender and sexuality has been an integral part of the politics intended to build the Islamic state and community. To be sure, any social construction having a patriarchal influence is necessarily a gender-loaded and misogynist process.

In this sense, it is remarkable to know that the utmost priority of the Islamic revolution in Iran in 1979 was the control of women. Within the first month of the revolution, Khomeini abrogated the family law that had previously given women more rights and ordered women to wear the traditional dress, the chador. One has to wonder why a political revolution that was supposed to redress the many economic and political problems of the country focused instead on dominating women. This obsession and focus on women is common to all cases of political Islam's rise to power. The rule of the Taliban in Afghanistan from 1996 to 2001 is a well-known case in which the Islamists institutionalized the deprivation of women's most basic human rights. Women in Algeria also paid a heavy price at the hands of Islamists following the national election of 1991. The Islamists had won the election but were prevented from taking power by the authoritarian rule, and the resulting conflict sparked a civil war in the country. Also, in the Islamic-ruled Sudan, the restriction of women's rights was accompanied by the enslavement of, mostly, women and children.

The Iranian model has also been replicated in Iraq in the aftermath of the Iraq War in 2003. Even when the country was in the midst of turmoil and confusion following the outset of the war, in December of 2003 the Islamists found the time, energy, and courage to abrogate the previous family law and propose a new law, law 137, which basically deprives women of their previously won rights. Only the strong opposition from women's organizations and the American intervention saved Iraqi women by preventing the Islamists from pushing this proposal forward. However, in the country's first national election in

2005, in which the politicization of religion, or rather the *religionization of politics*, played an influential role, the Islamist religious parties have been, naturally, triumphant. This gave these parties the opportunity to impose their explicitly misogynist agenda on society. The constitution that was drafted following the election clearly states that personal and family issues are under the jurisdiction of the religious laws applicable to any particular community. This represents a major reversal in the status of Iraqi women and the abrogation of one of the most progressive, by the region's standards, family laws in the Middle East that had been effective in Iraq since 1959.

The Islamists in Jordan are strong opponents of pushing forward a parliamentary government bill of law to stiffen the punishment for cases of honor killing, which represent extreme violence against women. The Islamists in Yemen are actively opposing the banning of child marriage, which subjects females to extreme physical and sexual violence. The Islamists in Morocco were not happy with the recently introduced improvements in women's status in the country. The Islamists in Egypt are also constantly arguing about issues concerning women from a conservative and misogynist standpoint. Thus, these experiences with Islamic rule and politics clearly show a positive correlation between greater involvement of Islam in politics and increased control of and violence towards women. The track record of Islamists regarding women's rights protection is extremely poor. By institutionalizing the inferiority of women and sexual discrimination, Islamists encourage a culture of violence towards women in all realms of society including state, community, and individual interactions.

The Islamist rule in Iran has undoubtedly increased violence and discrimination against women in society. The following incidents have occurred under Islamic rule in Iran. "On August 15, 2004, 16-year-old Ateqeh Rajabi was hanged in public in the northern Iranian town of Neka. Her crime was to have sex with her boyfriend. She had no lawyer, nor could her family find one willing to defend her." "In December 2004, Leyla, a 19-year-old girl with a mental age of eight, was sentenced to death for an 'act contrary to chastity.' The sentencing judge ordered her to be flogged before execution." "Thirteen-year-old Zhila Izadi also received a death sentence—later commuted—after being impregnated by her older brother." "On January 7, 2006, an Islamic court in Tehran passed a death sentence on an 18-year-old girl, identified only by her first name, Nazanin. She had stabbed an assailant while fighting off three men who attempted to rape her and her

16-year-old niece. Reports suggested their attackers were members of the *Basij*, a radical militia charged with upholding Islamic principles."[13]

According to the Campaign to Stop Stoning in Iran by Human Rights Education Associates, there are 11 people, 9 of whom are women, waiting to be stoned to death for the accusation of adultery (*zina*). The Iranian penal code stipulates the stoning of married individuals who have committed adultery. This law states that the stones should be "big enough to cause pain, but not big enough to cause instant death." Most of those who are stoned in Iran are women. On July 5, 2007 Jaafar Kiyani, a husband and father of two, was stoned to death after being charged with adultery, while his partner, Makrama Ibrahimi, is currently being held in jail awaiting the same fate.[14] Within the Islamic context, the punishment for having a relationship out of wedlock is 100 lashes if the woman is single and death by stoning if she is married.[15]

Human Rights Watch reported on the case of two sisters, Zohreh, 27, and Azar Kabiri, 28, who had been convicted of adultery in Tehran. They have already received 99 lashes for "illegal relations," based on accusations made by one of their husbands. Yet they were tried again for the same crime after additional accusations surfaced; they have now been sentenced to death by stoning.[16]

According to one Iranian dissident, "being born female is both a capital crime and a death sentence." According to the Women's Forum against Fundamentalism in Iran, two out of every three Iranian women have experienced serious domestic violence. Eighty-one percent of married women have experienced domestic violence in their first year of marriage. Rape victims and suspected prostitutes are quickly jailed, repeatedly raped, and are often impregnated by their guards. In 2004, nearly 4,000 women were arrested in Tehran alone; 649 of them were girls under the age of 14. In the summer of 2005, a court in Tehran barred a young woman from working outside the home after her estranged husband complained that she had disobeyed his order that she was only allowed to be his housewife. This same woman had fled from the marriage two years earlier after being battered by her husband, yet the court confirmed her husband's right to bar her from working outside the home. In November of 2005 an 80-year-old husband clubbed his 50-year-old wife to death, "because he could not tolerate her wearing makeup outside the home."[17] Increasingly in Iran, women are publicly hanged or are slowly and painfully stoned to death for alleged adultery or for having been raped.

The rise of Islamism and the dominance of religious militia and religious political parties reflect the intensified anti-female violence in Iraq. Basra, the second largest city in Iraq, was once a religiously mixed and tolerant community. The city is now practically ruled by religious militias and organized gangs. Here, violence against women has dramatically increased in recent months to the point that women are forced to stay indoors. Replicating the theocratic regimes of Iran and the Taliban in Afghanistan, these extremists are imposing Islamic life on the people of Iraq by strictly forbidding music, cinema, theater, certain types of hairdressing, and the selling of alcohol. They impose strict and rigid moral codes and the veiling of women, called *hijab*, on all of society, including non-Muslim minorities. The United Nations reports that graffiti warning messages have appeared in many areas of Basra. For example, one piece of graffiti in the city center reads: "Your makeup and your decision to forego the headscarf will bring you death."[18] Youssif had an encounter with extremists one day in May of 2007, which motivated him to flee the city with his family. Gunmen stopped him as he and his wife were walking. They asked her about her clothes and why she did not wear a *hijab*. "We were beaten so badly that day when I told them that we are Christians and they threatened to kill me if I would not respect Islam in this city."[19]

Several Muslim and non-Muslim women were not even given the chance to flee the city as they were killed on sight for not abiding by the newly enforced dress code and were subsequently discarded in the garbage. According to official figures, "at least 10 women are killed monthly; some of them are later found in garbage dumps with bullet holes while others are found decapitated or mutilated. The figures are much higher as more cases go unreported by their families who fear reprisals from extremists."[20] Another government figure reports that 133 women were killed in Basra alone during the year 2007. Seventy-nine of these victims were deemed by extremists to have been "violating Islamic teachings." Another 47 victims died in honor killings.[21] The new extremist culture imposed on society supplements an already existing patriarchal culture that tolerates and condones domestic violence towards women. This extreme culture, however, represents a scenario that is even worse for Iraqi women, considering this comes after years of suffering at the hand of a ruthless dictatorship.

World Corporal Punishment Research reported cases of 17 women in Munwashi, Sudan who have been tried for adultery and sentenced to 100 lashes of the whip each. They were tried under Article 146 of Sudan's penal code stating that an offending adulterer shall be punished with execution by stoning if the offender is married or one hundred lashes of the whip if the offender is not married. None of the women were legally represented at their trials, and their punishments were carried out on the same day as their sentencing, denying the women the opportunity to seek legal advice or to apply for an appeal. No men were punished in connection with these convictions.[22] On December 8, 2001 a criminal court in Nyala, Southern Darfur sentenced 18-year-old Abok Alfa Akok, a Christian woman from the Dinka tribe, to death by stoning after finding her guilty of adultery. She was pregnant at the time of her conviction and was not legally represented during her trial.[23]

A number of government directives in the Sudan require that female students and teachers conform to the Islamic dress code in public places and in government offices by wearing head coverings. A Khartoum court ordered 25 students from Ahlia University be flogged for charges of disturbances and obscene acts. The obscene acts referred, apparently, to the female students' wearing pants.[24]

Although Sudanese law prohibits slavery and forced labor, slavery does persist and affects mostly women and children. The taking of slaves and transporting them to parts of central and Northern Sudan continues, particularly in war zones.[25] Despite the law banning slavery, speaking out against slave raiding and slavery is taboo in Sudan, where slavery is very much alive and state-tolerated. A UN report from the International Labor Organization states: "Many women and children abducted in Sudan during the civil war have been reduced to a state of slavery. Very often they fall victim to torture and cruel treatment, including rape. They were then forced to work for their kidnappers or are sold as slaves." Not only are forced labor and slavery severe and ongoing problems in the Sudan that the government fails to take seriously, but slave raids are carried out with the support of government forces. However, the Sudanese regime has dismissed these reports as "mere media propaganda."[26]

A report published by the UK-based organization Anti-Slavery International summarizes the situation of slavery in Sudan. According to their statistics, between 5,000 and 14,000 people—mostly women and children—have been abducted in Sudan since 1983. The Sudanese government was "failing to take adequate steps to end raiding and slavery."[27] In the Sudan, systematic, repeated, public gang rape is also used as a weapon of war. Because tribal honor is bound to female chastity, this is a tactic used to destroy not only the individual woman but her entire social fabric. Many women do not report being raped for the fear that their families will ostracize them, or perhaps it is even because they also blame themselves for the shame they have brought on their families and tribes. According to Amnesty International, eyewitness-survivors have seen girls as young as eight repeatedly gang-raped. Witnesses also report that the girls would have their limbs broken by their captors if they tried to escape. Women and children have also described being kidnapped and kept as domestic and sexual slaves and of being gang-raped every night in captivity. The janjaweed militia accused of committing these atrocities is a government-backed militia.[28] Clearly, the rule of the Islamists in the Sudan has not only failed to improve the situation of women, but has made it even worse, to the point of reintroducing slavery in the modern age.

As far as women are concerned, Algeria's history is a history of betrayal. The active involvement of Algerian women in the fight against French colonialism has not been appreciated or recognized by those who have ruled the country since its independence in 1962. The authoritarian nationalists' betrayal of gender equality was continued by militant Islamists during the civil war, since 1992, when authorities cancelled the general election that was dominated by radical Islamists. These Islamists have been accused of committing serious atrocities against women during their struggle against the government.

Militant Islamists' raping of Algerian women, known as "terrorist rape," has become such a serious problem that the highest religious body in the country has ruled that women who have been raped by "terrorists" are actually allowed to have their pregnancy ended, even though abortion is not allowed in most of the Middle East. There have been an estimated 1,600 known cases of rape, while many others remain hidden in order to avoid family shame. Many girls have also been kidnapped by militants and forced to act as sex slaves. Often, they are killed following the ordeal, usually by having their throats cut. "There were frequent reports of young women being abducted and repeatedly raped, often for weeks at a time. The abductors sought to justify this sexual abuse by referring to it as 'temporary marriage.'" Meriem Yasmina, described how she was held as a sex slave with seven other girls before she managed to escape. She was kidnapped in September of 1997 during a massacre in her village of Tabainet, Medea. During nearly six months of captivity, she was raped repeatedly by about 40 rebels who were 20 to 70 years old. Another three girls told the story of how they escaped from another similar group. They explained how they had to abandon a young girl fleeing with them. She had been seven months pregnant and could not keep up with them as they made their escape in the mountains of Western Relizane province.[29] Even though kidnapping and rape are not the fault of these women, the outcome is usually grim when these victims come to face their families and society. When women are raped by these terrorists, they are often expelled by their families for dishonoring the family.

According to Algerian police records, there were 8,000 female victims of violence in 2006, 7,400 in 2005, and 5,845 in 2004. Domestic violence has led to the death of 36 women and 8 men in 2006. Lamia' is a 35-year-old woman who had tolerated her husband battering her in front of her young children for five years before she was kicked out of the house. Even her natal family rejected her. Her children were subjugated to sexual abuse from the husband's relatives, as custody remained with him. Fatiha, another 35-year-old woman was so severely battered by her husband that she was hospitalized for three months as she suffered from fractures and severe wounds. Her crime was that she wanted to be a singer. The constant violence committed against her also caused her children psychological trauma. One of her daughters even attempted suicide.[30] Despite their sacrifices in Algeria's struggle for independence, Algerian women have been let down by both the nationalists and the Islamists.

Discrimination and segregation of women exists throughout the Middle East; however, in Saudi Arabia it is worse than average. Whereas the political experience of Saudi Arabia is different from the other cases discussed in this chapter, the strong presence of Islam and the ideology of the political regime warrant its inclusion in the discussion of Islamism and women. Saudi Arabia is the only country in the world that prohibits females from driving. Some of the women who drove cars in Riyadh in 1991 in protest of this law were suspended from their jobs for several years. A Saudi woman commented: "It's safer and more Islamic for me to drive myself than to sit with an unrelated male driver."[31]

A recent event occurred in February of 2008 in which a 40-year-old married woman, who was a mother of three, a business partner, and a financial consultant for a reputable company in Jeddah, was incarcerated by religious police for having a cup of coffee with a colleague in the family section of a Starbucks located in the same building as her office. Family sections are the only places where men and women can sit together in public establishments in this country. Her husband reacted to the situation disapprovingly: "I look at this as if she had been kidnapped by thugs."[32] In 2002, in Saudi Arabia, religious police prevented 14-year-old schoolgirls from leaving a burning school building because they were not wearing their headscarves. Fifteen of the girls died.[33]

Official religious police armed with clubs roam the streets and shopping malls in Saudi Arabia, enforcing a strict interpretation of Islamic law. In an attempt to imitate this, the conservative Islamists in neighboring Yemen are reported to have been pushing for the establishment of religious police in the country. Religious gangs of bearded men have also begun to appear in public to police social mores and to punish men and women for walking together on the streets.[34]

The "Qatif Girl" is a case of gang rape that has instigated a debate regarding the judicial system and women's rights in Saudi Arabia. In June of 2006, a Saudi girl, 18 years of age, and the man she was with were gang raped by seven men in the city of Qatif, in the eastern province of the kingdom. The rapists were sentenced to various terms of lashing and imprisonment. But the rape victims were also sentenced to 90 lashes each for what is called *khulwa*, being with an unrelated male. The two were sitting in a car in a shopping mall parking lot when the incident occurred. The law prohibiting mingling between the sexes is very strict in segregated Saudi society. Her sentencing implies that it was her fault for being outside her home with an unrelated man, which had led to the rape. However, when she appealed the verdict, the appeals court not only increased the assailants' sentences, but also increased the victims' sentences to 200 lashes as well as a six-month term of imprisonment. The reason given for doubling the victims' punishments was that the girl had tried to "aggravate and influence the judiciary through the media." What she had done was take her case to the press. Moreover, the lawyer of the victim was also accused by the judges of being "disruptive to the court, disrespectful and showing ignorance of the court procedures." For this accusation, his license was suspended and he was ordered to appear before a disciplinary committee at the Ministry of Justice.[35]

The Human Rights Watch reported the case of Fawza Falih, a Saudi woman who was convicted of "witchcraft" and is awaiting execution. The judges relied on her coerced confession and statements of witnesses who said she had "bewitched" them in order to convict her in April of 2006. She said that her interrogators beat her during her 35 days in detention with the religious police. At one point, she had to be hospitalized as a result of these beatings. Earlier, her interrogators blocked her access to a lawyer. "The religious police who arrested and interrogated Fawza Falih and the judges who tried her in the northern town of Quraiyat never gave her the opportunity to prove her innocence against absurd charges that have no basis in law. . . . The fact that Saudi judges still conduct trials for unprovable crimes like 'witchcraft' underscores their inability to carry out objective criminal investigations." An appeals court ruled in September of 2006 that she could not be sentenced to death for "witchcraft" as a crime against God because she had retracted her confession. However, the lower court judges then sentenced her to death on a "discretionary" basis for the benefit of the "public interest" and to "protect the creed, souls and property of this country."[36]

The same organization also reported the case of a Saudi court that forced a married couple with two young children to divorce in response to a lawsuit brought by the wife's brothers. Officials placed the woman and her young son in detention and threatened to detain her husband. In August 2005, a court forcibly divorced the lawfully married couple. The court ruled that the husband's tribal lineage was socially inadequate for him to be acceptably married to his wife. Essentially the court declared that the marriage could harm the reputation of the wife's family because the husband was from a lower social class. The Riyadh Court of Appeals upheld the verdict.[37]

According to Human Rights Watch reports, Saudi Arabia enforces a strict regime of male legal guardianship over women. Saudi women must obtain a male legal guardian's permission to work, study, marry, and receive health care or access to many other public services. Without such permission, government agencies can bar women from exercising these rights. Women's legal guardians can include their husbands, fathers, brothers, and even male children.[38] Women do not have the right to move within the country nor to live in apartments or hotels without male escorts. It is mandatory for women of all ages to have a male guardian. A report prepared by the UN Committee on the Elimination of Discrimination against Women (CEDAW) states that women in Saudi Arabia are victims of systematic and pervasive discrimination across all aspects of social life. The Commission for the Promotion of Virtue and Prevention of Vice, a religious police commonly known as *muttawa*, is responsible for committing serious human rights abuses including harassment, threatening and arresting women who "deviate from the accepted norms."[39]

Yet this criticism from the United Nations incited a livid reaction from Omaima al-Jalahma, a female member of the King Faisal Faculty and member of the Shoura (Consultative) Council. She wrote an article titled "As a Proud Saudi Woman, I Speak," in which she rejected the "unfairness of CEDAW's report against a country where women are given their rights fully, unlike women in many other countries, including those in the West." After defending the mandate for male legal guardians, she continued: "I wish that women around the world could find a tiny bit of the pampering I receive here being a Saudi woman."[40]

Luckily, there are other forms of public female agency found in Saudi Arabia. Rania al-Baz is a celebrity TV host who was the victim of her husband's brutal beating, which nearly killed her in April of 2004. Her husband had savagely assaulted her, slamming her face against the marble-tiled floor of their home until it suffered 13 fractures. He left her unconscious for a couple of hours while he showered and changed then bundled her up in a sheet and put her in the family van. He was disposing what he assumed to be her dead body when she showed signs of life and, panicking, took her to a hospital, where doctors gave her only a 70% chance of survival. After four days in a coma and following 12 operations, she survived. She decided to give her permission to allow the photos that showed her grotesquely disfigured face to be published. This act effectively shattered the wall of silence surrounding domestic violence in Saudi Arabia.

Yet there was a price to pay for Rania's courageous efforts. Because she had gone public with the case, she had little choice but to publicly pardon her husband, allowing his original sentence of 300 lashes and six months of jail to be halved, in exchange for divorce and the custody of her three children. Even so, this was a very rare achievement for a divorced woman in this country. However, the ordeal did not end there. Having planned to return to work as soon as she recovered, she found herself unwelcome on television. Rania says: "I feel completely outside my own country and society, because of what it is, and because of what I did."

However, the positive side of this story, thanks to her stand, is that the first ever research study on domestic violence in Saudi Arabia was completed at King Saud University in Riyadh, in May of 2005. This study uncovered that 90 percent of the women interviewed had seen their own fathers violently abuse their mothers. Thus, her agency has made a difference by fundamentally challenging the culture of silence regarding violence against women in a conservative and male-dominated Saudi society. Rania al-Baz said: "I had two choices before me in life: to live as a typical, good Saudi woman, or live life as I wanted to live it, as I would like to live it. Even before my accident, I had decided to do the second."[41]

CHAPTER 5

Gender Alienation

> The devaluation of femininity has been a necessary step in human evolution.
>
> —*Simone de Beauvoir*

GENDER SEGREGATION AND DISCRIMINATION

The cultural values of the Middle East influence the social construction of gender roles, which is the foundation for gender alienation in the region. Gender alienation profoundly affects the development of the inner self, the perception of the other, and the relationship of the *self* to the *other*. These developmental consequences are detrimental to society as a whole. Gender alienation is a process that degrades and devalues the *self*, distorts the *other*, and affects the relationship between the *self* and the *other* in a damaging, coercive way. The alienation of women in Middle Eastern society is the outcome of several factors: the cultural preference for males, unequal treatment of boys and girls, gender seclusion and segregation, and social control over women.

Middle Eastern culture's preference for males forces women into an unfavorable and disadvantaged beginning the day they are born. Because the preference for males leads to the exclusion of women, it is a clear case of discrimination. Discriminatory cultural practices, consequently, degrade and devalue the unpreferred sex. From the perspective of the cultural value system, the only connoted meaning of *female* is *not male*. Society lacks appreciation for females, considering them inferior and unworthy creatures or, worse, considering them a burden, a reminder of bad luck, a boy that was not born. In this situation, a girl is thought to have taken the place of a potential boy. Her birth is a transgression, and therefore the girl is despised and rejected. Inevitably, treating individuals as unworthy, trivial beings ultimately is the basis for violence, which occurs at the individual level, between couples, or at the societal level.

The cultural fixation on the male sex is so extreme that men often take for granted the simple fact of life that the other sex is needed in order to produce male children in the first place. This unjustified obsession with males is naïve to the point that if this logic were followed to its natural conclusion, it would certainly lead to the extinction of the society. No doubt that biology requires both sexes for reproduction, and both sexes must be appreciated to maintain a properly functioning, healthy society. As previously stated, the reverse side of male reverence is female undesirability. As Beauvoir notes, girls are born on the wrong side of the line.[1] The cultural message girls receive, that they were born wrong or by accident, has severe, lasting effects on women. A study of Iraqi women concludes that being born female emotionally affects most women.[2]

This problem continues to grow, beginning in childhood when boys and girls are treated unequally by their parents and the extended family. Vieille expresses: "parents accept joyfully the trouble he provokes, but take badly that given by the little girl. The girl is considered to be made for obedience, the boy for pride and independence."[3] Reflecting on their study of Morocco, Davis and Davis point out: "The difference in mother's treatment of male and female children is a major lesson each child learns about the role of the sexes in society."[4] Thus, discrimination between boys and girls, or even among members of the same sex, becomes an ordinary fact of life and is therefore internalized and accepted. Boys are always preferred over girls; however, even among male siblings there is always one that is preferred over the others. Men and women become accustomed to this fact throughout their lives and will most likely reproduce these circumstances within their own families.

The important question to ask is: How do girls and boys cope with this situation? From early childhood on, children struggle with injustice and discrimination within the family. This struggle deeply affects the development of their personalities and consciousnesses, as well as their *inner selves* and how they relate to the *other* and the outside world. When protesting and resisting discrimination are discouraged or suppressed, feelings of bitterness, anger, insecurity, and injustice become deeply entrenched in the subconscious minds of children. This also has a harmful effect on these unfortunate children's development later on in life. This is no trivial matter, considering that this predicament affects the majority of children, all of the females and most of the males. What is more, the gender structure denies even the most preferred boys the ability to be fully effective in their position of privilege, as healthy and spontaneous development of their personalities is inhibited by being surrounded by all the other unfavorable females and males the system has produced.

For girls in Middle Eastern societies, reaching the age of puberty marks the beginning of a process of strict regimentation and signals the start of a life of anguish. Society confines them to the home and prevents them from playing with boys. High schools segregated by sex reinforce this reality. As puberty brings significant physical and hormonal changes to the lives of girls they are in need of the support of others, openness, understanding, and friendly discussions. Instead, the social demands and expectations of the dominant culture burden girls even more as they experience these changes. Menstruation is a terrifying experience for girls because of the socially instilled fear of losing their virginity, since both are associated with blood. Social control worsens at this age as girls' freedom is more explicitly and more forcefully restricted. Puberty is a girl's wakeup call to the bitter realities awaiting her. Gregg illustrates: "Girls experience a growing discontinuity between their skills and importance to the household on the one hand and their inferior status in it on the other. During late childhood, girls gradually find themselves more segregated from boys, restricted to the household and its immediate vicinity, burdened with longer hours of work, and increasingly subservient to the men of their households."[5]

Studying the attitudes of Egyptian adolescents, Mensch et al. agree: "As girls enter puberty, they experience an abrupt shift in what is considered appropriate behavior, and at that point, if not earlier, they become aware of the restrictions placed upon them as women."[6] Around the time of puberty, girls are expected to display increasing modesty and to withdraw from some of the public spaces to which they have access as children. "For girls puberty leads to a greater restriction on mobility."[7] Once girls reach puberty, cultural norms do not allow them to act as children anymore; however, their brothers are unaffected by these norms and continue to play outside and act as children. It is a brutal demand to require a girl to relinquish her childhood *when she is, in fact, still a child.* This is a violent act of killing all that is innocent

and child-like in young girls' lives. In the words of Patai: "Innocent
childhood is corrupted by the differentiation between the sexes, with
different status and privileges for boys and girls. This fact is affecting
the childhood itself and its true meaning. In fact, there is no real childhood; it is a boy life versus girl life. Boys and girls do not live their
childhood in the proper sense of the word."[8]

The simple liberty to life as a child is no longer possible for young
women. Aspects of life that were taken for granted merely days before
are no longer proper for a young lady's conduct. As Gregg argues,
ethnographic studies show that the traditional milieu of adolescence
is brief for most boys and nonexistent for most girls.[9] Telling her own
story, el-Saadawi reflects: "my childhood was over, a brief, breathless
childhood. I had scarcely been aware of it before it was gone, leaving
me with a mature woman's body carrying deep inside it a ten-year-old
child. My childhood had been wasted fighting against my mother, my
brother and myself."[10] "And so here I was, a child of twenty-five want-
ing to play, run, fly and love."[11] Indeed, this illustrates how the absence of a proper childhood leads to lifelong conflict and struggle for
women.

Indeed, the conflicting tension between nature and social conditioning is detrimental to the development of a girl's free and spontaneous personality. From the other side of the spectrum, girls' withdrawal
from the streets also affects the life of boys. Boys' relationship with
the *other*, girls, is affected as well. Separating the girls from the boys,
when they were only recently playing together, is damaging to the relationship between the *self* and the *other*. Removing girls from previously
mix-gendered streets leads to coercive and unnatural ways of separating
the *self* from the *other*. In fact, such a coercive withdrawal of the *other*
from the domicile of the *self* tends to create a relationship of animosity
and conflict between the two. In practical terms, men and women are
unable to experience childhood and adolescence freely and properly.
When children are finally relieved of direct parental control, which is
their entrance into adulthood, the first thing they do is try to compensate for their missed childhoods. The constant animosity, immaturity,
and irrationality that are rampant throughout political and social life
are prime illustrations of this late-coming adolescence.

The consequences of the gender segregation system are felt by men
and women even after school graduation and the start of adulthood.
In fact, the negative effects of this system persist until the very end of
men and women's lives. When young girls and boys mature and enter
adulthood, irreversible damage has already been done. Moreover,

these young people bring into their adult lives all of the complexities and frustrations that have been enforced on them in childhood, ensuring an unhealthy start to adulthood. In fact, the apartheid system of gender separation is the reason young people are so ill equipped to cultivate meaningful relationships between the sexes.

Even though university education and work life are co-occupied by men and women, at least in most of the Middle East, this does not help counterbalance the corrupted and damaged relationship between genders and between the *self* and the *other*. On the contrary, mixing the sexes after such a long, unnatural, and coerced segregation adds to existing frustrations. These new experiences of interacting with the opposite sex ultimately lead to the reinforcement of the dominant cultural, patriarchal social values in society. The disappointments that result from these few, hasty experiments with these sorts of relationships form the misconception that all the lessons learned from patriarchal ideology are justified and real. Thus, the ideologies that were initially enforced by society are internalized by the young generation to the extent that these concepts become their own convictions. Patriarchal ideology becomes the reality men and women live in, regarding their experiences with "free" mixing of the sexes in their adult lives. These disappointments with their new experiences along with enforced gender values are what young adults will eventually bring to their marriages.

NATURE AND SOCIAL EXISTENCE

The social construction of femininity in these societies does not necessarily reflect the true nature of women. El-Saadawi remembers: "I wept over my femininity even before I knew what it was; the moment I opened my eyes in life, a state of enmity already existed between me and my nature."[12] The artificial contradiction between the true nature of the female *self* and feminine social existence clearly affects the spontaneous development of the psyche, or the *inner self*. The socially constructed gender structure denies girls the conditions needed in order to solidify their subjective individuality. Quite the contrary, all conditions compel women to deny their basic right to individuality and natural existence. The patriarchal construction of gender relations is a process of dehumanization that creates violent social relationships between the sexes.

This process of alienation and dehumanization is, in fact, an act of violence and aggression against the *self* and individuality—an act that induces insecurity, passivity, aggressiveness, and violence in the development of adult personalities. Galtung reasons that alienation is synonymous with spiritual death, it is violence.[13] "A violent structure leaves marks not only on the human body but also on the mind and the spirit."[14] The *inner self* has no chance of maturing in a healthful way if women are treated with contempt and considered to be burdensome and inferior. "To be feminine," Beauvoir argues, "is to appear weak, futile, docile, and to repress spontaneity."[15] Al-Khayyat spotlights the fact that since a girl is often rewarded for being submissive and obedient; she will tend to develop a passive or negative personality.[16] El-Saadawi adds:

> The education that a female child receives in Arab society is a series of continuous warnings about things that are supposed to be harmful, forbidden, shameful or outlawed by religion. The child therefore is trained to suppress her own desires, to empty herself of authentic, original wants and wishes linked to her own self, and to fill the vacuum that results with the desires of others. Education of female children is therefore transformed into a slow process of annihilation, a gradual throttling of her personality and mind, leaving intact only the outside shell, the body, a lifeless mould of muscle and bone and blood that moves like a wound up rubber doll.[17]

Alienation of the female body is also a manifestation of gender alienation. Mackenzie states: "A person becomes an object for herself when she experiences her body as alien to her subjectivity, rather than as the direct expression of her subjectivity."[18] Best also stresses this fact, stating that "when women are perceived solely as objects of the male gaze, when their bodies are so regulated and culturally controlled, they are robbed of their subjectivity, of their identity, and, ironically, of the very sensuality for which they are imprisoned."[19] Beauvoir points out: "The young girl feels that her body is getting away from her, it is no longer the straightforward expression of her individuality: it becomes foreign to her; and at the same time, she becomes for others a thing."[20] "The gulf existing between the body-for-the-self and the body-for-others seems to be impassable."[21] In this process women become both obsessed with and fearful of their bodies.

Indeed, this alienation of the body is twofold. It is the alienation or separation of the body from the *self*, and the *self* from the body, as well as the alienation of the body from the body. Thus, the body is not only poised against the *self* but also against the natural body and hence, against nature itself. Consequently, a conflict is imposed between the body conditioned by nature and the body conditioned by culture and society. It is difficult for women to reconcile the socially reconstructed female body with the physical nature of the female body. It is difficult to determine which interpretation of the body is real and which is only perceived to be real through the eyes of the prevailing cultural values. This causes immensely disturbing confusion in women's understanding and the experience of their existence. Beauvoir hints: "Not to have confidence in one's body is to lose confidence in oneself."[22] Moreover, alienation of the body leads to sexual control over women and the alienation and degradation of sexuality as well.

The cultural necessity to control the female body is related to its relative closeness with nature. Ortner discusses the notion that women are being identified or symbolically associated with nature, as opposed to men, who are identified with culture. More precisely, it is the perception of women as being more rooted in, or having more direct affinity with, nature. This perception of the affinity with nature is common in every culture, giving credential to a universal devaluation of women in all societies.[23] Abu-Lughod adds that women's association with nature, which is a source for both positive and negative values, is seen as a handicap to their ability to attain the same level of moral worth as men.[24] While this closeness to nature could be a source of power for women, society regards it as a threat. In fact, it is this perceived threat that justifies the alienation and degradation of the female body, in which pitting the body against itself seems to make sense.

Actually, this artificially constructed dichotomy between nature and culture is intended to crush the power women derive from their closeness with nature. The strength associated with nature is interpreted through the patriarchal lenses as women's dependence on nature, a weakness, and therefore justification for female oppression. Potency that is associated with nature is a limitation in the political-economic system. Therefore, the process of subjugating and controlling nature, the creation of culture, is in reality the gradual alienation and control of women. Since the alienation of women, which is the result of cultural and economic forces, is by implication the alienation of men, it leads to the alienation of everyone. A process that aligns the creation of culture in opposition with nature and women is a violent cultural process that necessarily leads to the alienation of both women and nature.

Development of humanity and social existence has been a process of subduing nature through the advancement of culture and economy.

The triumph of culture and economy over nature is also reflected in the ascendancy of male power at the expense of female power. It seems odd that a society would have room for only one form of power; however, any power other than male power is perceived to be redundant and therefore should be suppressed. From this perspective, in order to master nature, everything associated with nature, including women, must be mastered. Therefore, a system of male domination and female subordination is created. Interestingly though, when the process of domination over nature was only in its initial stages, women were more valued and respected. Society's fear of nature generated a respect for nature and therefore women also.

Conversely, to act against nature is to act against women. These two dimensions work symbiotically to damage both realms. As women were degraded and devalued so was nature, leading to grave pollution and environmental destruction. However, the outcome of both destructive forces calls into question the alleged rationality of culture and economy as well as the rationality of men. Taking into consideration these damaging outcomes, one must scrutinize the concepts and processes that are the foundation of this culture. Why and how has this culture become hierarchical to the extent that it excludes women? Why has culture become a process of social degradation of woman and all that is associated with them? Why has the rationality of culture failed to embrace and nurture an entire half of society?

However, gender alienation and the denial of a healthy existence for women forced women to internalize their situation. Mackenzie states: "Oppression structures the psyches and the bodies of women."[25] Beauvoir also argues that oppression becomes naturalized by being internalized when the young girl in the end has agreed to her femininity.[26] The social denial of women leads to women's own internal denial of the *self*, or in Tarabishi's words: "She will internalize oppression and end up becoming her own oppressor."[27] Internalization is the process through which that which is socially constructed appears natural to the individual.

To live under the influence of the prevailing cultural values is a negation of a woman's natural existence. Sanday argues that as a result, a relationship between representations and self-representations materializes.[28] Very often, this relationship embodies a woman's reaction against her own true nature, rather than against her culturally designed social existence. Consequently, women tend to internalize this conflict, resulting in the rejection of their nature and of their true selves. Women accept their social existence as the true and genuine expression of themselves. Mackenzie argues that the process of internalization is a psychic alienation that tends to alienate women from their subjectivity:

> Oppression works best when the process of naturalising oppression actually structures both the oppressed's beliefs about themselves and their modes of relation to the world, that is, when the oppressed constrain their own possibilities while believing that these possibilities are constrained by some natural, inescapable facts about themselves. In other words, *the hallmark of oppression is its invisibility to the oppressed.*[29]

THE *SELF* AND THE *OTHER*

Unequal treatment of children and gender segregation reinforce a certain kind of a relationship between the *self* and the *other* that severely affects children's later development. The dominant cultural values imposed on girls at a very early age restrict their ability to concentrate on the *self* and from allowing the *self* to be full or pure. Instead, they become preoccupied with an inferior, unworthy, and distorted sense of *self.* These values force on women a new dimension to deal with, the preoccupation with the *self* in relation to the *other.* The *other,* in this situation, is the favored, over-valued, more worthy brother. Thus, in the socially constructed gender structure, girls are never free to devote their attention to the *self.* This creates a relationship between an inferior *self* and a superior *other.* While the development of the *self,* in relation to the *other,* is a natural and healthy part of personality development, it becomes unhealthy and destructive within the prevailing gender structure in these societies.

Thus, a relationship of conflict and animosity towards the *other* forms deep in the subconscious, which will eventually color the way people perceive and deal with the *other* in the outside world. Is it merely a coincidental fact that the Middle East is known to always be in conflict with the outside world, the *other?* The superior-inferior relationship imposed on brothers and sisters is severely damaging. Because of this unnatural and damaging relationship with the *other,* the *self* is subjected to a grim and utterly confusing situation, which causes the *inner self* to fall short of its full growth potential. The explicit expressions of male preference in the daily life of the family not only promote women's distorted and unhealthy relationships with the *other* but also prevent these females from developing healthy and free *inner selves*. Studying Iraqi women, el-Khayyat concludes: "More than half of the women said they wished they had been born a boy. Many related their wish to the oppression women suffer in society."[30] One Iraqi woman said "I wished I'd been born a boy because whatever I did they said, 'You're a girl, don't do that.'"[31]

The preferential treatment of boys does not mean that boys are necessarily dealt a better hand through the process of gender alienation. While it is true that objective conditions provide boys with an advantage as they develop their *inner selves*, the very same conditions distort any potentially healthy use of this advantage. Gender alienation, without exception, does not nurture a healthy development of the *inner self* for anyone involved in these circumstances. Because girls are exposed to and conditioned by the process of alienation and degradation, boys share the outcome by implication. Since relationships with the *other* are introduced at an early age, the alienation of one end of the relation affects the other. The very same culture that denies their sisters a healthy process of development effectively does the same to boys, only from a different angle.

According to cultural norms, the honor of men, and with it the honor of the entire family, depends wholly on the sexual behavior of sisters and female cousins. The resulting social and cultural system is linked exclusively to women's behavior. In order to protect itself, this system strives to strictly control women in order to ensure their conformity, submissiveness, and obedience. Therefore, one important social function of men is policing the conformity of their sisters or cousins. Speaking of her life experience, Khouri says: "My brothers stopped being friends, and turned into guard dogs."[32] The behavior of sisters and female cousins becomes a more vital issue to men than their own behavior. Consequently, this process affects the development of men's *inner self* and causes men to develop an unhealthy relationship with the *other*. The position of control, dominance, and violence that men have in relation to their sisters may even affect relationships between men as well.

As both girls and boys conform to their respective designed social roles, an enormous amount of extra pressure is added to the existing pressures. The behavior of females becomes the concern of the brother, father, mother, and the extended family. Living with the constant fear that a female might do something wrong in the eyes of others exerts a huge burden and stress on women. The strict control imposed on women by male relatives is miserable. Beauvoir states that for a female, discovering that men control the world modifies her concept of herself.[33] Consequently, this situation compels both sexes to drift away from the *inner self*, thus sacrificing the individuality of each to accommodate the requirements of the gender roles they are forced to play.

Socially constructed gender roles tend to create confusion regarding gender, the *self*, and an individual's relationship with the other sex. From their study of societies in which female freedom is severely constrained, as in Morocco, Davis and Davis conclude: "There is a relatively high degree of ambivalence by both sexes about their gender roles. There is also an indication of ambivalent and negative feelings about the opposite sex."[34] Khouri also reflects on her relationships with her brothers: "By the time we were eighteen; the emotional distance between us and the males of our families had grown to an insurmountable gulf."[35]

Gender alienation and segregation create a social contradiction. Because of the gender processes, the *other* is forced into the lives of men and women early on in a very unnatural and unhealthy way. At the same time, the natural needs of this *other* are denied. Access to the *other*, or having a relationship with the *other* is only permitted if the relationship is one of control, power, conformity, obedience, and submissiveness. There is no doubt that a more violent and authoritarian society emerges from these negative features of human relationships as they extend into adulthood. Because social gender negation of the *other* affects how society regards and deals with the *other*, appreciation, respect, and tolerance towards the *other* are not qualities promoted within society.

Naturally, the relationship to the *other* is an integral part of the development of the *self*. Healthy, culturally unconstrained interactions with the *other* require first a healthy social existence of the *self*. Having a healthy socially existing *self* and unconstrained interactions with the *other* are both basic human rights that any society should guarantee to its citizens, regardless of their sex. Yet culture and religion devalue the *self* and negate the *other*. They transform relations with the *other* into interactions with a shadow, someone devoid of real existence, integrity, or individuality. The realm of the *other* is strongly linked to violence and power. The *other* is central to the gender game and gender violence, as the *other* is the target of violence for both males and females.

As we have seen, fear of the *other* is strongly linked to violence against the *other* and is, in fact, an expression of it. Ignorance of the *other* breeds prejudice, misunderstanding, mistrust, and false perceptions, which are barriers to tolerance and reconciliation. The development of free, spontaneous, and creative personalities is hindered by the concerns of *others* that are brought into the lives of young boys and girls by the dominant culture and gender system. Tradition and conservatism foster unhealthy personalities and, hence, create the foundation for an unstable, intolerant, and divided society. Society as a whole is at great risk when individuals' *inner selves* are either lost, distorted, or both.

Femininity and masculinity are socially constructed through complex processes involving: gender alienation and segregation, gender assignment, and the relationship between the *self* and the *other*. These gender constructions exaggerate the differences between the categories of passive females and active males as well as the opposition of the two. Goldner et al. imply that learning to be masculine comes to imply learning to be "not-feminine."[36] One could also add that learning to be feminine comes to mean accepting the inability to enjoy the privileges associated with masculinity within society. Maynard and Winn point out: "Masculinity is a form of power and, to the extent that it is formulated in opposition to femininity, masculinity enables men to act out this power in the subordination and control of women. In one sense, then, to become masculine is to become an oppressor."[37] Mustafa Hijazi concurs:

> In order for the man to be transformed into the embodiment of the "macho myth," it becomes necessary for the woman to be weak and oppressed. She becomes the articulation of suffering who is in dire need of a supporter. She takes on the role of the emotional being, while the man is rational; she is in the home, he challenges the world; she surrenders, he is empowered and capable; she becomes the symbol of shame and need, he the symbol of pride, self-fulfillment and power; she is the dependent follower, the obliging servant of the master, he the master whose word is obeyed. She dies in her psyche that he may gain the illusion of life; she is crushed that he may gain the mirage of self-fulfillment.[38]

According to the cultural and social constructions of femininity and masculinity, women are emotional by nature while men are more rational. Thus, the culturally constructed and enforced opposition between masculinity and femininity creates an artificial separation between emotionality and rationality. This is seen as further justification for the superiority of men and the degradation of women. However, this separation is unnecessary because of the fact that every person, regardless of sex, is both rational and emotional at the same time. Furthermore, rationality is not an absolute term; it is a relative concept that cannot be generalized in this way. People are not irrational by nature; however, the construction of gender relations that forces people to behave irrationally in their gender roles is irrational.

If men are considered to be rational, reasonable, and wise, then how does one account for all the obvious irrationality in political and public life, which is dominated by men in the Middle East? One also wonders why, in Middle Eastern societies, where men's world dominates, conflict, decline, and misery are always present? Moreover, culture and economy, which are dominated by supposedly rational men, have been strongly criticized for being violent and wasteful systems. These cultures are also consistently associated with wars, conflicts, militarization, pollution, colonialism, and the debasement of women. It is no wonder that this realization is leading to the demand for a better system in which gender equality and the inclusion of women, among other things, are integral parts. Certainly, wisdom and rationality are of no use if they do not help *all citizens* develop and prosper within society.

PART TWO

POWER, VIOLENCE, AND GENDER

CHAPTER 6

Gender and Power

Denied power in the real world, they scheme and compete, using whatever means are available to them, in order to attain a measure of control over their destinies.

—*Amal Rassam*

UNACKNOWLEDGED POWER

Within patriarchal social structures, women find themselves inferior to men, as men use their position of power to dominate and control women. Women are degraded and presented as the weak and powerless sex. Yet one wonders why such a woman, in her marginalized and socially trivial state, would need to be so strictly controlled and dominated. Does a debased or marginalized person pose such a threat as to warrant this harsh control? In fact, this is a contradiction. Assuming the weaknesses of women, this need to control them so strictly does not make logical sense. On the other hand, it makes more sense to argue that stern control, in fact, produces weak and marginalized women, showing that women are not inherently weak but instead that weakness is the end result of gender control. In this sense, stringent control of women both acknowledges women's power and strength and at the same time acts as a mechanism to neutralize that power and strength. Thus, control over women does not necessarily deny women power or a role in society; rather, it is intended to bring female power under male control.

Patriarchy and the control of women, reinforced by monotheistic religion, emerged together with the rise of the state and the accumulation of wealth. This process bore witnesses to the birth of the elite, a minority of the population that formed a distinct group in terms of wealth and power. The majority of the population, whose marginalization was gradually increasing with their loss of power, authority, and wealth, sought to regain authority through the marginalization of another, women. This became an important process, as it provided a counterbalance to the social displacement produced by the emergence of the elite. The marginalization of women became an important way for men to regain the power and authority they had lost through the process of social polarization. Furthering this process, monotheistic religion has helped strengthen the patriarchal context that supports domination and control of women.

Thus, the first process of polarization, based on wealth and power, has led to a second level of social polarization based on gender. Yet both levels of social polarization embody repression, exploitation, and control. The control of women is a process through which women's power is deformalized, leaving only one permissible form of dominant, formal power, male power. This process ensures the supremacy of male power, and by controlling women, eliminates any challenges to this power. Because this process elevates one power and at the same time suppresses another, it is a process of violence.

One important consequence of this process is that female power, which cannot be expressed formally, must be expressed in alternative ways; hence, female power becomes an informal, traditional, and unacknowledged power. Female power is power that lacks the sanctioning of social, cultural, and religious legitimization. It is an unsanctioned and culturally illegitimate power. Rosaldo suggests: "Women may be 'anomalies' because societies that define women as lacking legitimate authority have no way of acknowledging the reality of female power."[1] Green argues: "There are a number of different kinds of power. Yet by focusing only on formal power, we fail to understand the full set of resources employed by women. Because men are backed by societal authority that ignores women's social needs, many women have chosen to employ unorthodox forms of power."[2]

Power relations are significant in any social structure. Foucault claims that power exists everywhere, both the dominant and the subordinate produce power, and power and resistance are closely linked.[3] Thus, while the definition of gender as a power relation in which men are dominant and women are subordinate is still valid, it nonetheless needs to be modified in order to accommodate for the power of the subordinate, the power of women.

Rosaldo comments: "Social scientists have largely taken male authority for granted; they have also tended to accept a male view that sees the exercise of power by women as manipulative, disruptive, illegitimate, or unimportant."[4] On the other hand, Rassam, in her study on Morocco, contends: "It is generally conceded that although women may have no authority in a society, they do not necessarily lack influence or power. A closer examination of the structure and operation of the household reveals the presence of a considerable measure of 'unassigned power,' which women compete for and utilize to further their own needs and wishes."[5] In her study of power and resistance in Cairo, MacLeod remarks: "Women, even as subordinate players, always play an active part that goes beyond the dichotomy of victimization/acceptance, a dichotomy that flattens out a complex and ambiguous agency in which women accept, accommodate, ignore, resist, or protest; sometimes all at the same time. Power relationships should be viewed as an ongoing relationship of struggle."[6] Friedl, in her study of the sources of female power in Iran, concurs: She notes that reports of women's position in Middle Eastern societies

> contain a seeming paradox; women are said to be subordinate to men, second-class citizens, oppressed, veiled, and confined, unequal to men legally and in access to resources. Yet, on the level of everyday life and popular culture, women, especially mature matrons, are widely perceived as "powerful." No matter how contradictory the concept of the oppressed-yet-powerful woman might seem, the contradiction is contrived. Indeed, I will even argue that subordinated people, women in this case, not only can be both oppressed and powerful simultaneously, but that they can derive power to effect changes in their own and in others' affairs from the very relations of inequality that define their position: from concrete, adversarial circumstances in their lives, from the existential conditions to which they are confined, unfavourable as they might be.[7]

Thus, because official power excludes women, female power manifests in the informal domains. To put it differently, the absence of female power in the public domain does not negate the fact that women do have power in the domestic or traditional spheres. Studying low-income districts in Cairo, Singerman insists that it is a type of myopia to suppose that if women are seldom visible in the upper echelon of the state bureaucracy, the military, or among the elites, then they must not be engaged in politics.[8] However, she continues: "If one investigates politics at the level of the household and community, women are obviously engaged in decision-making processes, distributional activities, and in informal institutions. The everyday activities of women, although undertaken in the household and community, are not simply concerned with 'domestic' affairs; rather, they are involved in wider matters of power."[9]

According to Hijab, three factors were usually used to assess how much power women have. First is the participation in the democratic process, that is, having the right to vote, to be elected, to be a member of government, and so forth; second is the legislation on matters of personal status; and, third, is women's access to education and paid employment. Using these indicators, women were believed to have low status and little power in the Arab world.[10] Hijab continues: "Access to parliaments or to the wage-labour force were insufficient measures of power: low representation in parliaments did not mean that women had no power in their community; low participation in the wage-labour force did not mean that women had no money or no control over income."[11] In the same vein, because it is only the minority elite that dominate the struggle for power, most men do not access power within the public sphere. Conventional spheres of political and economic life exclude the majority of men. Therefore, one must admit that the general perception that the public domain is dominated by men is in abstract terms only.

Men's presence in the public domain does not automatically translate into the ability to access power and wealth. It is thus equally valid to argue that the absence of women from the public domain does not necessarily measure the power that women hold in society. Conversely, Caprioli states: "The percentage of women in non-democratic parliaments does not reflect their greater equality, because members of parliaments in non-democracies exercise minimal power even though the percentage of women in such parliaments is often high."[12]

Even so, in terms of measuring women's progress, the spheres of politics, law, and economics are too relevant to dismiss altogether. Simply because they fail to measure the traditional power of women is not a justifiable reason to exclude these spheres from the analysis of female power. They are useful in showing that women's progression toward equality in the Middle East has been relatively unchanged. Within these crucial domains, women do not yet have power. Moghissi warns against adopting a position that "celebrates women's agency and empowerment within a protected and narrowly defined women's space, but neglects more crucial spaces, larger socio-cultural structures, and religious and politico-legal institutions in which women are robbed of both agency and any prospect for meaningful change."[13]

Thus, indicating that women have informal power in the family or community should not be regarded as vindication for their lacking official and formal power. It is equally misleading to argue that because most men also lack power in the public domain, which is an undisputable fact, it is pointless for women to compete for power in this domain. Framing the matter in this way is misleading and counterproductive in the advancement of women's status in society. Therefore, to claim or admit that women have informal power should not be perceived as an obstacle for women seeking to enhance their formal power. After all, Afsaruddin reminds us: "Empowerment is the carving out of public space by women for themselves."[14]

Even so, we are right to acknowledge that if power exists in the public sphere, it must also exist in the domestic sphere, and since female power is absent from the public domain, women are limited to exercising their power in the domestic sphere. Nelson points out that the whole discussion of power in Middle Eastern societies is influenced by categorizations of public/private spheres.[15] However, several authors criticized the dichotomization of public and private spaces.[16] Khoury contends: "The household encompasses such seemingly 'public' spheres as production and political alliances. Clearly, the dichotomy between public and private has to be modified."[17]

Although the spatial divisions within Middle Eastern society do, to a certain extent, reflect the lines of gender, the rigidity of this demarcation is undoubtedly in question. Public and private spheres exist within each gender domain. The household is not entirely, nor exclusively, a private space because it is open to all other women, neighbors, and relatives. Local streets, quarters, and the various community networks also function as public spaces for women. Yet the dichotomy of public and private spaces has been used to support the erroneous conclusion that women are nearly powerless in these societies.

It would be at the risk of supporting another extreme position to conclude that exclusive control is ascribed to women in the domestic domain, however. The fallacy of this assumption is at its worst when women's supposed control of the domestic domain is seen as a counterbalance to men's power in the public domain. This argument exaggerates the power of women in the domestic domain by supplanting the extreme stance that there is *no* space for female power with another extreme that ascribes *all* power and control to women.

Rassam underlines "the importance of distinguishing in the domestic sphere between kinship as politics, which is the prerogative of the male, and kinship as household management and organization, which is left to the females."[18] Complex power relations are imbedded into the structure of domestic space. While it is true that women have power and control regarding the management of daily life and issues of domesticity, final authoritarian decision-making power lies with men, not women. This fact is reinforced, if not dictated, by dominant cultural norms and religious sanctions. The task of providing for the family, which is chiefly restricted to the husband, reinforces the imbalance of power between partners. Maintaining control of finances is the source of ultimate power for the husband. This control and authority far exceeds the power held by women within the domestic sphere.

To see the domestic realm as an autonomous, isolated, or self-contained unit is an exaggeration of the power of women. Although men are absent from the domestic sphere most of the time, they still exercise their power in family affairs. Rules and customs that are present in the public sphere, where men spend most of their time, influence men's behavior. Men tend to reflect this in their authoritative form of involvement in domestic life. In this way, family and domestic life are not exempt from the heavy-handed influence of the state and its legislation. The domestic domain does not function in isolation from the public sphere and the authoritarian rules that govern it; because of this, women's power in this domain is neither absolute nor uncontested.

Additionally, it has been argued that instead of stressing the exclusion of women from public space, a better angle of analysis is to acknowledge male exclusion from certain domestic spaces. In support of this, Nelson points out: "The segregation of women can alternatively be seen as an exclusion of men from a range of contacts, which women have among themselves."[19] Makhlouf, who studied women in Yemen, proposes: "One can venture that in fact the men are excluded from the female world, as much, if not more, than females are excluded from the world of the men."[20]

It is true that an alternative reading of the gender structure can confirm the exclusion of men from domestic space; yet, if taken too far, this line of argument can also be used to draw other erroneous conclusions. Rather than challenging gender segregation by acknowledging it for what it is, an apartheid leading to the exclusion of both sexes, conclusions of these sorts of arguments suppose segregation is a fair and balanced arrangement. In this way, the exclusion of women is not only justified, it is considered to be counterbalanced by the exclusion of men from domestic spaces. Yet if women's exclusion is initially met with resistance, wouldn't men's exclusion warrant the same reaction?

One might assume that because men have power in the public sphere, women necessarily have power in the domestic space, because it excludes men. This is seen as a natural division of power between men and women, as if these two powers are equal in status. This perspective depicts power in the domestic sphere as a compensation for women lacking power in the public domain, or as an "equal," "fair" division of labor between the sexes in terms of power.

HIERARCHIZATION OF POWER

The argument that a fair distribution of power between the sexes would relegate male power to the public sphere and female power to the domestic resonates with the Islamic religious ideology that men and women's roles and responsibilities should be distinctly separate. The form of power distribution religion ascribes is derived from the natural differences between men and women, and as the logic follows, in a perfectly natural world everyone would be content with his or her share of power. Yet one of the fundamental ideologies regarding gender in Islam, as with many religions, is an inherent inequity between men and women. This inherent gender inequality is at least explicit in the dominant conservative and misogynist version of Islam, a version of Islam that has recently been challenged by Muslim feminists. And logically, this kind of hierarchization of the sexes naturally leads to a hierarchization of the power associated with each sex. Thus, mirroring religious gender hierarchization, men are at the top of the social power structure and females are at the bottom.

However, religious justification for this disparity in the status and power of men and women fails to address the impacts this ranking has on everyday life. Male supremacy is the basis of decision-making power in the public sphere, regardless of the fact that decisions are made in this sphere that affect the lives of women in every way possible. The exclusion of women from the public domain is effectually the exclusion of women from the process of decision-making all together.

In this sense, any power or status that women acquire in the private sphere is certainly an insufficient compensation for the exclusion of women from the public domain and, therefore, from politics. The

structure of the public domain is still an unjust and exclusionary social arrangement. Therefore, power and status held within the private
domain should not serve as an alternative to the power and status employed in the public domain. This is a fragmented social arrangement
in which individuals are only able to have power either here or there,
never comprehensively. In fact, to recognize the power women have
in the domestic sphere as a substitute, or at best a complement, to the
power of men in public life, in a way, confirms and reinforces the dichotomy of the private and public spheres within society.

This dichotomy is neither an optimal nor desirable social arrangement of gender roles. In this power hierarchy the power associated
with the public sphere, male power, is the highest power in society.
Women are excluded from this sphere and have little or no power,
influence, or impact. On the other hand, female power associated with
the private domain is inferior power and is always subject to the influence of men, and in many crucial instances, to the decisions made by
them.

Along these same lines, the male dominated state has a considerable
impact on the family and domestic politics. Despite arguments that
men are mostly excluded from the domestic realm, dominant religious
and cultural ideologies also grant men power and control over women
within the private sphere. Therefore, in contrast to nearly complete
exclusion of women from the public sphere, men are still a significant part of the private domain. Society also sanctions and legitimizes
men's power over women in the private domain. In fact, the authoritarian or theocratic regime's monopoly over politics, wealth, power, and
decision-making in all aspects of life leaves most men with no power
to exercise except within the private domain.

Thus, even in the domestic domain, "natural" power resides with
men, not women. Female power in the private sphere is always conditional and dependent on male consent. Religion and culture reinforce
the power hierarchy by legitimizing male power, whether in the public
or private domain, and by invalidating female power. The sanctioning
and legitimization of power significantly influences the way both male
and female power is perceived and exercised.

According to Karmi: "it is important to realize that the 'power'
wielded by women in the patriarchal situation is not power in the formal sense but only influence. There is no structural basis for female
power in a patriarchal society, and whatever power women are able
to achieve by manipulating the system can be taken away from them
by men at any time."[21] Rassam also comments that although women

try their best to manipulate men to their own advantage, the ultimate decisions almost always mirror the desires and needs of the males.[22] Thus, from their position of relative weakness, women can only achieve power by manipulating the authoritarian man. Because of this, female power is a manipulative and weak form of power and is always subject to the will of men. In her study on family relations in Iran, Kousha observes: "Even for husbands who regarded their work and careers as more important than their families; such fathers delegated responsibilities and decision making to their wives because they saw children as being the mothers' domain of influence and too unimportant for the fathers' precious time. Nevertheless, all actions had to have the father's stamp of approval."[23]

Popular history in the Middle East also reflects male conditioning of female power. Combs-Schilling argues that the female in the *One Thousand and One Nights* remains dependent on the male for her existence, for her life itself. Her ability to bring the man pleasure, to entertain him, can give her a degree of worth in his eyes and therefore some influence on him. However, her influence is indirect and subordinate, dependent on his whim, while his control is direct and forthright.[24]

In contrast to the public sphere, the domestic sphere encompasses the struggle for power between men and women. The power of men in the public domain is practically uncontested, whereas power in the domestic space provides an opportunity for men to directly contend with women and assert their superiority. Therefore, one can argue that the hierarchy of power between the sexes exists within both the public and private domains and crosses in between.

However, abu-Lughod warns: "Power relations take many forms, have many aspects, and interweave. By presupposing some sort of hierarchy of significant and insignificant forms of power, we may be blocking ourselves from exploring the ways in which these forms may actually work simultaneously, in concert, or at cross-purposes."[25] Though this point is valid, the hierarchy of power does not exclusively deny power to women, but instead highlights the unbalanced relationship between the power of women and the power of men. Recognizing hierarchy does not necessarily justify it; rather, recognition is a significant step towards altering the hierarchy.

Hierarchy and issues of power and control are also central aspects of the relationships between women. The role of the mother-in-law, for example, embodies the aspects of hierarchy, power, control, authoritarianism, and violence. In fact, the foundation for the role of the mother-in-law is the hierarchy of her power and status in relation to the new bride's. This illustrates the fact that power hierarchies do not negate power altogether. Although there is a ranking order of the public and private domains, there is also a structure of hierarchy within them both. A division of power within the spheres reflects this. Within the domestic sphere, men have the final say in key decisions, while the less important daily decisions are left to women.

This does not mean that this division of power within the private domain is rigid or strict, however. Göcek and Balaghi explain that the boundaries of power are unendingly negotiated.[26] The process of negotiating and renegotiating the relationship of power occurs on a daily basis between the sexes. Domestic space is where this contest for power is played out. When power is exercised, the consequences of agency of one sex affects and is affected by the other sex. Nelson argues: "By re-evaluating the notion of power from the standpoint of reciprocity of influence, one can say that women can and do exercise influence over men."[27]

In this way, women achieve a certain level of power in the domestic sphere. However, this should not obscure the reality of unequal and unjust relationships of control and domination that exist between the sexes. Even though women's place in the patriarchal gender structure, and in all related activities, is based on degradation, there is nonetheless an elevation and appreciation for the world of men, where negotiations and decisions regarding politics, economy, and culture take place.

Because domesticity is considered to be part of the female world, the gender structure tends to trivialize the domestic sphere, deeming it unworthy of the attention of men. In her study of Persian folktales, Friedl explains: "Men are especially reluctant to interfere in their daughters' or wives' relationship with other women. To meddle in women's affairs, to take sides in their quarrels, is beyond the duty and dignity of a man."[28] Cultural and religious values ensure the exclusion of men from feminine space by declaring this domain unmanly. In turn, women play an active role in reinforcing the cultural exclusion of men from the private world and use it to their advantage. Furthermore, the failure of marriage to establish a healthy relationship between partners reinforces the situation.

The exclusion of men from the private domain does not inherently reflect the power of women; instead, it can also be seen as the process of social degradation and marginalization of the domestic sphere. It is true that, on the one hand, socially constructed divisions of space give women some control over family life and their children. None-theless, ultimate power, authority and control reside with men who are, in turn, happy to not be bothered with the insignificant and trivial aspects of the domestic sphere. Makhlouf remarks: "While the men are busy in the market, the office and the mosque, involved in those economic, political and religious activities that are defined as central in the culture, the domestic orientation of women seems irrelevant to the progression of activities 'outside' in the society. As if, by so clearly defining the feminine space, culture was setting women apart into timelessness."[29] Thus, in the domestic domain, female power is per-mitted or tolerated, whether women function in this sphere as queens or servants, simply because the domestic domain, the world of women, is downgraded.

It is curious why women's traditional, domestic power has not yet translated into more power in the public sphere, considering what happens in these spheres has tremendous direct and indirect effects on women's lives and that their absence is a missed opportunity to in-fluence this. Why is it that we expect women to settle for only trivial power rather than aspiring for equal power in society? Assuming their social inferiority, is acquiring the minor amount of power granted to women in the gender structure considered to be their ultimate con-quest? Exaggerating and celebrating the meager power women exer-cise in the private sphere runs the risk of confirming the inferiority of women. Instead, we should consider this traditional form of female power as a positive starting block for the next step, strengthening this power by extending it to other spheres such as the public and political realms of society. This extended power should then be used to make tangible improvements in the lives of women. Rather, women remain excluded from the domain where politics, economics, and legisla-tion are negotiated and shaped. Considering this, one might wonder whether the traditional power of women at the domestic level func-tions as a pacifying or compensating mechanism for their lack of power in the public domain.

Another factor affecting the power of women is the role of the state. State and nation-building in the Middle East, not unlike in other re-gions, has initially excluded women. Women's roles, interests, and as-pirations have been absent from the initial formation of the modern state. The incorporation of women has come later on in the process of nation-building. Only after the authoritarian and theocratic re-gimes felt it necessary to incorporate women in order to complete the state's domination over society did they begin to include women in the process of state-building. Paradoxically, this incorporation of women has also come with an increase in violence and authoritarianism.

Economic policies implemented by the state also discourage any serious opening of the labor market to the employment of women. These policies prevent women from acquiring larger shares of formal power. Essentially, the nature of the state and the political process hampers the objective of elevating women from their submerged world of domesticity into a more balanced life orientation by limiting the options available for women's empowerment. Further, the state's failure to implement economic and political reforms and to provide a decent level of services, living standard, and human capital development forces social institutions such as the family, religion, tribe, and sect to play a more significant role in society. In fact, these other social units provide spaces for protection from control and domination by the state. Thus, while these social units can be a source of power for women, they simultaneously reinforce patriarchal gender relations and the unequal status of the sexes. The failure of the state to improve economic conditions also makes the duty of providing more difficult for males, which affects domestic life and the structure of the family. While this might shake the imbalance in the relationships between men and women, it very well may increase violence between the sexes within marriage as well. In contrast to authoritarianism, a more productive social contract would, or should, include women in the nation's efforts. Women should not be content with their traditional power and space. Instead, they should aspire to be empowered at the formal level.

CHAPTER 7
Power and Price

Games are always in some sense contests, even if only with the self.
—*Sherry Ortner*

THE GENDER GAME

Although female power may be underappreciated, it is real and present in various forms. What we are concerned with here is how this power manifests within the patriarchal context and whether the use of this power truly serves the interests of women. The traditional structure of society does not encourage women to exercise power and agency in a meaningful, positive way. Marital relationships clearly demonstrate this in the manner in which females are allowed to contribute to the relationship in terms of power and agency. To be sure, both men and women exercise agency and power in their marital relationships. However, not unlike men, women do not necessarily use or invest this agency and power constructively or toward the end of fostering a better partnership, an investment that would benefit both partners. On the contrary, more often than not, women, like men, utilize power and agency in a game of gender relations, the result of which is mostly negative and destructive. According to Ortner:

> One of the central games of life in most cultures is the gender game, or more specifically the multiplicity of gender games available in that time and place. The effort to understand the making and unmaking of gender, as well as what gender makes, involves understanding the workings of these games as games, with their

inclusions and exclusions, multiple positions, complex rules, forms of bodily activity, structures of feeling and desire, and stakes of winning, losing, or simply playing. It involves as well the question of how gender games themselves collide with, encompass, or are bent to the service of, other games, for the gender is never, as they say, the only game in town.[1]

In terms of social gender polarization, the relationship between men and women is a zero-sum power game in which any gain on behalf of one side is considered a loss to the other. The relationship of power between wife and husband embodies this kind of gender game. Money and sex exchanged between partners are integral components of this game. These classic and ever-present ingredients of the gender game are not only found in the Middle East, but worldwide. Money and sex are the two most frequent issues that appear in marital conflict.

Religion also plays a significant role in defining the terms of the gender game between partners. Islam excludes women from matters of family finances through the Islamic sanction that men are to provide for women, thereby giving men the upper hand in this respect. Thus, Islam in this regard imposes a strong and forceful patriarchal aspect on the relationship. Both religion and culture require that the husband be the provider for the family, not both partners, even if the female is financially capable of doing so. Thus, Islam encourages women to keep their wealth for themselves, and this is said to illustrate that women are highly valued in Islam and are accorded with high status and respect. In reality, however, this works against the interests of women and tends to limit the choices available to them in life. As the provider, the husband's control over the family's finances is a tremendous source of power used to ensure the submission of his wife. Furthermore, because having control over one's finances is a defining feature of maturity, the wife's lack of financial independence prevents her from becoming a fully developed individual. It is this immaturity that induces the wife to actively engage in a subversive gender competition with her partner, the gender game.

Lacking monetary control, a wife's best card to play in the gender game against her husband is the ownership of her sexuality. In general, women's relationship to their sexuality is said to reflect a more natural state, whereas male-dominated culture and civilization are associated with the suppression of sexuality. Sex is often used by women as leverage to gain money and resources. Sexual power becomes a counterbalance to the financial power of the husband, and, therefore, sexuality becomes a power struggle between partners. Keddie and Beck express that another traditional reaction by females to subordination is manipulation of sexuality.[2] Minces agrees: "One of her main trump cards is manipulation of her husband's sexuality; she will 'punish' him by refusing her favors under various pretexts, depreciating his virility."[3]

Thus, sexuality is exercised in the gender game as a tool for manipulation. In fact, the religious and patriarchal exclusion of women from the financial world leaves women with very little choice but to use sexuality as a bargaining chip in this way. Yet, to be fair, even the male's obligation to provide for the family is, in reality, an exercise of manipulation and control of women. As both sex and money are reduced to tools of manipulation and control, violence and conflict in marital relationships increase.

Even though it is commonly employed by women in gender relations, the use of sexuality in the gender game is rigorously restricted by religious prescriptions. Islam confiscates this source of female power by sacralizing female sexuality as a religious duty owed to her husband. Thus, women's position in the gender game is strongly weakened because of their inability to support the family financially and the religious control over their sexuality that can pose serious limitations for women using their sexuality as a tool of manipulation. When men have the upper hand and women are weakened, the opportunities for compromising are limited. This huge gap in the power structure between men and women and the diminished ability to compromise is also a source of increasing conflict and violence in Middle Eastern families.

However, women have other means of procuring their power in this gender game. Vieille argues: "It is an act of hypocrisy and duplicity, when a woman submits herself to marital and masculine authority and to the dominant values, which are defined by men and, at the same time, plays her own role inside the institutions that deny power to her. One example of this behavior is the game of the woman inside the family, particularly in relation to her sons."[4] A woman will manipulate the special relationship she has with her children, particularly her sons, as a way to counter the position of her dominating husband. Therefore, her relationship with her sons becomes a part of the power struggle with her husband. Yet exploiting her relationships with her children in this way will prove to be negative and harmful for everyone in the long term.

There is another method of influence women use to affect their situation. In her study of Saudi women, al-Torki explains: "Married women who are in conflict with their husbands sometimes manipulate the security and support inherent in the father-daughter relationship in that a wife may threaten to return to her natal household."[5] However, natal family involvement is one of the major obstacles that make it difficult for new families to ensure their maturity and independence. Therefore, employing traditional methods of relying on the maternal family as a strategy for women to gain some leverage in the gender game can prove to be counterproductive in the end. This form of resistance is limited in its effects and tends to support the same traditional, patriarchal system of values that has cornered women in the first place.

The gender game does not necessarily result in equality between men and women. In the domestic sphere, the gender game reflects the disparity between the legitimate, authoritative power of men and the illegitimate, manipulative power of women. Relationships between partners within the domestic space are focused on control and conquest. Yet since women are absent or excluded from the public sphere, it is hardly a fair competition for the female gender to even play in the public domain. Male power in this domain is nearly uncontested and unchallenged. The upper hand that male power has in both the private and public spheres completely overshadows women, forcing them into a precarious situation, and as Beauvoir comments: "She is obliged to offer the man the myth of her submission, because he insists upon domination."[6]

In that sense, the private domain is where the gender game clearly manifests because it is in this space that the game influences, challenges, and contests female power. It is possible, though, that the satisfaction felt in playing the game and the little gain that women can generate by playing prevent women from challenging the gender game altogether and the social structure that supports it.

INFORMAL POWER

When female power lacks public recognition, it becomes informal, indirect, and limited. In her study of Persian folktales, Friedl explains that a woman's personal influence is the only influence she has because women usually do not fill a position in the power hierarchy.[7] In her ethnographical study of an Iraqi village in the 1960s, Fernea also observes: "In spite of the relative obscurity in which these women lived, I came to realize how much they influenced men, their husbands and especially their sons."[8] Joseph, on the other hand, stresses the role of sibling relationships in reproducing patriarchal power relations. Not only do brothers exert power and control but "sisters also [have] some power over brothers. Women have numerous avenues for involving their brothers in their lives. Because a woman's behavior immediately reflects on her brothers' honor, dignity, and sense of self, she [can] enhance or detract from her brothers' status by her actions, potentially compelling her brothers into action."[9] Studying Moroccan proverbs, Dwyer notes that there is also the image of the strong-minded and manipulative Middle Eastern woman, maneuvering in the family sphere with her informal powers and her noticeable self-assurance.[10]

Female power is also related to the formation of informal networks of relatives, neighbors, and friends. These networks serve as a support system for women as well as a medium for conducting and organizing marriages, a significant aspect of social life in the Middle East. Al-Torki contends: "Separation of the sexes leads to the radical seclusion of women from public life. This segregation finds its cultural compensation in the elaboration of formal and informal networks of friendship and kin. Social visits are the major means for women to reduce their isolation. It is thus not suspiring that they are more elaborate among women and are taken more seriously by them than by men."[11] She continues: "The very seclusion 'shielding' women from public life also excludes men from a domain affecting their public concerns. It is precisely this seclusion that gives women information about marriageable girls unavailable to the men but needed in the formation of kin groups."[12]

Forming informal networks and contracting marriages reflects a form of female agency and power in society. Nevertheless, these networks are still a part of the traditional system that ensures the structural control and oppression of women. In the words of Ortner: "It is the creativity of the women within the limits of their traditional politics."[13] Informal networks operate within patriarchal settings and are permeated by patriarchal values and norms. While women temporarily benefit from these networks, in the end it is a traditional system that also reinforces and strengthens the patriarchal gender structure, which is ultimately destructive toward women's interests. Therefore, these networks are a positive aspect in the short term but negative in the end. The small gain of informal power is also a loss for women because the end result of this form of female power strengthens patriarchy.

A conflict is thus created between immediate gains of agency and status for some women and the collective social agency and status of women as a whole. This form of individual female agency is expressed by playing an active role in enforcing patriarchal control over other subordinate women. Females often help enforce patriarchal control by intervening in the lives of other women and policing their behavior. These exercises in female power inevitably evolve into degrading and dehumanizing acts against other women. As a result, the relationship between women and the agency they invoke depreciates, becoming a negative aspect in the patriarchal context. In addition, female gathering is not only a source of negative power but also a source of gossip, teasing, and conflict, which also reflects women's disadvantaged position and lower status in society. A Moroccan proverb reads: "The quarrel of women is a trouble, and their trouble will not be forgotten."[14] Patriarchy is a system that denies women access to positive and meaningful forms of agency and participation, and the choices that are offered to women by the patriarchal system are very limited, conditional, and counterproductive.

There are various reasons why women seek informal networks and social visits. One reason is because they are excluded from public affairs where their energies and initiatives are neither needed nor welcomed. However, a more productive and inclusive public sphere and a democratic state project that could appreciate and absorb the energies and capabilities of both men and women would have a different impact on the patriarchal gender structure of society.

On the other hand, women also seek the formation of these networks because they live in loveless, dull conjugal relationships. However, if women were to strive for better relations with their husbands, rather than investing heavily in traditional networks, their efforts may very well lead to more positive outcomes in the domestic realm. Even though the public domain excludes women and confines them to the domestic sphere, women could choose to conduct themselves differently within this domain. Women do have a choice as to where they invest themselves. They can invest mostly in externalities, but they can also invest in developing healthy relationships with their husbands. While it is true that by seeking traditional networks women are given the chance to display agency and resistance, it is also true that women could also display agency and resistance by striving to improve their marital life. Agency that could revive the quality of marital relationships is a positive form of agency, and improving marital relationships would also be a positive form of power.

Paradoxically, adopting a strategy of improving women's relationships with their partners would first require women to relinquish their central role in arranged marriages, one of the significant sources of female power within the gender structure. Yet arranged marriages are one of the crucial social features that ultimately contribute to the failure of marriages. Women's involvement in marriage organization is clearly a type of female power that damages the interests of women in the long run. Choosing a wife and arranging a marriage is very often linked to the authoritarian role of the mother-in-law, and is also a mechanism for the natal family to maintain control over the newly wedded partners.

Informal female power is the product of women's segregation and seclusion from public life as well as loveless, dull, and dysfunctional marriages. Networks and social visits are more of a compensation for their unfavorable circumstances than an indication of active agency. All-female gatherings tend to be more intense and take on a different meaning in the context of a segregated world. These gatherings become the limits of the female world. In fact, they become women's entire world. A study conducted by Mensch et al. on Egyptian adolescents concludes: "The important task of adolescent socialization, particularly for girls, is learning how to mobilize social networks rather than becoming independent from the older generation."[15] To argue that women are segregated yet powerful is questionable indeed.

Unmarried women have very little or no status in these societies that only recognize women as individuals when they have married. Yet women achieve this minimal recognition at the price of submitting to the control and domination of the husband, as a servant of his will. When a woman has children, particularly boys, her status elevates greatly. However, this increase in status is also accompanied by the burden and misery of the fact that she alone will be in charge of caring for all household members, husband and children, and doing endless household chores. A mother's increased status is also always vulnerable to the will of the husband and is constantly at risk from the uncontrolled right of men to divorce. Given this, the role of the mother-in-law is the highest status a woman can achieve in a patriarchal structure. Nonetheless, this role is contingent on the support and tolerance of men. This position is also associated with the miseries and insecurities of the new family, as well as an obligation to impose violence on another woman by demanding her submission.

Because women's status and power is greatly constrained by religiously and culturally sanctioned patriarchal male domination, women are in conflict with men's status in society and in the family. Rassam points out: "It is clear that the woman's status is, largely, dependent on how well she assesses and manipulates her ties to the males in the household."[16] She continues: Unlike men, "women have no inherent rights to power; what little they do manage to accede to is both limited and transitory as it is contingent on their fulfillment of the roles of wife, mother and mother-in-law."[17]

What is more, the patriarchal gender structure does not allow women to actively initiate an elevation of their status. Spellberg explains: "Women are not active in promoting or attaining honor, but demonstrate only passive proof of its maintenance in the public vigilance of male control and protection."[18] From studying Persian folktales, Friedl concludes that in the tales, a woman's destiny is usually dependent on the actions of men who have authority over her, like a father or husband.[19] It is obvious in all instances within the prevailing gender structure that women inevitably behave negatively following an elevation in their status, simply because few other options exist. Even the agency granted to women in the role of the mother-in-law has its limitations and conditions.

It is important to add that although it is often claimed that Islam grants women in the Middle East dignity and respect, this does not translate into tangible rights, status, or power for women. In fact, substituting *respect* in place of status and power only aggravates the miseries of women in these societies. This claimed respect for women also stipulates the unquestioned, normalized subjection of women to utter obedience and submissiveness. It is noteworthy that Middle Eastern cultures are not troubled by this paradoxical contradiction of bringing together such obviously disparate social values. Respect and obedience are, of course, mutually exclusive, and the existence of one negates the other. One can find this same tendency in the Islamic and cultural sanctioning of the obedience of children as a show of respect toward their parents. Respectability can lead to a better life and higher status for women *in concept only*. Women's limited basic human rights contradict any notions of respectability and appreciation of women in these societies. In this regard, it is possible that the high level of respect for women that is touted in the Middle East is, yet again, a case of the broad disparity between empty rhetoric and the dim reality that is found in the region.

FRAGMENTED POWER

Rassam is a proponent of the argument that women's gains in power and status cause power to become fragmented, which may, in fact, damage women's interests overall. She argues: "It is my contention that the inevitable competition for domestic power which takes place among women in the patriarchal extended household prevents the potential formation of any alliances among these women and weakens their position vis-à-vis the men. In addition, the fragmented and varying nature of the power, which is available to women, prevents any one woman from gaining and holding onto too much power at any one time."[20] The traditional social system, in which sons bring wives into the households of their mothers, allows each woman only partial access to domestic power. Through such fragmentation of power, women are unable to consolidate too much power at any time, thus contributing to the maintenance of male dominance.[21]

These fragmented sources of power, in which women maintain a little power here and there, do not add up to an integrated and comprehensive form of power for all women that could have a potentially positive impact on women's status in the public domain. One concrete example of fragmented power's detrimental impact is the formation of informal female networks. Even though these networks tend to benefit and support the women involved directly, this nevertheless comes at the expense of forming formal networks that would benefit the advancement of women in society as a whole. It is true that under authoritarian control, the lack of freedom and ability to express opinions prevents and weakens civil society, as well as women's participation in public life. However, explaining this situation is not so simple.

Reality proves that men do not monopolize rationality to the extent necessary to legitimately justify their dominance in the public realm. Equally, reality also proves that women do not lack rationality, wisdom, and sound judgment, which would certainly prevent them from participating in the public sphere. In *One Thousand and One Nights*, one finds that rationality and wisdom are not necessarily associated with the ruler in the story, Shahrayar, or men in general, but with the female character, Shahrazad. The ruler's reaction to his wife's act of betrayal is emotional and lacks wisdom, a reaction associated with the natural reaction of a female. His reaction is extreme, brutal, and violent, which are the very indicators of the lack of power. These stories portray male power as weak and present female weakness as a form of power and wisdom.

The indirect power of women is a reality that is difficult to deny. Yet it is important not to interpret this power as a balanced compensation for the subjugation and oppression of women, but rather of its existence in spite of being subjugated and oppressed. It is in the interest of women themselves to transform their fragmented power into a more formally recognized power, which would guarantee better human rights for women and a higher status in society. Conversely, the feelings of contentment and satisfaction that women derive from their fragmented and limited powers within domestic space work against their own interests in the long run. It is important to recognize the agency that women do have in gender relations, but it is equally important to ask: To what end does this agency serve?

Power and agency have a mutual and dialectic relationship. Agency that secures a power gain in the short run, but fails to improve the situation of women in society, is agency that does not necessarily secure real and lasting power. In her study of Iraqi women, al-Khayyat draws attention to the fact that: "Although many women were conscious of their oppression, they all saw this as an individual problem and their everyday behavior merely encouraged such oppression."[22] Rosaldo adds: "As long as the domestic sphere remains female, women's societies, however powerful, will never be the political equivalents of men's."[23]

The line defining power and weakness in gender relations is not easily drawn. For example, one could look on the role of the mother-in-law, the highest-ranking female power for a woman, from different angles and see a very different picture. On the one hand, one can see this role as an illustration of female power and resistance to the gender system. On the other hand, it can also be seen as weakness and complicity with the dominant patriarchal ideology, which reflects both women's power and weaknesses at the same time.

This situation induces women to take advantage of whatever opportunity the gender system offers or tolerates, regardless of the cost or whom it may harm. Aspiring for something different, or nurturing a form of female power that could challenge women's situation, is not a tolerated option in patriarchy. Friedl observes that women "can be expected to continue to try to use traditional means to create power, such as resistance, in conducting their lives, even to intensify these power tactics when other sources of power are curtailed."[24] MacLeod, in her study of the women of Cairo, elaborates: "The resilience of power relations can be explained, not as something which happens behind women's backs, but as the result, in part, of the way women struggle."[25]

The inability to mobilize women to challenge the patriarchal structure of gender relations is a controversial issue in the discussion of female power. Not only does female power fail to challenge the gender process, but much of this power is, in fact, derived from conformity with the system. Friedl contends: "A willing, cooperative, and competent housekeeper, a woman can gain considerable manipulative power."[26] "Accepting the male paradigm, women paradoxically can turn the male view into a source of power for themselves in relation to others in low positions."[27] Assia Djebbar states: "Muslim women are all too often silent, and they appear to be so all the time. The assumption, sometimes overstated, that they exercise a measure of authority behind the scenes is small consolation and one, which is generally offered to oppressed minorities."[28]

Thus, these forms of female agency and informal power do not help to improve women's situation. Female participation in the Middle Eastern labor market is still around 25–30 percent at best, which is the lowest rate of female participation in the world. This disparity in the public realm was also made evident in recent political elections held in the Middle East, in which women failed to be elected despite the fact that they represented more than half of the electorates. Women still constitute less than 10 percent of representatives in Middle Eastern parliaments, the lowest percentage worldwide. One wonders, though, why female power, influence, and agency in the domestic sphere do not translate into success in the public sphere, even at a minimal level. Kuwaiti women's struggle for political rights persisted a long time before women were finally permitted to participate in the political system; yet, even so, not a single woman has been elected thus far. This has occurred in other Gulf countries as well. In Bahrain two parliamentary election sessions did not result in the election of any women to parliament. Only after an official decree accorded women a quota of seats in Iraqi parliament were 25 percent of the votes secured for women. Even then, most of these "elected" women were staunch advocates of the patriarchal and misogynistic ideologies that counteract efforts toward the empowerment of women. Furthermore, a 2006 Gallup poll in eight predominantly Muslim countries found that the majority of women in Saudi Arabia still do not agree that women should be allowed to hold political office. In 2005, 500 women addressed a letter to the Saudi King asking him to save the country from the onslaught of Westernized ideas regarding women and to uphold the ban against women driving and working alongside men.[29]

The power that women do have in the domestic domain is exercised in the form of violence, particularly against other women. In this sense, the expression of this power is an opportunistic act of violence against weaker individuals in a social system that insists on hierarchy, control, and submission. Agency used to perpetuate the cycle of violence and victimization that contributes to the subordination of women is itself violent and destructive, despite the fact that it comes from women themselves.

The role of the mother-in-law is the highest position of control, power, and status a woman can achieve in the patriarchal power structure; however, it is only a fragmented power. Therefore, even in its pinnacle form, female power that can be exercised partially here and partially there fails to aggregate a power forceful enough to challenge the very rationale and structure of patriarchal ideology. Thus, the lure of power, fragmented as it is, is self-defeating, self-damaging, and counterproductive. The patriarchal system tolerates this kind of power solely because fragmented power fails to present any serious challenge to the foundational premises and values of the system. Patriarchy has a built-in mechanism for tolerating limited, fragmented female power. This minor toleration ensures the conformity and compliance of women as well as female active participation in the patriarchal system. Therefore, this minor tolerance of female power proves to be in the interest of the patriarchal order. This system of tolerance and compliance also helps to explain the survival, persistence, and durability of the patriarchal system.

The patriarchal system guarantees whatever limited, fragmentary power women manage to gain is lost because of the fact that the system becomes even more durable as the result of tolerated female power. Of course, the question is whether or not this is a fair trade-off. The other question is whether or not women have any other choice. For sure, patriarchy limits women's choices to only those that support patriarchal structures. Yet one wonders why the patriarchal system is allowed to continue defining the social existence of men and women. Because these minor patriarchal gains for women did not, and do not, inspire any serious change in the position and status of women in society, is it not high time to question the very rationale and values underlying patriarchal ideology?

CHAPTER 8

Violence, Victimization, and Conformity

The hallmark of oppression is its invisibility to the oppressed.
—*Catriona Mackenzie*

VIOLENCE-POWER NEXUS

It is crucial in order to understand the ways in which violence is exhibited in society to have a theoretical framework regarding the subject of violence. Galtung has made a prominent contribution in this regard. According to Galtung: "Violence is present when human beings are being influenced so that their actual somatic and mental realizations are below their potential realizations. . . . Violence is here defined as the cause of the difference between the potential and the actual, between what could have been and what is."[1] "Increased violence may come about by increase in the potential as well as by decrease in the actual levels."[2] Galtung makes several other distinctions regarding violence such as the distinction between physical and psychological violence; intended and unintended violence; manifest and latent violence; and direct and indirect violence, that is, whether or not there is an actor directly engaged in violence.[3] Galtung also stresses the connection between personal and structural violence, arguing: "There is a personal element in structural violence while on the other hand there is a structural element in personal violence. Thus, personal violence works not only on the basis of individual deliberations, but also on the basis of expectations impinging on the actor as norms. When one husband beats his wife there is a clear case of personal violence, but when one million husbands keep one million wives in ignorance there is structural violence."[4] Structural violence is a key concern in analyzing gender relations because the gender structure creates and is created by structural violence.

Structural violence is a mode or a system of domination, dehumanization, and debasement. It is violence generated by the social system irrespective of the will and intentions of individual actors. Physical violence is a direct and overt manifestation of structural violence, whereas structural violence is much deeper and systemic. Galtung also contends: "The 'tools of oppression' may have internalized the repressive structure to the extent that their personal violence is an expression of internalized, not only institutionalized, norms."[5] Participants in direct violence are unconscious of the underlying structural violence in their society. Considering this, it is important to stress that an analysis of structural violence does not excuse or justify physical violence towards women.

In another study, Galtung also distinguishes between direct, structural, and cultural violence. "Direct violence is an event; structural violence is a process with ups and downs; cultural violence is an invariant, a 'permanent', remaining essentially the same for long periods, given the slow transformation of basic culture."[6] He adds: "With the violent structure institutionalized and the violent culture internalized, direct violence also tends to become institutionalized, repetitive, and ritualistic."[7] Thus, members of society can use cultural violence to justify and legitimize direct and structural forms of violence by making it look, or even feel, right or at least not necessarily wrong. Generally, a causal flow of violence can be identified from the cultural, via the structural, to direct forms of violence. Galtung continues: "Culture preaches, teaches, admonishes, eggs on, and dulls us into seeing exploitation and/or repression as normal and natural, or into not seeing them at all."[8]

Violence is also strongly connected to power. Discussing this violence-power nexus, Mason contends: "Violence, as an instrument of power, intimately and inextricably entwines with power."[9] "Violence is neither indispensable to, nor exempt from, a given power relation."[10] Goldner et al. express: "Violence is simultaneously an instrumental and an expressive act; its instrumentality rests on the fact that it is a powerful method of social control."[11] In this way, violence is an expression of authority and power aiming to ensure control and domination.

More specifically, violence relates to the domination of men over women. Mason emphasizes this, stating: "Violence connects to patriarchal power, which is a form of domination that subjugates women by blocking them from doing certain things or thinking in certain ways; women are controlled through demands for social conformity and obedience. Violence is both an effect of male power and crucial to the continuance of that power."[12] Yodanis argues that in male-dominated institutions, "violence is a tool that men can use to keep women out or subordinate and thereby maintain male power and control."[13] "Violence is not solely explained by men's individual characteristics, attitudes, and experiences. Rather, violence against women is linked to structures of male dominance."[14] Moreover, Maynard and Winn suggest: "Violence is both a reflection of unequal power relationships in society and serves to maintain those unequal power relations. It reflects and maintains the power that men have over women in society."[15] Thus, violence is a crucial element of the dominant-submissive power relation found in the gender structure; it is a means of maintaining and reinforcing male power and the subjugation of women.

Interestingly, though, Mason points out a conceptual contradiction in the feminist approach to the violence-power nexus. He states: "On the one hand, feminist theory tends to assert that violence is a manifestation of male power. On the other hand, violence is said to be the product of the difficulty that patriarchy has in maintaining this power."[16]

One of the ways patriarchy manages its difficulty with maintaining power is to reify women's subjugation. Mernissi argues: "In order for power to exist, it is necessary that the dominated person suffer the mutilation of certain attributes previously shared with the dominator. The reification of woman is a necessary condition for patriarchal domination."[17] Thus, degradation and reification of women's subjugation are necessary to sustain and justify patriarchy's power and domination as well as violence against women.

The social construction of gender in Middle Eastern society is a clear-cut illustration of prevailing structural violence. Battering of women exists in all societies; however, Middle Eastern cultural values go further in justifying and legitimizing violence against women in this region. To be a woman is to be the subject of violence, control, and intimidation from all angles. Everyone, including males and females, participates in this "party of violence": the husband, father, mother, brothers, uncles, aunts, sons, and parents-in-law. In contrast to other forms of violence, society tolerates violence against women and considers it to be a legitimate, honorable, and heroic type of violence. This pattern of direct violence, which has become firmly institutionalized, as Galtung advocates, "could be referred to as 'ritualized', or 'institutionalized' violence. That type of violence tends to be accepted socially as part of 'human nature' or social reality."[18]

The natural question one may ask in this regard is: While all these people partake in gender violence, who is left to defend and support women and redress the extreme injustices against them? The ritual-ization and institutionalization of gender violence in patriarchy leave no room for any perception of injustice against women and lead to the normalization of this violence in society. And yet if everyone is indifferent toward women's suffering and society as a whole func-tions against them, what choices do women have, given these circum-stances? Dominant gender ideologies leave women with no option but to resign and surrender to their fate. Any alternative that runs the risks of disgrace, prostitution, even honor killing presents itself as a far worse option. Not only do women surrender to their fate, but they, in fact, participate in this ceremony of violence. Patriarchal gender ideology is an open system of aggression and violence that can coerce an entire society into acting as its accomplice. This ideology fails to recognize women as worthy human beings, thus violating their basic human rights. According to Green, gender violence is centrally posi-tioned within the overall context of gender relations.[19] Galtung also emphasizes this fact:

> Failure to perceive the reality of patriarchy in human society can perhaps best be explained as an example of cultural violence at work. Patriarchy, like any other deeply violent social formation, combines direct, structural, and cultural violence in a vicious triangle. They reinforce each other in cycles starting from any corner. Direct violence, such as rape, intimidates and represses; structural violence institutionalizes; and cultural violence inter-nalizes that relation, especially for the victims, the women, mak-ing the structure very durable.[20]

Thus, the everyday manifestations of violence are conditioned by the structure of society and gender ideology, which facilitates the pro-duction of oppressive gender relations. A repressive model, according to Mason, is one that sees power as a matter of prohibitions and limits that are placed on desires and actions of human beings.[21] Therefore, relationships between the sexes are portrayals of violence, control, and power relations. Green states that at the individual, interpersonal, and institutional levels, gender violence, which is a mechanism of control, works to entrench control over females.[22]

Direct violence against women takes many forms such as female genital mutilation, rape (including marital rape), honor killing, wife battering, and so forth. Galtung affirms that rape, whether committed as a violent form of obtaining sex, or a sexual way of committing violence, is an important aspect of the violence against women.[23] The woman's body becomes an object of conquest for men, and the interpersonal relations between men and women come to reflect the violent gender structure and ideology. Violence is not only expressed in physical ways; it can take on many different forms. One Iraqi woman says: "He never allows me to express my opinion when we're with others; he always shuts me up and disagrees with anything I say. He always makes fun of me."[24] Al-Khayyat insists that women suffer from steady feelings of guilt without necessarily having committed any dishonorable act.[25]

Communication between husband and wife becomes violent as well, supporting the dominant-submissive power relations in family life. The sexual power relations, Green explains, "focus on the family as a site of gender violence, which is perpetuated by the silence that protects 'traditional values' and the sanctity surrounding the family."[26] She continues to say that control can be forced through direct as well as insidious means. The most insidious forms of violence do not involve overt brutality but psychological cruelty that results in anguish and the disintegration of the self.[27] Galtung adds: "When the other is not only dehumanized but has been successfully converted into an 'it', deprived of humanhood, the stage is set for any type of direct violence, which is then blamed on the victim."[28]

The flip side to the control over women in the home is the exercise of violence as an expression of male domination in society. There is a strong link between violence, power, and the construction of masculinity. Violence and masculinity are intertwined and mutually reinforcing. Prevalent gender ideology causes the construction of masculinity to embody gender violence. Beauvoir argues that a male feels hostility towards women because he is afraid of them, and he is fearful of them because he is afraid of the personage, the image, with which he identifies himself.[29] According to Yllö: "Violence against women is a part of male control. Violence grows out of inequality within marriage, and reinforces male dominance and female subordination within the home and outside it."[30] To summarize, Maynard and Winn argue that male violence is not merely a result of women's subordination in society but also contributes to the construction of that subordination and is thus instrumental.[31]

However, despite the preponderance of daily acts of violence and society's tolerance of it, one cannot say that violence is biologically inherent in the nature of men. There is nothing normal about violence, whether it is committed by men or women. It is equally important to stress that there is no justification for a society's tolerance of it. However, the structure of Middle Eastern society tends to condition individuals to accept violence and submission. Yet both nonviolent men as well as unsubmissive or even violent women exist in these societies. If direct violence is mostly represented by male violence, structural violence represents the agency of both sexes. Women undoubtedly play an integral role in maintaining the structure of violence in society.

VICTIMIZATION AND AGENCY

To assume women are necessarily weak, passive, or victimized would be a misleading approach to understanding gender relations. To claim that women are inevitable victims, Kelly, Burton, and Regan argue, is to confuse empirical reality with the construction of identity.[32] Yllö asserts that the feminist focus on women as a victimized class has masked the diversity among women as well as among the men who perpetrate the violence.[33] Goldner et al. stress the need to move beyond "the reductionist view of men as simply abusing their power, and of women as colluding in their own victimization by not leaving. This description casts men as tyrants and women as masochists and deprives both of their humanity while simultaneously capturing a piece of the truth. While gender inequality is a social reality, at the same time, reciprocities and complementary patterns in the couple's relationship are implicated in the cycle of violence."[34]

Women too are the victimizers, at times, playing an active role in perpetrating various different forms of violence. Regarding women as perpetual victims tends to reinforce and legitimize the patriarchal premise that women are weak creatures by nature. Yet women are, in fact, not always weak, passive, or victimized. On the contrary, they are strong, active, and can play a positive role. But the nature and structure of patriarchal gender relations prevents women from taking on a more constructive role in society. In fact, the gender structure allows or encourages women to behave violently and destructively.

Although it is true that women are often victims, men are also victims of the patriarchal gender structure. There is no direct link between passivity and being victimized; victimhood and agency work together at the same time. According to Kelly: "A focus on women as victims of violence that comes to constitute a denial of women's agency is a misleading approach. In this construction, women's agency is recognized only when women act in ways, which resemble traditional male behavior. In this restriction of the meaning of agency, agency appears to reside solely in the actions of the violator; thus, the position of agent for women is confined to perpetration of, or support for, violence."[35]

However, women in the Middle East have always been depicted as powerless victims. Göcek and Balaghi insist: "The assumption that tradition-bound societies leave little room for female participation in society tends to portray a passive image on women in the Middle East, as mute followers of tradition, bound to a static and powerless existence."[36] Afshar also contends that the romanticized images of the gentle victims of the harem are contrasted with everyday reality, which bears little resemblance to the perfumed undulating sexual prey. Middle Eastern women have for long found effective strategies for accommodating and playing a fulfilling role within a marriage, and even coping with polygamy.[37] MacLeod agrees: "Women in the Middle East are often pitied as the victims of an especially oppressive culture, generally equated with Islamic religion. Women are depicted as bound to the harem, downtrodden and constrained. Yet this picture cannot be reconciled with the assertive behavior and influential position of women in many Middle Eastern settings."[38]

Thus, while it is true that women are victims of gender relations, their victimhood is not an absolute or constant state. Not only are they victims, but they are also abusers who contribute to, sustain, and even increase the intensity of violence in society. Kelly criticizes the common conception of female victimization arguing that gender analysis is predicated on leaving out women as perpetrators and supporters of violence in both interpersonal and inter-group relations.[39] Loseke also contends: "Because feminist theories begin with the a priori labeling of women as victims and men as offenders, they also are unable to conceptualize women's violence toward men except as violence done in self-defense."[40] Furthermore, Jackson states: "Radical feminist perspectives are often misread as essentialist, as implying that men are naturally sexually violent and predatory, and that women are innately loving and egalitarian."[41] Rather, it is the case that men and women are both victims and abusers within the patriarchal gender structure.

Violence is not monopolized by men; women also help facilitate the perpetuation of structural violence within gender relations. In this regard, one can say that female violence negates the concept that social violence is exclusively a male phenomenon. It also invalidates the conceptualization of women as passive victims and establishes the truth of their agency and active involvement in perpetuating violence. Including women in the category of perpetrators reveals that the perpetuation of violence is a comprehensive or inclusionary process that both sexes contribute to. Moreover, female violence is exercised within the context of the patriarchal gender structure and the dominance of male power. Therefore, female violence inherently supports the oppressive gender structure and, ironically enough, strengthens male power.

As Galtung argues, violence breeds violence.[42] Although it is true that female violence is a reaction to the violence brought against them, whether it be direct or structural, it is not a passive reaction but an active involvement in violence. In other words, while female violence is apparently an attempt to redress injustice brought against them, women's role in the perpetuation of violence tends to exacerbate the situation. Minces contends: "Older women transmit men's authority and are thus equally important in maintaining customs. Their authority over their own domain is often as despotic as the men's and they will exercise every means of pressure at their disposal to ensure that the established order is respected, formally at least."[43] Thus, women act as violently as men do in domestic family life. The role of the mother-in-law is one institutionalized mechanism for dispensing extreme female violence. Mernissi argues that if a woman is impelled to rebel against the constraints, her enmity to the system is explicitly destructive to the surrounding order.[44] Beauvoir concurs: "Even her outbursts of violence rise from depths of resignation. . . . She may hope neither to change the world nor to transcend it, she can only destroy."[45] "Woman is deprived of the lessons of violence by her nature; her muscular weakness disposes her to passivity."[46] Beauvoir continues: "She can do away with this inferiority only by destroying the male's superiority. . . . All oppression creates a state of war, and this is no exception. . . . She replies to his lack of confidence in her by assuming an aggressive attitude. Here two transcendences are face to face; instead of displaying mutual recognition, each free being wishes to dominate the other."[47]

CONFORMITY AND COMPLICITY

Female victimhood and violence are not absolute, exclusive features of women's condition. Conformity and resistance are other aspects of the role women occupy in the gender structure. Men and women also negotiate authority, status, and power within the gender structure. However, the only way women are able to do this is to conform to the established social norms and cultural values. For a woman, having the ability to negotiate her own status and power is a matter of guarding her virginity until marriage, producing sons through marriage, and seizing the "opening" in the patriarchal power structure in her role as the authoritarian mother-in-law. Any other sort of status negotiation within the gender structure is not only unconceivable but self-afflicting.

Oppression cannot work, Mackenzie proposes, if the oppressed decline to identify with the oppressor's definition of themselves; such refusal would signal the onset of hostilities between the oppressor and the oppressed.[48] Kandiyoti adds that the control of women is a type of social control that may bring forth a populist consensus from both male and female constituencies.[49] Beauvoir also concurs: "It must be admitted that the males find in women more complicity than the oppressor usually finds in the oppressed. Yet this is how a woman is brought up, without ever being impressed with the necessity of taking charge of her own existence. So she readily lets herself come to count on the protection, love, assistance, and supervision of others."[50] Finally, MacLeod comments that although these women definitely struggle to amplify their options, they also play a real part in upholding the social context, including power relations that limit women's opportunities.[51]

It is interesting to explore the question of why women comply and conform within the gender structure when it is clearly detrimental to their own interests. One of the realities that tends to reinforce the conformity of women is what Ortner calls "socially engendered conservatism" and the traditionalism of women's thinking. "She is almost universally socialized to have a narrower and generally more conservative set of attitudes and views than men, and the limited social context of her adult life reinforces this situation."[52] Mann also brings to our attention that a woman is not just the embodiment of this system, but the transmitter of its values.[53] Kousha concurs by referring to "the irony that lies in the fact that while it is the patriarchal structure that determines women's status, it is often the mother who carries and passes on to her daughter a devalued view of the feminine and of women's role in society. Socialized according to dominant gender roles, mothers pass on a cycle of powerlessness that becomes instrumental in perpetuating the patriarchal structure where masculinity and its attributes are more valued."[54]

By transmitting the values of the social system, women themselves act as accomplices to the patriarchal system. It is inconceivable that one could transmit social values without accepting these values first. Playing the role of value transmitter reinforces the subjugation of women as well as their acceptance of this situation. In order to be able to transmit social values, women need to make sense of these values and to make sense of their miserable situation. The only way to do this is to internalize the very same values that oppress them. Many of these oppressive controls, Green reasons, may or may not be perceived or experienced as controls.[55] Zuhur states: "Women may not view themselves as being sexually oppressed."[56] "Women educate their daughters in survival techniques adapted to the degree of patriarchy prevalent in each era."[57]

There are great pressures placed on Middle Eastern women to conform to the patriarchal reality. Apart from the few various ways of subverting the system, women have little choice but to comply, and they do so to the extent that they internalize the values of patriarchal gender ideology as their own. Even though women suffer from gender violence, they tend to idealize violence. For instance, it is perceived to be humiliating for women to not be married to *real* man. Yet a real man, in the patriarchal context, is highly masculine, authoritarian, and expects servitude from women. The opposite type of man is considered by women themselves to be feminine. It has been pointed out that during the civil war in Lebanon 1975–90, the many warlords interested in maintaining ongoing war received much admiration from Lebanese women, and many weddings occurred between these leaders and beautiful Lebanese women.[58] The ruthless and violent dictator, Saddam Hussein, was also admired by many Iraqi women as a true and strong Iraqi man. A similar admiration for the heroism and manhood of Osama bin Laden was found throughout the Middle East. Yet this region is not alone in this tendency, as this phenomenon has been observed in Germany regarding Hitler as well as with Italy's Mussolini. It seems that men who are perceived to be attractive and desirable by women are those who are violent. Al-Khayyat argues that women "strongly supported the traditional notion of masculine superiority because women are socialized to believe that a strong dominant man is the ideal."[59]

Therefore, conforming to the exigencies demanded by gender relations is a part of life in this gender structure. The same mechanism that induces male violence against women, as well as the submission of women to male control and power, also induces women to exercise violence against other women. Consenting to subordination and violence becomes justifiable to women when they act as both perpetrators

and victims in this process. Women not only conform to gender ideology, but they become an integral part in enforcing control as well.
Controlling and policing women in society is the duty of both men
and women. "All older women are expected to be sexually inactive,"
al-Khayyat states, "and as women get older they can be trusted more
by men in the family, and they start policing younger women to meet
the same expectations of trust."[60] She continues to say: "This oppression is practiced upon women by both sexes. In fact, women probably
feel a greater direct oppression by members of their own sex than by
men, as women practice social control by adopting male ways of thinking and male roles in policing each other."[61]

Self-policing is a virtue and a necessity for women in the gender
structure. In this sense, self-policing and the participation of women
themselves in the control over other women limits males' control of
women's lives but do not result in less control over women overall.
However, women's involvement in self-policing is only possible by
internalizing the mechanisms of control, sharing the responsibility of controlling women with men. Thus, male control is replaced
with self-control and external control with internal control. This self-
policing creates the appearance that women are taking control of their
own lives and resisting the power of men. In reality, however, by self-
policing, women act as men's accomplices by promoting strict conformity with the unjust and oppressive gender structure. The destructive
side to this strategy is self-evident. Internal control is even more powerful than the external control in the subjugation of women. Internal
control requires the highest level of internalization, acceptance, and
conformity, thereby worsening women's already wretched experience.

Because of the effects of this process, escaping this situation is even
more difficult and complex, considering especially that in some ways,
this conformity is beneficial to women. Al-Torki in her study of Saudi
women remarks: "Whereas women complain about parental control
and restrictions on their mobility, many see advantages in the financial
and emotional security, which their networks of kin and friends grant
them."[62] The same observation was made by Mohsen about Egyptian
women, that while they are expressing their discontent with the old
ways, blaming them for all social evils, these women are unwilling to
risk losing the security of the old system.[63] Calling it the "convenience
of subservience," Jalal also emphasizes this fact: "Submission can be
socially rewarding. Women are accorded respect as well as a modicum
of privileges within the sphere of the family and, depending on their
generational and marital status, also in wider social networks."[64] She

adds: "As beneficiaries of social accommodations worked out over long periods of history, middle and upper class women everywhere have a stake in preserving the existing structures of authority, and with it the convenience of a subservience that denies them equality in the public realm but also affords privileges not available to women lower down the rung of the social hierarchy."[65]

Conformity provides some advantages to women, which in turn make it easier for them to accept their submission. These advantages help ensure a rank of power in the social structure that allows some women to enjoy a certain level of power. Zuhur argues: "Some degree of female support or passive acceptance of the patriarchal order occurred over time, but we do not know if female power existed despite it or because of it."[66] Undoubtedly, the task of challenging the social system is difficult, making conformity the easier option for women. Some level of intimacy with the husband, marriage commitment, family, and the presence of children make it all the more difficult for women to show resistance. As Mackenzie warns, complicity is easier than the arduous task of resisting oppression and accepting responsibility for one's own freedom.[67]

However, if women support and participate in violence, they should at least admit their involvement, whether it is direct or indirect, as well as their responsibility for perpetuating the violent system. In support of this point, Jalal contends:

> There is a gap between individual awareness and collective action. This is precisely why the role of relatively economically privileged and educated women in the reproduction of the gender biases underpinning their subservience has to be plainly acknowledged. Refusing to accept an element of complicity on the part of women is tantamount to viewing them as passive victims acted upon by social forces over which they have no control. Holding them responsible, might serve as a goad for some and confirmation for others to undertake the critical self-evaluation that is so essential if they are to realize their potential as active agents with choices in shaping the processes of social change.[68]

CHAPTER 9

Gender, Resistance, and Subversion

Shahrzad's own story contains a hidden theme, old and timeless—the theme of what can happen when reality closes all doors; when life seems uncontrollable and unchangeable: when life means death; when one's own life appears to be an insoluble puzzle and only one's own imagination can lead one out of a predicament.

—*Azar Nafisi*

RESISTANCE AND POWER

Gender relations are constructs that emerge through the complex, multidimensional interplay of power and resistance, aspects that are strongly linked and inseparable. For this reason, gender relations are never one-sided or one-dimensional. According to Foucault, power exists everywhere and is strongly connected to resistance. "Where there is power, there is resistance, and yet, or rather consequently, this resistance is never in a position of exteriority in relation to power."[1] Abu-Lughod, on the other hand, inverts Foucault's statement, saying that where there is resistance there is power. She also advocates the use of resistance as a diagnostic tool for understanding power.[2]

Resistance can actually be understood as a form of power. However, this raises the question as to whether resistance as a form of power generates its own resistance. Considering the linkage between resistance and power, is it outrageous to expect that men would also resist female resistance, which we now recognize as a form of female power? In fact, this power-resistance struggle is an example of a vicious cycle of power reacting to resistance, reacting to power, or in other words, power and reciprocal power or resistance and reciprocal resistance. Power produces resistance, and the power of resistance forces the dominant to react to this new, challenging power; thus the original source of dominating power also invokes the power of resistance. Power and resistance interlock in a never-ending game in which actors change places in reaction to one another other. Yet in the end, all are losers.

Because the resisting power of one gender spawns the resisting power of the other, there is no easy way to dichotomize power and resistance in this analysis. To say that the role of exercising power is delegated to men, while resisting is the women's role, would be misleading. Both sexes exercise power and resistance at the same time. However, this is not to say that men's power and women's power are equal; they are not. For instance, a woman could attempt to resist her husband by leaving him, yet in the Middle East this approach is a fatal attempt if the women's husband refuses to divorce her; neither can she simply remarry or start her life all over again. This form of power and resistance is carefully controlled and severely punishable at the hands of legitimized superior men. In fact, it is this very imbalance of power between the sexes that leads to resistance in the first place.

According to Friedl, "Power differences between dominants and subordinates inevitably lead to resistance against demands, controls, and restrictions. Dominants in turn perceive the resistance as attempts to challenge, even usurp, their power (in a Zero-Sum game). Resistance therefore can, and often does, lead to more suppression: to punishment, discreditation, loss of honor, and confinement rather than freedom, choice, or autonomy."[3] Friedl continues: "Open disobedience of male orders leads to conflict, hidden disobedience to distrust. Both conflict and distrust lead to greater oppression and tighter control, thus creating a vicious circle of tyranny and rebellion."[4] Mason adds: "Violence emerges out of a struggle between power and resistance. . . . Violence is thereby conceptualized as an instrument for maintaining existing relations of domination and subjugation."[5] In this violence, Mason continues, " individuals continually resist and subvert the effect of violence."[6] This raises the critical question of whether violence increases or decreases as a result of this perpetual cycle of power and resistance, or whether in the end, resistance promotes the interests of women.

The relationship between resistance and power is related and bound to the social gender structure. Even if women's main method of gaining power is through resistance, the fact remains that they still achieve power within the oppressive gender system. Female power and resistance are linked to the traditional structure that has led to their oppression.

Friedl implies that while resistance, based on the acceptance of male rule in government or in the family, may lead to small personal victories for individual women, it cannot be expected to alter the tilted power balance between dominants and subordinates in general.[7] The question is, then, why should the terms of the patriarchal gender system be the ultimate limit placed on women within this region? Why should women, after centuries of oppression and segregation, settle for such low gains and such minimal power that results from their surrender to the same gender structure that has oppressed them for centuries?

Resistance does not make the social system acceptable. Resistance cannot transform an unjust gender structure into a fair and balanced system. Middle Eastern gender relations continue to be oppressive to women, despite their resistance. Resistance does not negate subordination either; rather, resistance and subordination exist alongside each other. Essentially, resistance does not necessarily negate relationships of power and control; resistance is *a part* of these relations. The story of Shahrazad, the heroine in the legendary *One Thousand and One Nights*, is a story of a woman who becomes a symbol of women's resistance in the historical accounts of Middle Eastern societies. However, this does not negate the fact that hundreds of women before her were met with a brutal end at the hands of a ruthless autocrat. The callousness in the story reflects the fact that resistance does not necessarily reduce brutality in the real world. The relationship between ruthlessness and resistance is not that simple.

Where there is gender violence and oppression, there will always be resistance. *One Thousand and One Nights* is an early work documenting female resistance to gender injustices and the suppression of women in the Middle East. The major storyline that frames the work follows the main character, Shahrazad, a woman who gains power and influence over a despotic man. Her story is a message of resistance to extreme gender violence. In the story, Shahrazad's resistance is portrayed as successfully ending the violence. Yet we cannot forget that, in the end, the ultimate word, decisions regarding life and death, rested in the hands of the man, not the woman. Female power is dependent on the will and the mood of the man as he has the ultimate authority and power. However, power cannot exist outside human interaction and communication, and the interactions between individuals will always reflect the agency of both people. Within these instances of human interactions, together, power and resistance act, react, and may even change places.

Female resistance to unjust power in gender relations is not simply the only fact of the story, however. In some ways women themselves support the unjust power and control from which they suffer. This paradox reflects the dialectic relationship between resistance and support. The dialectic unity of resistance and support is not confined to gender relations only but is characteristic of all power relations that involve domination. Resistance is understood in less absolute terms when actors' support for the system of injustice is brought to the discussion. In order to make sense of violence, suffering, and subjugation, women internalize the dominant system of social values as their own. In this process, women adopt the traditions that form the basis for their subordination and oppression as their own traditions.

Women actively participate in and support violence, which initiates the process of internalization that actually reinforces conservatism in society. According to Ortner, this internalization becomes a considerable impetus for a woman to collaborate in her own subordination and control.[8] Green also emphasizes this fact: "Given their crucial role as socializing agents, women also play a crucial part in defining certain acts as legitimate. Often, when a particular practice is the norm, even the victims of violence have internalized it and accepted it as legitimate."[9]

Paradoxically, female resistance naturally supports the prevailing gender system as women employ the same traditional values, norms, and mechanisms established through gender relations to resist male power. Ortner argues: "Though this is a man's game, women often embrace these desires and restrictions as well, for there is always a chance that the game will work to their benefit, or that of their daughters."[10] Karmi suggests that the role of female subordination is crucial in supporting the patriarchal structure and ensuring its persistence.[11] Green also adds: "In many cultures where existence outside the family is unfeasible, 'established' women are often the most active enforcers and proselytizers of gender relations. Women become participants in the support, promotion and perpetuation of violence against other women."[12] Afary and Anderson concur: "Women are no longer seen as 'powerless and innocent victims of patriarchal social structures'; women themselves have been involved in the subjugation of other women, using privileges of class, race, ethnicity, and seniority associated with the patriarchal order."[13]

The other important aspect to explore regarding power and resistance is the relationship between resistance and victimhood. These are not mutually exclusive terms, and the relationship between them is quite strong. Thus, resistance does not exclude victimhood, and likewise, victimhood does not exclude agency and resistance. The social system neither necessarily expects nor requires its victims to express total capitulation and surrender. In fact, it is the feeling of victimization that leads to women's resistance of male control and power. It is important to emphasize, though, that resistance does not transform a victim into a nonvictim, nor does resistance invalidate a situation of victimization. In this sense, victimization is the source of and the motivation for agency and resistance.

However, we must be careful in this regard, because overemphasizing resistance and excluding the realities of victimization in the gender system may give the appearance of a balanced social system in which all parties involved acquire equal strength and power. Such a conclusion would be misleading and harmful to women in the end. Moreover, women's agency and resistance are not entirely positive features. Women can also be negative and destructive, making significant contributions to the already negative and oppressive gender structure, thus acting against their own interests. For instance, informal female gatherings can be interpreted as a sign of female power and agency. However, one of the main focuses of these gatherings is gossip. As al-Khayyat cautions, gossip functions as one of the strongest forms of social control, particularly in policing women.[14]

The ineffective and counterproductive nature of women's resistance in marital relationships is also present in abu-Baker's study of Palestinian women. She illustrates the fact that because Arab women's work "is regarded as secondary income, and because Islam requires the man to cover all his wife's expenses, married working wives use this against their husbands. During marital conflict they announce that they are not obliged to cover the expenses of the children. Thus, this acts as another source of pressure on the husband, a value on which the children are raised as if it were a legitimate source of conflict."[15] She continues: "The wife leaves her children in the marital home purposely in order to 'discipline' the husband and to cause him to have to 'suffer' with them so that he can appreciate her and her work in the role of housewife and mother."[16] Frequently, as a sign of resistance, women will return to their natal families as a means to punish the husband during times of marital conflict. Often women take their children with them, but sometimes they will leave the children behind as another form of punishment intended to teach the husband a lesson in managing all of the domestic responsibilities without her. This can also serve as a demonstration for her children, making them aware that they must appreciate the "indispensable" role that their mother plays in their lives. Of course, this appreciation is justified in the patriarchal domestic context that overemphasizes the role of the mother and housewife and marginalizes the role of the father in the domestic sphere. Yet we must ask whether this social gender arrangement is desirable. Does it support the well-being, security, and welfare of the children and can it impact marital relationships in a meaningful way?

There is a tendency to romanticize resistance. As abu-Lughod argues, this is illustrated by the tendency to read all forms of resistance as signs of the futility of systems of power and of the resilience and creativity of the human spirit in its refusal to be dominated.[17] Therefore, regarding gender relations, it is important not to see resistance as necessarily the opposite of power, in which resistance and power would be two equal, parallel, or separate poles with power at one end and resistance at the other. While resistance can secure certain advantages and elevate the power of women, it is misleading to consider their resistance, which is a reaction to male power, as an end in itself. Exaggerating the effects of resistance may very well lead to a sense of comfort and satisfaction that blurs the harsh reality of gender relations. Both power and resistance are areas of contention in society. While resistance can be emancipating in the sense of opposing domination, it can also strengthen existing power relations, thus becoming a part of the system. Resistance is linked to power and it both maintains and weakens power simultaneously.

SUBVERSION AND PATRIARCHY

The form that female resistance takes is not always direct and overt, but women have other ways of resisting male power. Abu-Lughod stresses: "What one finds now is a concern with unlikely forms of resistance, subversions rather than large-scale collective insurrections, small or local resistances not tied to the overthrow of systems or even to ideologies of emancipation."[18] Knowing this, we must consider whether emancipation within an oppressive system is possible, and consequently, what choices are available to women in this social system. Confrontation, resistance, subversion, conformity, and surrender are all options warranted to women. It is important to establish the fact that none of these options is necessarily mutually exclusive either. While it is true that any open challenge to the system is a risky and potentially costly option, actual complete or final female surrender is more of a myth than a fact.

Therefore, resistance is more of a middle ground, or a compromise between direct confrontation, on the one hand, and surrender on the other. As with any compromise, resistance is a contradictory option for women. While resistance generates some power and agency for women, it nevertheless tends to preserve the basic rules of the social gender system. Therefore, resistance is detrimental to the objective of establishing a new system of gender relations that values and respects both sexes. However, this claim is not meant to undermine the significance of resistance in gender relations.

On the contrary, resistance is certainly better than surrender and is necessary in a system that denies women a meaningful social existence. After all, the essence of the story *One Thousand and One Nights* clearly shows that resistance can counterbalance injustice and brutality. This story has become a part of the history and the collective social memory within this region. The fact that this story of resistance has become part of the collective awareness helps support resistance and the recognition of its significance and inevitability, even in the present-day situation. Again, though, we must consider what type of resistance is permitted or tolerated in society and whether this resistance helps women or not.

There is a Moroccan proverb that states: "The cunning of women is strong, and the cunning of the devil is weak."[19] One Persian story, presented by Friedl, that illustrates the cunningness of women is the story of a man with two wives. He eventually finds himself sleeping in the mosque because each wife refuses him a bed since he has another wife and need not bother her.[20] In the stories found in *One Thousand and One Nights*, female resistance is indirect and a form of guile, which, one could argue, reflects and reinforces the condition of female inferiority and is arguably condemnable because of this. Yet acting deviously seems to be the only choice left for women as they face their brutal, harsh destinies.

Successful, direct resistance to extreme gender violence is not simply a challenge for women but a challenge for society as a whole, including men. Resisting extreme violence requires the agency of an entire society. When danger and violence are not considered to be the problems of the entire society and resisting as a society is not a viable option, women are left alone to face their brutal destinies. Because of this, deviousness appears to be a rational and logical course of action. Survival instincts rule supreme over any sort of social construction, mythical or real. Considering this, what should be condemned, in this respect, is the entire political, social, cultural, and gender systems that permit and tolerate extreme violence in society.

Having established that, however, does not preclude the fact that acting devious and guileful is not the best or most desirable option available to women. It is merely the only course of action a weak woman can take in a social system that insists on maintaining her weakness and muting other, more radical options. Instead, it should be *the system*, which has created the myth of female weakness, that should be condemned rather than women's exploitation of this myth as a means of survival. Surely, the need to be devious or guileful would be minimized in a more just, less violent, and less politically authoritarian gender system.

Patriarchy is a system of social relations in which open, confrontational resistance is not tolerated. Treacher and Shukrallah point out that an informal level of resistance persists until women find the formal and public means of expression, space, and energy to bring these informal levels of resistance to the surface.[21] Under these circumstances, subverting the system appears to be the best option for women. Mernissi upholds the notion that femininity can only assert itself through means of subversion.[22] She continues: "Hypocrisy, deceit and duplicity are, in the end, the only weapons available, and many women do not hesitate to use them. Given the framework of relationships as defined by the system, no other behaviour is possible, since direct confrontation would be suicidal. This approach becomes second nature, to the point that even the least subordinate of women has recourse to it the moment she feels threatened."[23] Nafisi joins the discussion: "It can be argued that in order to survive, the weak has no option but to turn out to be crafty and cunning and that, therefore, to women who are treated as the 'weaker' sex, guile is a learned second nature."[24] It is clear that women's options are limited to these subversive modes of behavior in patriarchal systems.

Furthermore, Minces contends that "Despite the constraints of a male-dominated society, women have developed all sorts of strategies to reduce the effects of this domination; through gossip and intrigue, they can exercise a degree of control over the affairs of the men."[25] Keddie and Beck add that women exercise some control over men's affairs in the course of gossip, intrigue, and ridicule.[26] Mernissi concurs: "Wherever there is inequality, there is also dishonesty, subterfuge, hypocrisy, and a wish, whether acknowledged or not, for revenge. It is self-evident that in societies that give one sex but not the other the right to several partners, a more or less silent dynamic of strife must become evident and manifest itself in more or less aggressive forms of behavior. She resorts to trickery, which is the corollary of inequality."[27] Friedl argues: "Subversion, in the form of minimal compliance with controversial rules or the outright subversion of such rules is at once a form of testing the limits of the rules and the tolerance of the rule-makers and thus is an expression of one's dissatisfaction with them."[28] Additionally, abu-Lughod says that women take advantage of contradictions within their society to affirm themselves and to resist.[29] Finally, el-Saadawi confirms these conclusions as she reflects on her own story: "I began to search constantly for weak spots in males to console me for the powerlessness imposed on me by the fact of being female."[30] Clearly, even though directly confronting male power is strictly prohibited in Middle Eastern societies, women manage to assert themselves nonetheless.

Thus, women take advantage of contradictions and weaknesses within the system in order to subvert, but not necessarily challenge, the system that undermines them. One of the important ways women do this is by mocking these weaknesses. Makhlouf, in her study of Yemeni women states: "A deeper examination of the rituals of the female sphere reveals an autonomous female view of the world, which not only contradicts the male model but also often ridicules its main ideas."[31] "Thus, if we examine the content of the stories and jokes that are told by women during their visits and meetings, it becomes obvious that the image of men implied in them contradicts the cultural ideals of manhood."[32] Abu-Lughod, in her study of Bedouin women in Egypt, also states: "A form of women's resistance is sexually irreverent discourse, women making fun of men and manhood. Women seem only too glad when men fall short or fail to live up to the ideals of autonomy and manhood, the ideals on which their moral superiority and social precedence are based, especially when such lapses occur through desiring women."[33] Dwyer identifies a similar tendency in Morocco: "On these all-female occasions, however, women often emphasize the lowered male image. They often call male sexuality and intelligence into question, and laugh together at men who run after women and so show their foolishness."[34]

While this approach does take advantage of male weaknesses, it also embodies a serious contradiction. It's true that subverting the dominance of men gives women a sense of power; however, mocking men's weaknesses and unmanliness does not necessarily benefit women, and may even augment violence against them. Therefore the ends to which this subversion serves are questionable. From another perspective, it is true that women benefit from weaknesses in the system in some ways, but it is not necessarily true that mocking these weaknesses helps improve their situation. In fact, this approach may prove to be counterproductive.

Because female subversion is a form of power, it tends to generate a reaction of resistance from men. Men's resistance to this mocking may very well result in increased violence against women considering their masculinity and male ethos are at stake. They may feel forced into reacting violently in order to prove themselves or to hide their exposed weaknesses. Minces warns: "Women have learnt to play upon all the so-called weaknesses of their male relatives in order to reduce the oppression that weighs upon them, but in denouncing these weaknesses, they perpetuate their own oppression. They force men to be the male chauvinist autocrats, which this male-oriented society has produced."[35] Mocking male weakness results in a vicious cycle of increased violence towards women as well as the perpetuation of an oppressive system.

Attracting attention to the role that sibling relationships, particularly brother/sister relationships, play in the reproduction of patriarchy, Joseph discusses the ways women exploit male competition in an effort to enhance their own position in Lebanon. She states: "Young males emerging into their manhood might compete with their fathers for control over the family, using relationships with their sisters as a base of power, at times with the cooperation of their sisters and mothers."[36] However, the effectiveness of the strategy of achieving power by subverting the authority of the father is questionable. Replacing one control with another does not necessarily result in less control. A brother may begin to construct his masculinity by way of controlling his sister; however, this is not necessarily a better option for *her*. On the contrary, it may be worse. A brother's position is disadvantaged in the patriarchal generational hierarchy, vis-à-vis older males. The brother's underprivileged position may cause him to be even more violent towards his sisters. The brother is also eager to establish and demonstrate his masculinity, and the most accessible object for proving his masculinity is his sister. A man's control and authority over his sister will prove to be a useful exercise in preparation for eventual encounters with his wife.

Most often, a brother's control is the harsher option for women. Furthermore, helping the brother to empower and affirm his authority may very well add additional control over women's lives rather than merely replacing the existing control. What is worse is that by encouraging her brother's control, she empowers and legitimizes the additional control over her life. Obviously, the combined, cumulative control from both the father and the brother is a far worse outcome than the control of one single male.

On the other hand, the nature of the relationship between father and daughter is distinct from sibling relationships. Aged and beaten by life's problems and experiences, the father may offer a milder form of control over the life of a daughter than a brother would, even though both relationships are structured by honor and strict gender morality. While it is true that both sibling relationships and father-daughter relationships encompass the control and authority of one party, and the servitude and submission of the other, the special emotional relationship between a father and his daughter can affect or intersect with this structure. Fathers tend to romanticize their relationships with their daughters, in contrast to their stricter, harsher, less fulfilling relationships with their wives.

To conclude, any approach to resistance that perpetuates and strengthens the oppressive gender system is not in women's interests, despite any temporary gains or advantages procured through this method of resistance. Dwyer dwells on this saying that the sum total of women's beliefs supports some subversive activities while militating against protest that truly aims to generally increase women's life options. As a result, women's acts of protest have tended to remain individual and veiled.[37] From this approach, women do everything possible to mitigate, but not change, the situation that entraps them within the gender structure. In this situation, women have no choice but to subvert, resist, and be satisfied with ridiculing the oppressor or to be happy with the small amount of power allocated to them. Women invest in this approach to resistance because they are subdued into overlooking the expenses associated with participating in an unjust and cruel game for the sake of enjoying the small gains their acts of subversion and ridicule manage to achieve. This game, in which the potential gains are small, is played with women's destinies at stake. The gender structure as a whole and all the associated gender games, which lead to the degradation of women, tend to downplay any gains women make from playing. Taking pleasure in playing these games is based more on eluding outcomes than real power and control. One wonders why the power and control that is associated with the subversion and resistance of women has undergone little change with regard to the situation and status of women over the many centuries of history in Middle Eastern societies.

Subversion may provide women with false comforts that distract from the more desirable objective of challenging patriarchal ideology altogether. Moreover, this approach to resistance tends to neglect the fact that even men resist the gender system and the strict code of honor and morality that inhibit their sexual and emotional gratification. This is true despite the fact that the gender system and moral code in general represent power and control for men. In fact, the arguments raised against the use of subversion may take away any sense of agency and power women are able to gain in an otherwise oppressive and strict gender structure. Yet an approach to the situation that can identify a common ground with men, exploiting men's dissatisfaction with the gender system and morality code, as opposed to mocking men's weaknesses, arguably, would be a better solution for women in the long run.

PART THREE

IMPACTS OF FEMALE POWER AND AGENCY

CHAPTER 10

Status and Victimization

If so many Muslim mothers are possessive, even to an abusive degree, the reason is not to be sought elsewhere than in a system that denies them their most elementary rights.

—*Abdel Wahab Bouhdiba*

MOTHER-CHILD: AN OPPORTUNISTIC RELATIONSHIP

Marriage is the fundamental component that keeps Middle Eastern society functioning, and reproducing children within marriage is crucially important for everyone in the family structure. A Moroccan proverb says: "If a man leaves his substitute, it is as if he did not die."[1] Families tend to be large in the Middle East, and the cultural preference for boys aggravates the already high birth rate by increasing the number of children born in the family. A father and his extended family will not be satisfied until a baby boy is born. The reproduction of many girls is accepted or tolerated because it is regarded as a price necessary to pay for having at least one boy in the family. The status and social appreciation of the wife is highly dependent on producing male children. Patai argues that a woman who has only daughters is not much better off than a childless wife.[2] Society fails to recognize women as people and worthy human beings; their simple state of being goes unappreciated. Appreciation for women comes only from their ability to reproduce males. Having many children increases the chance of having more boys in the family; therefore, it is no surprise that women also desire many children.

Because the uncontested husband can easily break a marriage bond at his will, the wife's uncertain position in the household is an unpleasant reality. For this reason, Vieille contends that children are supposed to be "nails" that attach the wife to the home. After marriage, women themselves hasten to increase these ties, which guarantee them against repudiation.[3] This reality is also reflected in a Moroccan proverb: "A marriage without children does not last long for men."[4] Yet by having many children, women deepen their misery by increasing their work load. Having high numbers of children puts extreme pressures on women because the dominant cultural norms relegate the responsibility of rearing children to women, not men. Men are neither expected nor encouraged to assist with raising children. In fact, it is considered unmasculine to help the wife with either the children or household chores.

Other than guarding her virginity until her wedding night, reproducing male children is the only safe and sure way for a Middle Eastern woman to be able to negotiate her status and enter the realm of social power and authority. Thus, bearing children, particularly boys, improves women's status in the family. According to Bouhdiba, one valorises the mother by stressing the childbearing role of women. The cult of the mother constitutes one of the keys to an understanding of the basic personality of the Arab-Muslim societies.[5] "There is practically no other institutionalized social role accorded to women than that of mother."[6] It is this inability to access other institutionalized social roles that entices the mother to play a significant, even abusive, role in the politics of the family.

Mothers are heavily involved in the lives of their children. They are so involved that, as a Moroccan proverb says, "The child that loses its mother has nothing."[7] The mother-child relationship is the most significant relationship in the structure of the family; it is even more important, and rewarding, than her relationship with her husband. Her children will offer comfort and support to her that may help her endure the difficulties of her marriage. Both mother and child benefit from the symbiotic or opportunistic alliance that emerges between them. Children may receive less harsh control and restriction from senior males in the family if the mother intervenes on the children's behalf. Reciprocally, the woman may feel that she is understood and supported by her children when it comes to her relationship with her husband. Even though children are raised in the patriarchal context, male children tend to see their mothers separate from the archetypal patriarchal image of the female sex. They do not regard their mothers as inferior women, as they do regarding their wives or sisters, for instance.

In a patriarchal society where gender relations and relationships in general are hierarchical expressions of domination, control, and authority, it makes sense for the victims of patriarchy, women and children, to unite in this special way. This special relationship between mother and children helps them support each other, and even though it is sometimes unconscious, it allows them to find a common interest in opposing a common oppressor, the male father and husband. The bond of complicity between the mother and the child circumvents and compensates for the abuses of patriarchal male power as they jointly outwit or take revenge on the father. Here, complicity, Bouhdiba articulates, is tantamount to positivity, and, in the dialectic of intrafamilial relations, it establishes an effective negation of the negation.[8] Thus, patriarchal negation, negation here in the sense of denial, of a healthy existence for women and children is now counterbalanced by the agency of this alliance between the mother and her children.

Moreover, the special affinity and closeness the mother develops to her children reinforces her initial feelings that the husband was, and still is, a stranger and outsider to the family. The fact that the male is always out of the home and constantly absent from daily family life reinforces this feeling. The wife's lower status in the gender structure and in her unsatisfactory relationship with her husband are injustices forced on her. Yet this induces her children to sympathize with their mother and to show more understanding and appreciation towards her. This strengthens the special bond that ties the children to their mother even more. Her daily contact with the children and their dependency on her make it easier for the mother to communicate her situation of victimhood and suffering to them. The unique bond children develop to their mothers is a show of children's gratitude, understanding, and sympathy. Nevertheless, this situation is frequently manipulated either to the advantage of the mother or to the disadvantage of the father. Yet, according to Kousha in her study of family relations in Iran, there are psychological consequences that result from this: "The often powerless position of mothers in the marital relationship perpetuates a cycle of powerlessness in the female child and critically colors her attitudes toward the father and other men."[9] She continues: "Seeing daughters as an extension of themselves, some mothers tended to open up to their daughters and share with them their familial problems and marital unhappiness. However, this process not only hurts the child, it also brings the carefree stage of childhood to an abrupt end because the child's eyes are opened to the adult world where relationships take on a different shape."[10]

The existence of the especially strong relationship between mother and son is a well-known fact in Middle Eastern societies. It is also important to mention that, in principle, a strong relationship between a mother and her children is a positive aspect within the family. However, the development of this special relationship between the mother and her children necessarily comes at the expense of a better relationship between the children and their father. The children's relationship with their father is only superficial and is permeated with fear and hostility. It is worth considering in what ways society would be affected if these qualities were to dominate the relationships between men in the public domain? While children later on in life identify with their father, a symbol of authority, their relationship with authority in general is colored by fear and hostility, thanks to the complex intricacies of the politics of family relations they have experienced in their homes. This, however, can contribute to the significant gap between authority and society that exists in the Middle East.

Thus, through her relationship with her children, the mother instills distance and a quality of rigidity between the father and son, which ultimately reinforces the patriarchal nature of the family. In her study of Morocco, Rassam proclaims: "The mother is in a position to capitalize on the latent resentment of the son towards his father produced by a system that insists on giving all authority to the father and demands complete obedience from the son."[11] In fact, the distance between the father and his children created by the mother tends to split the family into two separate parts. On one side is the mother and the children, and on the other is the distant, excluded father. This demonstrates how politics of exclusion are not simply confined to the political realm of the regime but permeate the structure of the family and the relationships within it as well.

In contrast to the direct, approximate relationship children have with their mothers, father-child interactions are indirect, as the father typically relates to his children via the mother. The disparity between the indirect relationship of father and children and their direct relationship with their mother is not necessarily good for the family, considering that the state of the relationship between partners is already shaky. In fact, both relationships are unhealthy. Children are either too close or too distant to the parent; there is no middle ground. The relationship between the children and their father is filtered through the mother's experiences, motives, interests, dreams, miseries, as well as the quality of her relationship with her husband. This process of filtration can be manipulated quite easily. Kousha explains: "The family is divided into two fronts where the father resides in one, alone in tyrannical rule and the mother and the children, the powerless family members, occupy the other. This poisons the atmosphere in the house. Most often, children assume the mother's attitude and her beliefs toward the father before they ever get a chance to get to know him on their own."[12]

Although the mother experiences a sense of satisfaction from her children's appreciation and sympathy, this strong bond may be a compensatory process that ultimately discourages her from improving her relationship with her husband. This neglect is reinforced by social values that purport that the success of a marriage is dependent on factors such as producing male children, rather than on the level of understanding between partners. Women's status is also largely dependent on the status of her children. In this way, children are more important to women than their husbands are. Of course this negatively affects the relationship between a women and her husband, yet her love for her children, particularly her sons, compensates for her inability to love her husband that is derived from many sources.

The mother's closeness to the children is an indication of the hopeless, grim prospect of fostering a loving relationship between the husband and wife. The special relationship between a mother and her children is a consolation for the failed relationship with her husband. In reality, closeness to the children diverts attention and resources that could otherwise be invested in recuperating her relationship with her husband. The manipulative and opportunistic nature of the mother-child relationship is a part of the game-like relationship with the husband; this ultimately minimizes the chance of fully appreciating and nurturing more productive relationships with her children.

Naturally, one might assume that the children's sympathy and understanding for their mother could eventually influence the unjust nature of social gender relations in a positive way. It is true that the mother could very well take advantage of the opportunity these special bonds provide by nurturing a more humane value system and a sympathetic appreciation of the female sex in her children. She could help her male children to have a better and more meaningful relationship with their sisters and wives. As desirable as this would be, the reality is that the gender structure does not support this outcome. Gender relations and the politics of the family neither allow the mother to encourage this kind of relationship, nor do they allow children to consider it a viable option. Hence, the children's feelings of sympathy and understanding they have for their mothers do not extend to their sisters or wives and do not affect the general nature of gender relations. Vieille asserts that this special relationship between the mother and her children is a relationship of duplicity and hypocrisy, as she

> submits herself to marital and masculine authority and to the dominant values which are defined by men and, at the same time, plays her own role inside the institutions that deny power to her. One example of this behavior is the game of the woman inside the family, particularly in relation to her sons. On the other side, a woman is socially recognized through her sons; it is due to them that she derives a respect denied to the wife, the daughter, or the sister. It is at this point that the specific game of the woman intervenes: she expects from her son an attachment with which she will counterbalance the superiority of her husband in the household. She makes the son a rival of the father at the same time as she submits to him.[13]

Thus, strong relationships between mother and son inhibit males from developing healthy relationships with the opposite sex. The authoritarian mother-in-law role that she will eventually occupy in her son's life will also inevitably harm the relationship between the son and his wife. Davis and Davis, in their study of Morocco, observe that a mother's power and influence over her son is life-long.[14] In fact, men may develop a subconscious resentment towards the opposite sex because of this. There are several factors that contribute to the development of male resentment of females, which may eventually affect a man's relationship with his wife, most notably the daily over-involvement of the mother in her sons' lives, the strong mutual dependency of mother and son, and the use of the relationship to manipulate the mother's relationship with her husband.

Thus, the relationship between a mother and her children is, indeed, complex, and the mother's failed marriage affects the relationship even further. Likewise, strong mother-child relationships discourage the development of better relationships between husbands and wives. In this respect, a vicious cycle is created. To be sure, love of a woman for her children has two parts. One is real and natural motherly love and the other is the artificial love that compensates for the mother's lack of love and closeness to her husband.

Moreover, because this latter kind of love is compensatory, it is unreal and unnecessary. This excess love complicates and exaggerates the relationship between the mother and children even more. This undoubtedly affects the relationship in general as well as the party receiving this exaggerated love, the children. As they gradually mature, children discover that their mother's love is motivated by her inability to love the father, which causes children to doubt and question this love. This superficial side of a mother's love calls into question the totality of her love for her children, as they now feel this love is unreal and suspicious. Considering that love for the mother is nearly the only permissible and celebrated form of love in society, the pool of real love that can be drawn from in society is diminished and shaken. This will eventually make it much more difficult to initiate a loving relationship between a man and his future partner, particularly if he associates the shaken love of the mother with the female sex in general.

The dominant social and gender structures tend to distort the true meaning of fatherhood, motherhood, siblinghood, and particularly partnership and friendship between the sexes. These structures offer little help in the struggle to maintain healthy functioning relationships of motherhood or fatherhood. The concepts of motherhood and fatherhood are nearly devoid of meaning and value if parents fail to recognize their daughters as full human beings worthy of respect and recognition. In the dehumanization of daughters, the parental roles of mother and father, which are fundamentally human roles by nature, are also dehumanized. In other words, patriarchal ideology and the gender structure not only violate women and girls but also the very sense of motherhood and fatherhood as well. It is interesting to note that despite the emphasis of religion and culture on motherhood, patriarchy, which is also reinforced by religion and culture, seems to prevent the full realization of a meaningful motherly role. Yet the difference between actual and potential realization is also a form of violence. Patriarchal gender structure socializes women to be weak and dependent mothers. This inevitably has a negative effect on her relationship with her sons and daughters.

Thus, the dominant gender ideology is not only violent and aggressive towards women but also towards the humanly vital experience of parenting. It deprives girls of their humanity and dignity and deprives parents of what could be a healthy, mutually fruitful relationship with their daughters. Naturally, dysfunctional motherhood is detrimental to the welfare of the both male and female children. "It would clearly be desirable for the good of the child," Beauvoir advocates, "if the mother were a complete, un-mutilated person, a woman finding in her work and in her relation to society a self-realization that she would not seek to attain tyrannically through her offspring."[15]

MULTILEVEL DEPENDENCY

In the process of cultivating strong attachments with her children, the mother becomes heavily dependent on them, particularly the sons. Because a wife's status in the family is highly dependent on producing many children, boys in particular, an involuntary relationship of dependency between the mother and her children develops. The dependency of the children on their mother is quite natural and is to be expected. Yet this other unnatural sort of dependency exclusively relates to the social system and the dominant cultural values that socialize women to be dependent and weak. In a way, the mother's multilayered dependency on her children counterbalances the children's excessive dependence on her.

In fact, dominant cultural values and strict social control succeed in preparing woman for living in a perpetual state of dependency, which, in some ways, proves to be useful in her adult life as she will inherit multidependency relationships in married life. A married woman is dependent on her sons to advance her status in the family. A mother is dependent on her daughters to assist with the household duties of managing a large family. She is dependent on the husband for finances and major decision-making. She will eventually be dependent on her sons and their wives in order to acquire authority and power through the role of the mother-in-law. She will also be dependent on her sons for support later on in life when she is old or divorced.

These multiple forms of dependency cause women's position in the family to be extremely precarious and weak. While women manage to function in this situation of dependency, for the mother this is not necessarily the best option to pursue. Yet these dependencies themselves discourage women from pursuing more independent and constructive ways of surviving. This clearly shows how accommodating to the gender structure can cause an initial position of weakness to worsen, and a presumably positive relationship between a woman and her children to become a limitation. The ostensibly positive strength of the bond between a mother and her children may very well be a burden that discourages the woman from pursuing other, more productive options.

It is noteworthy to explore the various effects of this multifaceted dependency on the relationship between mothers and children. Does it induce differential treatment between sons and daughters? Does she appease her sons, frequently taking their side, and does she feel compelled to pay more attention to her sons than her daughters? Is the mother motivated by this dependency to become more sensitive to the needs, aspirations, problems, and dreams of her sons more than those of her daughters? Finally, is it the family's status and economic needs that force the mother to place her bets on the likely winner, which in the deeply patriarchal culture is always the son? It is, after all, the sons who women rely on for support when they grow old, not their daughters. Culture and economy ensure this fact. Sons are able to impose their mothers on their weaker partner; however, daughters do not have this same power over their dominant husbands. Sons not only have the power necessary to do this, but they can also afford the financial demands of this arrangement.

Mothers' differential treatment of their children is not surprising. After all, it is because of her sons, that a wife's status within the family structure can improve dramatically. Davis and Davis assert: "The male's relationship with his mother is close since the mother is likely to regard the son as a fulfillment of her destiny as a mother, a powerful insurance against repudiation by her husband, and a hope for support in her old age."[16] Therefore, a mother tolerates her son's carefree lifestyle and pampers him regardless of his actions. This is considered to be his reward for the higher status she has been granted because of his existence, a sort of show of gratitude for her, at last, being recognized by society.

Family structure causes women to be weak and dependent as they are forced to enter into an unequal partnership with her husband. A woman tries very hard in this situation to use whatever options are available to increase her status and ensure her survival. By doing this, she is merely playing by the rules of the system that she is entrapped by. Can she really be blamed for this? That is precisely how society expects women to behave. Naturally, this logic makes sense through the lens of the prevalent social system, where internalizing patriarchal values are central. Yet the important question is whether or not this is fair. Life is a series of choices a woman must make that determine whether she will survive or not. Although one can easily see the rationale behind the mother's behavior, these choices create misery for the next victims of the patriarchal system, her very own daughters.

MOTHER-DAUGHTER: RELATIONSHIP OF VICTIMHOOD

While it is clear that the mother plays to the side of the winner, her sons, it is interesting to see what kind of relationship she builds with the losers, her daughters. This is an interesting research question because it spotlights the relationship between two direct victims of the same social system. The way a mother deals with and treats her daughters, the way she regards their plight, is remarkable considering the mother herself has suffered from the very same social consequences her entire life. It is noteworthy to observe the relationship of the previous victim to the new victim, particularly observing what the learning process can look like in this regard. What sort of message is being transmitted from one generation to another? Is it a message of continuity or a message of change? Is it a message of resistance or a message of defeat and surrender?

The bitter experiences of being unwanted and unwelcome that women felt when they were young are reinforced again in the way they treat their daughters. A woman must first cope with being an unwanted girl and then is burdened by her production of other unfortunate, unwanted girls. Guilt, sorrow, and defeat are all feelings associated with a mother's experience in this regard. The wonderful, beautiful experience a woman can experience by carrying a baby in her womb for nine months and then bringing this human being into the world is brutally damaged and rendered meaningless by the dominant social values. It is an extreme case of violence not only against women but also against nature itself.

One Iraqi woman mentioned: "On many occasions I've wished I wasn't a woman, because they're oppressed in this society and denied their rights. Now I wish that I had a baby boy rather than a girl for the same reason."[17] These experiences of injustice, degradation, and marginalization directly and indirectly affect the feelings of the mother toward her daughter. Resentment toward her brutal situation in society is somehow protracted into resentment for her daughters who share this misery like all women do. This is a hidden, involuntary and subconscious resentment: Why have you come into this female-inhospitable world? This resentment and negativity is derived from the fact that the mother is the one who has brought her daughter into a society that is still not ready to accept her as a dignified equal. This resentment is also associated with the powerlessness of the mother to affect or change the fate of her daughter or herself.

Life experience teaches a woman that the fate of her daughters will not be better than her own. After all, her own fate is fundamentally no different from her mother's. Obviously, this realization affects the relationship between mother and her daughter. In fact, a mother has two options in this regard. Either she will support her daughter in a struggle against the prevailing traditional culture, achieving vindication for her own existence at the same time, or she will force her daughter, whether consciously or unconsciously, to surrender to the very same gender system that she herself has surrendered to, and in this way she will make sense of her own suffering. For the most part, this suffering is regarded as the inevitable destiny of all women.

There are reasons, however, for tolerating female children in a culture that prefers and idolizes sons. The help and support provided to the mother by a female child is very important, if not indispensable. A Moroccan proverb reflects this reality by saying: "He whose first child is one with a vulva was gladdened by God."[18] In her study of low-income districts of Cairo, Hoodfar contends: "Every single mother wishes to have at least one daughter. Some said, 'there is no woman lonelier than the one without a daughter.' The lucky woman bears a female child first, who can help with housework and child rearing."[19] Thus, it seems that daughters are instrumental in the patriarchal system. In order for the mother to manage all of the patriarchal burdens placed on her, she enlists the help of another female, her daughter. Patriarchal, religious, and cultural values and norms ensure that female children have no option but to comply and submit to this social arrangement.

Despite the need for daughters in the patriarchal context, the daughter is subjected to a harsh social existence. In this situation, the female child receives no support from her mother, even though she is the one naturally expected to help and support the child. As a woman surrenders to her enforced social existence, no room is left to support another female facing this same harsh existence, even her own daughter. Patriarchy conditions the mother-daughter relationship in a way that the social validation of one is the social negation of the other. The mother begins to gain recognition while the unmarried female remains inconsequential. In patriarchy, there is no room for both. The social validation and recognition of females comes only when they marry and reproduce children. Thus, females must wait for the recognition that will come later on in life. Regardless, though, this recognition is conditioned, controlled, and limited with little room for negotiation.

Even though she is dependent on both her sons and her daughters, a mother reacts differently to these dependencies. Dependency on the son induces the mother to help her son enforce his male authority over his sisters, his future wife, even over herself, and she encourages his rivalry with the authority of the father. Yet the mother behaves very differently toward her daughters. The dependency of the mother on the patriarchal servitude of her daughter to cope with the extremely frustrating tasks of managing the household and childbearing does not lead to any special status for the daughter. The help provided by the daughter within this relationship of dependency is not even recognized, let alone appreciated, by the mother. This is clearly an unfair double standard and a case of discrimination. It also clearly demonstrates hierarchization within the complex system of dependent relationships that govern family life. The attitude of the mother clearly reflects the patriarchal societal conviction that women are unworthy.

Al-Khayyat argues: "Since the mother's role is to bring her daughters up according to the values and standards of society, she herself must not adopt any constructively critical attitudes towards those standards. In order to fulfill her duty of socializing her daughters, the mother does not allow herself to become too close to them."[20] It seems that this has dual implications regarding the position of the mother, both of which negatively affect her relationship with her daughter. The first implication is that in order for the mother to be socially validated she must adopt an uncritical approach to the patriarchal gender values that dominate social life, even though these values are detrimental to the healthy, natural existence of women and their daughters. The second is that because the mother invests in the dominant male authority as a survival strategy she does not offer to help or support her daughter. Therefore, her relationship with her daughter grows distant. Emotional remoteness and depersonalization are unavoidable aspects of the victimization process. This is why the mother-daughter relationship manifests itself as a relationship of victimhood. Moreover, al-Khayyat also argues that because their mothers were totally submissive to their husbands, most of the women lacked any model of a strong female character on which to base their behavior.[21] Thus, a mother cannot be a role model for her daughter in the way the strong, authoritarian, and highly regarded father is for his son.

The mother-daughter relationship is framed by the same patriarchal standards and values that dominate gender relations in society. This is clearly reflected in what Middle Eastern women have to say about their relationships with their mothers. Telling her own story, one Syrian woman talks about her own mother: "I don't think she was malicious or did unkind things deliberately, but as a human being she needed outlets and there was no one around her on whom she could exercise authority except women. Even regarding the question of marriage, she tried to force me into an arranged marriage which she herself had rebelled against over 30 years ago."[22] Similar feelings were expressed by several Iraqi women as well. One Iraqi woman said: "I love my mother but I don't like the way she brought us up. She worried so much about our reputation and always warned us about this or that . . . It seems that all she had to teach us was how to protect the family honor." Another woman says: "My relationship with my mother was friendly and sympathetic but I didn't like her frequent complaints at home, as she didn't do anything about what was wrong apart from complaining." And another woman says: "Despite my mother's inexperience, she was rough and bad-tempered with us. We lived in an environment of threats and tension." And finally, another woman recalls: "My mother was unhappy in her life. She hated herself and she used to vent her anger on us. She never taught us the difference between right and wrong."[23]

Despite the extent to which aspects of the mother-daughter relationship are negative, it does not mean that the mother is altogether unaffectionate toward her daughter. Undoubtedly, affection does exist in these relationships. Yet the failure of the mother to overcome her own selfishness and help her daughter achieve a better outcome is remarkable. A woman is not entirely responsible for this failure; however, she shares the responsibility to address these issues with society and culture as well. Society discourages women from developing free, strong, independent, and friendly personalities, which would not only help women but would also help their daughters escape a similar fate if they were encouraged. The culture of violence and social control that ensures the submissiveness of women also causes the submissiveness of their daughters and granddaughters.

Although a woman's survival necessitates the preference of her sons, it is at the expense of her daughters. While boys are the center of attention, girls are neglected and marginalized, which is clearly unfair and unequal treatment of children. Yet this is the same exact story of the mother's upbringing, as she was once the neglected and devalued daughter. One is tempted to ask whether by neglecting her own daughter, the mother feels some sort of vindication or justification for the neglect and degradation she herself has suffered from in her natal family. From the mother's perspective, these earlier feelings of neglect finally make sense in this context; she now perceives this to be *the inescapable fate of every girl* in this society.

It is not easy to digest or reconcile injustices people experience. They continuously seek answers as to why they have suffered. After resigning to her fate, a woman must find an explanation or justification for her miseries. Sharing a common fate with all women is the only way to ensure a woman's acceptance of her circumstances. Because seriously challenging her fate is neither possible nor permitted, and because all of her hopes have been dashed, inner peace does come in the end and allows a woman to tolerate her miserable situation. Unfortunately, this inner peace comes at the expense of another female, her very own daughter.

CHAPTER 11

Patriarchy and Agency

What the devil does in a year, an old woman does in an hour.
—*Moroccan proverb*

THE MOTHER-IN-LAW: A PATRIARCHAL POWER NICHE

The way a woman negotiates the circumstances of her gender manifests in another important relationship besides her relationship with her parents, siblings, husband, and children—that is, her relationship with her son's bride. Within the marriage structure, the relationship of the mother-in-law adds a layer of difficulty to the already unequal and precarious relationship between the wife and the husband. Overall, this has a destructive influence in the new family. Mernissi points out that the entire structure conspires against the prospect of a loving relationship between the couple.[1] A mother's strong ties to her children have inhibited the development of an intimate and meaningful relationship with her husband, and as she sees it, it is her role to obstruct the devotion of her son to his wife.

By interfering in her children's lives in this way, she elevates her status, authority, and power. Women's status and power are dependent on having children; as noted before, however, birthing daughters is moot, as far as power and status are concerned. Bearing sons into the family is preferred not only because of the underlying patriarchal preferences in exclusive, discriminatory societies but because it will open up a new avenue of power and status for the mother that daughters cannot offer. The mother is the one who will choose a wife for her son and she is the one who will control, or at least influence and interfere with, the detailed affairs of this new marital unit. Zuhur discusses: "Mothers-in-law established their own dominance over young brides, utilizing the power of age and status along with the patrilineal definitions of influence."[2] Mohsen adds: "The power of women in the household is a function of their age and the stage of developmental cycle of the family and it reaches a climax when she becomes a mother-in-law."[3]

Reproducing children for the sake of raising the mother's status is not a positive or efficient course of action. She cannot guarantee her promotion in this way because she has little power or control over the outcome of reproduction. Therefore it offers her little to no real choice or agency, even though socially, it is a biological necessity. On the other hand, the status associated with becoming a mother-in-law is a completely different avenue for a mother to gain control and power. Now it is her time to create a role for her in the gender structure, and in this case, society accepts and tolerates this role. Female initiative and agency are clearly exhibited by the mother-in-law in her role in the family. By accepting the rules of this patriarchal gender game from the beginning, she adopts the cultural preference for male children, which in the patriarchal context brings her one step closer to power. In doing so, she ensures not only a higher level of power and status for herself, but perhaps for the first time in her life she also secures a forceful niche within the patriarchal structure.

The initial instance in which a woman's status is elevated is the birth of a son, a symbol of power and status of the male sex. The second status advancement comes from her domination over her son's new bride, a female and a symbol of weakness and degradation. As she sees it, if a woman's own daughter is unable to help her achieve higher social status, then someone else's daughter will. While a mother's relationship to her son is the association of a weak and insecure mother with the symbol of power and status, her relationship with her daughter-in-law is essentially the inverse. The difference between these two cases is that in the first the mother is the victim and in the second case she is the victimizer. Both are integral roles females play within the same system of power, intimidation, and control.

A mother-in-law's imposition on her son's family is an opportunistic exercise of power considering it creates yet another weakened victim of this system. It is a clear example of how women use the patriarchal world and the mindset imposed by men to their own advantage. Women eventually succeed in finding a niche for themselves within the system, while at the same time transforming their position from victim to victimizer. And to be a victimizer is, of course, a symbol of power, authority, control, and status. It is interesting to note the association of power and status with the process of victimization. Patriarchal gender ideology instills an inextricable relationship between power and status and victimization. These facets become interlinked in the patriarchal context, and the only way to achieve power and status appears to be through violence and victimization.

Studying Moroccan society, Rassam argues: "The mother-in-law's power derives from her virtual monopoly of domestic information and skills, her access to the father-patriarch, and close ties to her son; power which she jealously guards from the wife whose only power derives from her sexual and procreative functions."[4] The asymmetrical imbalance of power between the mother-in-law and the daughter-in-law is the source of control for the mother-in-law. However, the true status and power advantages associated with this role are ultimately derived from the mother-in-law's access to male authority. This parallels the authoritarian principle that the source of status and power is mostly associated with proximity to the authoritarian ruler.

While a mother also exercises control over her own children, it is different from the control over her daughter-in-law. In contrast to her relationship with the daughter-in-law, an outsider, her children are special and closer to her and therefore her control over them is softer and gentler. If the bride is a close relative of the family it may ease the situation slightly, but it will not dissolve it completely. Studying Turkish society, Kiray mentions: "As a bride she is an outsider and is always made to feel so."[5] The mother-in-law's need to take advantage of this opportunity to dominate and control that is offered through the arrival of the new bride is so great that she will not waste this chance regardless of the consequences or whom she may harm.

In the patriarchal context, this seems rational granted the new bride's arrival represents practically the only real opportunity for women to exercise power and status in the dominant gender structure. The daughter-in-law will become a woman's first and only real victim that will allow her to fully express her power and domination. The fact that the victim is a female, an insignificant being within the patriarchal context, makes it easier for society to tolerate any injustices that this relationship might entail. The mother, who is herself a victim of the gender structure, is now the abuser. When society victimizes and perverts the female sex, the sense of control and power a mother-in-law wields in her position becomes even more important for women who would otherwise remain powerless. It is not by chance that the conflicting relationship between mother-in-law and bride is legendary in Middle Eastern culture, and in cultures around the world, for that matter.

The relationship between a mother and her daughter-in-law is indeed a noteworthy and interesting relationship within the dominant gender structure. Control, power, and hierarchy permeate this relationship even though both are victims of the same set of cultural values. This relationship is an example of a social structure that permits, sustains, and supports oppression and injustice. In fact, it is this avenue of power and control that makes an otherwise intolerable social system seem tolerable to women.

Within the dominant social and cultural system, motherhood is a woman's final surrender to her miserable fate. Motherhood signifies the resignation of any hope of radically changing her situation. This surrender leaves her with no other choice than to play by the rules of the patriarchal system. Not only does a woman thereby accept defeat, she herself begins to participate in this ceremony of violence and victimization. Keddie and Beck contend: "The middle-aged woman may have the chance to become household tyrant and relieve herself of the most unpleasant household chores. Once she has lost the possibility of staining the family line her status in many ways approaches more closely that of the man."[6] Living her entire life deprived of power, authority, and control over her own fate, the new position of the mother-in-law radically alters her state of victimization as she becomes the abuser and oppressor. After all, her previous experiences have taught her that status, power, authority, and control are necessarily associated with oppression and domination. This transformation into a state of power and control gives women a sense of worthiness and importance in an otherwise hostile and discriminatory social system. Increased female power and control justifies the social system in the eyes of women. It is only because this avenue exists that oppressive gender relations are tolerated by the women it enslaves.

CYCLE OF PATRIARCHAL VICTIMIZATION

From the mother-in-law's perspective, life now makes sense. The system that has oppressed her does not seem as entirely unjust or disadvantageous as before. While it is true that she is, or was, oppressed by the system, this same social arrangement has also allowed her to become an abuser herself. In the mother-in-law's eyes, patriarchy is not such a horrible system after all. She has been made to suffer continuously from birth until now, but has finally received her reward in the end. Everything seems logical and rational from her perspective. When it is finally her turn to exercise power and authority, she becomes convinced of the "fairness" and "justice" of the patriarchal system. Now that she is in a position of power and authority, all of the miseries, injustices, and sufferings society has inflicted on her, first as a child, and then as a young girl, and later on as a wife and mother, have been forgotten and forgiven. All her previous doubts, questions, and resistance toward the dominant patriarchal gender structure that she harbored as a victim no longer make sense or appeal to her.

Achieving power and authority as a mother-in-law makes her previous sorrows and sacrifices seem worthwhile. Shedding the memories of her previous suffering and oppression, she begins to approach the system in a new way. She now judges the system through the lens of the mother-in-law, a position of control and power. This opens her eyes to a new reality of the system, in which everyone "wins" somehow. Following the logic of this new perception, it seems normal to begin life as a victim as long as you *end up a victimizer in the end*. Victim and victimizer exchange places in the course of patriarchal life. The previous victim becomes the victimizer of a new female in an interminable cycle of violence and victimhood. Kandiyoti argues: "A woman's life cycle in the patrilineal extended family is such that the control and authority she will have over her own daughters-in-law eventually supersede the deprivation and hardship she may experience as a young bride. The powerful postmenopausal matriarch thus is the other side of the coin of this form of patriarchy."[7]

Thus, the mother-in-law completes the patriarchal cycle of life. Living most of her life as a victim, it is her turn now to play the role of the victimizer and complete her life process, the patriarchal life process. Both roles of victim and victimizer are justified within the patriarchal gender system as well as by a woman's previous misery and suffering. Both occur in her lifetime, and she understands them as the natural stages of her life. This outcome is strongly facilitated by the fact that the mother-in-law has already internalized the values of patriarchy and its gender structure. In this system there are no complete victims, nor are there complete victimizers. Instead, women are both, and both are "normal." Reflecting on a true story from Morocco, Dwyer remarks: "Her own past reflects the same unhappiness with her mother-in-law experienced in the new home. And yet Aisha prepared to become the most potent force in subjugating her daughter-in-law."[8] Thus, her previous experience of being a victim justifies and motivates her performance as a victimizer. This change in a woman's position feeds the cycle of violent gender relations *where the aspiration of the victim is not to achieve justice but to further injustices that will benefit her.* To be sure, the mother-in-law, who has by now absorbed and internalized patriarchal values and norms, does not think she is acting unjustly toward her daughter-in-law. Instead, she thinks that she is acting justly within the system that she is entrapped by, a patriarchal justice par excellence. She does not see herself as an abuser but a defender of values of honor and traditions. At this stage in her life, a woman's objective is not to make the system less violent, which would result in fewer victims; instead, her only intent is to become an abuser herself. This process is a natural part of ordinary life in Middle Eastern societies. Society exposes its citizens, in one way or another, to this absurd cycle of victimization in which everyone, in reality, is victimized in the end. Overall, it is society as a whole that pays the high price for this violent absurdity.

The fact that a woman's daughter has become *someone else's* daughter-in-law and not her victim, does not relieve her guilt in having a hand in the system of power, authority, and control that her daughter is now the fresh victim of. The mother participates in this gender system of domination and suppression despite the fact that it creates misery and desolation for her own daughter. The mother selfishly perceives the fact that because her daughter is now not her own direct victim, this will result in, perhaps, a less painful and more tolerable life situation. Whatever amount of control over her daughter's life the mother forgoes by abandoning her daughter to her fate of subordination in the new family is replaced by the mother-in-law's control when the daughter arrives as the new bride. With the arrival of the daughter-in-law, the mother-in-law's status within the family structure is elevated and her level of power and control inevitably increases. Thus, it is the arrival of a new victim, the daughter-in-law, that makes it less painful for a woman to tolerate the unjust gender structure.

From the daughter-in-law's perspective, whose life has so far been controlled mostly by men, the cruelty of her mother-in-law is what finally convinces her that both men and women contribute to the ruthlessness of the system she lives in. For the daughter-in-law, not only is the world of men oppressive, but now the world of women is likewise tyrannical. Yet she also starts to perceive this situation as a natural part of her life and her inescapable destiny. As a result, she will surrender to the system. Rather than resisting her fate, she waits her turn to become the abuser as a mother-in-law to the brides of her sons. It is important to notice that even daughters and daughters-in-law eventually become a part of the perpetual cycle of violence as mothers-in-law, women with power and control. Kandiyoti affirms: "The cyclical nature of women's power and their anticipation of inheriting the authority of senior women encourage a thorough internalization of this form of patriarchy by the women themselves. Subordination to men is offset by the control older women have over younger women."[9] Rassam too stresses this cycle of control: "The woman begins her career as a wife at the lowest status position, and then slowly makes her way up, gaining respect and a certain de facto power with time. The cycle of a woman in a traditional household is embodied in her successive roles of bride, mother, and mother-in-law, each with its own basis of fragmented power."[10]

These observations regarding the stages and cycles of women's status and power are interesting for several reasons. A woman's investment in the prominent mother-son relationship now makes complete sense as a mother-in-law. By building a special relationship with her son, in reality the mother is investing in her own future power and authority. Moreover, the status and power of the mother-in-law, permitted only through men's acceptance and cooperation, is in some way a reward for her sacrifices and her services: performing sexual and reproductive duties, managing the household, performing endless household chores, and raising children. The subjugation of her son's wife is woman's reward for all of these services, a patriarchal-style retirement. However, is this arrangement a fair trade-off for women? It is important to note the fact that almost every woman, by having at least one boy, ironically, supports the patriarchal system by exercising her gained control and authority.

Is this really the only kind of relationship a mother-in-law can have with the wife of her son? Is this built-in conflict between the wife and her mother-in-law truly inevitable? Is it inconceivable to think that the mother and the bride, both of whom are oppressed by the same social system, could find a common ground against the control and power of the son or husband? The negative, destructive nature of this conflict between the mother-in-law and the new bride is one of the reasons that feelings of empathy and solidarity are lacking between members of the same sex. Friedl indicates: "The relationships between mothers-in-law and daughters-in-law, and among sisters-in-law, are potentially so fraught with tensions that solidarity seems to be hard to attain."[11]

Similar to the relationship between the mother and her own daughter, the relationship of the mother-in-law to the bride clearly illustrates betrayal of the oppressed in favor of the oppressor. This relationship is mostly negative, destructive, and violent, regardless of whether these features are overt or hidden. This relationship does not offer solidarity, empathy, or understanding to either woman. The same bitter experience the young bride had felt in her relationship with her mother are repeated in her relationship with another woman, her mother-in-law, another member of her own sex. The fact that this control and intimidation comes from a member of the same sex makes it even more difficult for the wife to accept.

There are several reasons for a new bride to resist the control of the mother-in-law. One reason is that women expect other women, more than they do men, to show empathy and solidarity; therefore the wife has a difficult time digesting the animosity of her mother-in-law. The other reason for resisting the role of the mother-in-law is that this role is derived from the weaker and inferior sex. This motive for resisting the power and authority of the mother-in-law is a clear illustration of how the perceived inferiority of women is internalized by women themselves. According to Rassam: "Women resent submission to the mother-in-law, for as the wife puts it, 'she is only a woman.' The prerogative acquired by the mother-in-law is recognized as being temporary and a function of her having attained a specific status in her domestic life cycle; they are not viewed as being inherent to her. Men's authority and prerogatives, on the other hand, are considered to be 'natural' and inherent to their 'maleness.'"[12]

MOTHER-IN-LAW, SON, AND BRIDE: A TRIANGLE OF CONFLICT

The relationship between the mother-in-law, the bride, and her husband is an interesting, complex situation that has a deep impact on the family structure. A Moroccan proverb says: "If a man with his mother [alive] marries, he goes to trouble by steps."[13] Rassam states: "Caught between these two women is the male in his dual role as husband and son. While competing for his attention and loyalty, the women make contradictory demands: the wife tries to isolate her husband from his natal family to form her own, while the mother seeks to keep him integrated in hers and minimize his involvement with his wife."[14] In their study of Lebanon, Keenan, el-Hadad, and Balian also state: "Husbands must balance the demands of their wives and mothers, who both demand respect and obedience, particularly from a young wife. Many husbands resorted to violent outbursts directed toward the wife when conflicts occur."[15]

This situation not only leads to a lack of understanding and empathy between women, but it also works to the advantage of the husband, who finds a source of comfort, worth, and satisfaction in this contest. This conflict between women over the loyalty of a husband or son, in fact, strengthens the control and authority of men in the end. This conflict precludes any possible process of internal contemplation or reevaluation of the patriarchal construction of gender roles on the part of either the men or the women. In this respect, this conflict functions as an external force hampering any internal questioning of the gender situation that could possibly result in a desirable outcome. Therefore, the status quo is maintained that prevents any opening or crack in the gender structure from forming. However, if it were possible, the desirable outcome of questioning the system might result in a lesser form of male control and might challenge the very rationale of the patriarchal system.

While men take advantage of this contest between the wife and the mother in order to receive better treatment from both, men also consider this trivial fight to be indisputable proof of the inferiority of women. This strengthens the overall patriarchal social mentality. Kandiyoti asserts that there is little doubt that what is being played out in the mother-son-bride triangle forms a central structural component of a much broader patriarchal scenario.[16] Gregg concurs: "For both men and women, the role changes in midlife present both developmental challenges and opportunities for empowerment and individuation. Paradoxically, however, senior women's power ultimately tends to support the patriarchal system, as they exercise their power largely to safeguard and perpetuate it."[17] This maze of relationships is not only a good illustration of how patriarchal structure and the patriarchal mentality work, but these relationships also reinforce this structure. The triangle of relationships between the husband, the wife, and the mother-in-law is indicative of a society in which conflict and animosity dominate, and because of the gender structure a lack of solidarity and empathy exists between individuals.

Rassam argues: "It is important to note that in this triad it is the mother and not the wife who is the legitimate and culturally approved object of the man's overt affection and tenderness, qualities that are generally assumed to be nonexistent in his relationship with his wife."[18] Religion sanctions love and affection toward one's mother and emphasizes obedience towards one's parents as religious duties. Religion also stresses the role of the mother, who demands respect, care, and obedience from her children. These religiously sanctioned and culturally encouraged duties do not simply end when a son marries; rather, these are lifelong duties.

The relationship triangle forces a man into a situation where he must choose whether his love will go to his mother or to his wife. There is no middle ground to be found or compromises to be made. As the pool of love in the patriarchal context is minimal and limited, there is no clear distinction between various categories of love. There is only one love and the receiving parties compete for this undifferentiated love.

However, one wonders why the mother-in-law insists that only her love, and not the love of a wife, will guarantee the happiness of her son. Why is it that the mother-in-law considers her imposition on the life of her son after his marriage to be the only way to ensure his happiness and comfort? Is it similar experiences she has had with her own husband that motivates and guides the actions of the mother-in-law regarding her son's married life? In her mind she knows very well that marriage is not about love, and her own marriage experience tells her for sure that a mother's love of her son is the only source of love available to men in loveless, miserable marriages. She knows a wife cannot love her husband in the patriarchal context and therefore her own love is an attempt to compensate for the love that the wife cannot provide. In the same vein, her life has shown her that a husband cannot love his wife either, and therefore she, not the wife, is deserving of her son's love. Likewise, the bride's experiences will eventually induce her to adopt the same attitude of betrayal and indifference toward her own daughter. Thus, a cycle of betrayal and a lack of solidarity and sympathy for members of the same sex are established in the domestic family structure, which perpetuates the unhealthy gender structure in society.

This dispute over a son's limited love relates to the aspect of loyalty that is a subject of contest and manipulation. Both of the competing sides expect and demand a show of loyalty from the son. Loyalty, in this sense, is perceived as one-dimensional, straightforward, unhesitant, and undivided. There is no room in patriarchy for multilayered, multidimensional loyalty. Differing loyalties are only recognized as conflicting loyalties. The exclusiveness of loyalty necessarily means a son's loyalty to his mother leaves no room for loyalty toward the newcomer. Equally so, to be loyal to his wife would require severing any previous or existing loyalties. This patriarchal perception of loyalty defines it as a simple and static concept. In reality though, loyalty is as complex and dynamic as social life is.

The issue of who is most deserving of a son's loyalty is also affected by the relative proximity of family members. The mother's claim over her son's loyalty is strong because he is her immediate biological family, while the son's loyalty to his bride is questioned because she is an outsider and not an immediate part of the natal family. The bride, in this respect, is perceived as an outsider aiming to steal the son away from the family, and therefore is a suspicious intruder and a troublemaker. It is only natural in this case that the mother should do her best to protect her son by guarding his goodness and loyalty to his natal family. The same tribal sense of logic is present in authoritarian politics in which there is always an enemy conspiring to steal the wealth and honor of the nation.

It is no wonder that the mother-in-law role not only supports patriarchy but also strengthens authoritarian practices in society. Naturally, by "protecting" her son, the mother tends to control him. She performs an authoritarian role in her son's life through violence and pure, simple control. The mother draws on an arsenal of religious, cultural, and patriarchal values, as well as authoritarian practices, to control her son. Not unlike her selfish behavior toward her own daughter, by controlling her son the mother forces him to revolve his life around her at the expense of his ability to build a meaningful attachment to his partner. This follows the logic that if the mother controls the son, then it is acceptable for the son to control his wife. Thus by supporting the control of her son over his wife, the mother-in-law supports male authority and control over another female, even though she has also suffered from patriarchal control. Regardless, she helps her son smother any sign of protest and resistance from the new bride, forcing her to resign to his control. Thus, the daughter-in-law's resistance to the control of her son is unacceptable in her eyes. What she has considered to be a legitimate course of action in her own life is now wrong in her son's wife's instance. The mother-in-law's behavior illustrates how women support male authority and control over other women. Perhaps, in this respect, the role of the mother-in-law is matched only by female politicians and parliamentarians who advance patriarchal male power in society by preaching gender inequality and the inferiority of women while claiming to represent women's interests.

AGENCY AND PUNISHMENT

It is interesting to note that the role of the mother-in-law is perhaps the only, or at least one of the very few, positions in which women actively employ power, control, and domination. Yet considering the nearly universal negative perception of the mother-in-law in Middle Eastern culture, and in other cultures as well, it is clear that in the few instances of female power and domination, women are still met with animosity and rejection within the patriarchal system. This is very different from the perception of men's power and domination. Is this bad reputation a punishment for the agency and power that females achieve in this system?

Mature or older women are exceedingly portrayed negatively in Middle Eastern cultures. Westermarck collected several Moroccan proverbs that display the evilness of the old woman: "When a woman becomes old, nothing remains in her but poison and the color of sulphur"; "The tears of an old woman are hidden behind her neck (not to be trusted, because they come easily)"; "If you see an old woman with a rosary, know that she is truly a devil (old women are hypocrites)";[19] "An old woman is worse than the devil."[20] Westermarck's collection also includes the following:

> There is a saying that when a boy is born a hundred jinn are born with him and that when a girl is born there are born with her a hundred angels; but every year a jinni passes from the man to the woman and an angel from the woman to the man, so that when the man is a hundred years old he is surrounded by a hundred angels, and when the woman is a hundred years she is surrounded by a hundred devils.[21]

Friedl finds a similar pattern in Persian folktales where Old Woman appears as a favorite folk character in tales, jokes, and conversation;[22] "While the stereotypical old, poor man can be humble, desperate, kindhearted, generous, industrious, dedicated or dumb, his counterpart Old Woman is usually simply greedy, hungry, and open for purchase for any service."[23] Thus, Middle Eastern folktales punish female agency by portraying the mother as a conspiring old woman meddling in the happiness of the newly wedded partners. Her bad reputation is the price a woman pays for her increased participation, agency, and self-confidence in patriarchal society.

It is interesting that this negative female stereotype includes such a large number of women, involving even young or middle-aged women. This popular portrayal of women has little to do with age per se and more to do with agency. It is also remarkable that a mature woman's increased agency comes at a stage in her life that is also perceived to be negative. *Sin al-ya's*, as it is called, is the age of despair and hope-lessness, when women are no longer able to reproduce, or are no lon-ger sexually attractive to men. However, this is the stage in a woman's life when she not only is able to participate in enforcing control over the younger female generation, but her control over her own life in-creases. In her study of Moroccan proverbs Webster indicates: "A sort of self-fulfillment attends the prophecy of increasing evil with increas-ing age, for as aging, experienced women lose their sexual power over men, they turn to other strategies for survival and security."[24] Only when the patriarchal functions of a woman are exhausted does she find her niche that provides her better status and higher authority.

The control and violence the mother-in-law brings to her son's new family increases conflict and violence within it. She prevents the cou-ple from creating conditions needed for a loving and meaningful re-lationship to develop between the new partners. The mother-in-law's involvement can make the already difficult early years of marriage even more adverse, if not completely miserable. It is this negative and destructive aspect of the mother-in-law's role that spurs the wife and the son to feel a mix of overt, hidden, conscious, and unconscious re-sentment toward the mother-in-law.

While it is true that her negativity is directed at the bride, her son suffers greatly as a result. Meddling with her son's happiness via the bride leads to resentment from the son as well. Because sons are re-quired to show obedience and respects to their mothers, for the most part, their resentment is hidden and subconscious. One wonders if this resentment adds to the unpopular image of the old woman in the col-lective popular conscious. The punishment of the old woman stigma that is associated with women in social life stems from two sources. The first is women's increased agency in the patriarchal context that debases and marginalizes other women. The second is the fact that this agency manifests in a negative and destructive way, affecting many people, particularly the younger generations.

While patriarchal ideology is ultimately responsible for miserable gender relations between the sexes and the difficulties that arise from it, it is the mother-in-law who is blamed by society, rather than patri-archy itself, despite the fact that she is only acting within the confines of the patriarchal structure. The fact that women are degraded and treated unequally also contributes to the highly disagreeable image of the old women. The weakest sections of societies always pay the high-est price. Yet, on the other hand, the damage that a mother-in-law does to the gender relations of the new family is real and significant.

The case of the mother-in-law clearly illustrates the fact that women are not only victims of the gender structure but perpetrators of violence also.

In their study of domestic violence in both Muslim and Christian low-income Lebanese families, Keenan, el-Hadad, and Balian conclude: "Conflict with a husband's family was another frequent cause of violence, particularly in younger families; conflict may arise because of a husband's strong allegiance to his mother; interpersonal stress between a husband's mother and the wife was common."[25] The real stories told by Lebanese women are very revealing in this respect: "My mother-in-law expected me to do all the housework. I couldn't finish on time. He came home and beat me because his mother told him I am slow"; "My mother-in-law instigated my husband by saying I did not wash my brother-in-law's clothes. She also told him I waste a lot, so he got upset and beat me"; "We lived with his mother and she told him I did not listen to her orders. He hit me. One year later, I went shopping to buy the children clothes and didn't get permission from his mother. I also did not ask her to go with me. When she told him, he beat me badly"; "My mother-in-law doesn't want me to visit my parents. I got upset and cried, so he beat me."[26]

The active role and agency of the mother-in-law reveals a power structure within the world of women that is not unlike the power structure that dominates male-female relationships and also male-male relationship for that matter. The female power structure that dominates the world of women is constructed within the patriarchal context of hierarchy, domination, and submission. This is the very same structure that has created women's miseries in the first place, the same structure that women complain of and suffer from. It is important to emphasize that even though the mother-in-law represents female power, authority, and status in a patriarchal system, she is also the pinnacle form of their weakness and surrender to the system. Certainly, resisting the demands of the social system, or attempting to change the rules of the game, would result in a better outcome *for all women and men alike*.

PART FOUR

PATRIARCHY AND AUTHORITARIANISM

CHAPTER 12

Authoritarian Family Structure

In everything there is partnership with the exception of marriage.
—Moroccan proverb

MARRIAGE AND CONFLICT

In Middle Eastern cultures, aside from bearing sons, marriage is the most important personal and social objective. Much suffering, restriction, and control are tolerated with the hope that marriage will lead to better circumstances and a different social experience than childhood and adolescence. Yet no matter how strong or high these expectations are, marriage is not free from the contradictions, inequalities, and relationships of power and control that dominate society. In fact, premarriage experiences socialize both men and women to perceive the other sex as different, unequal, and even acrimonious. As a result, both partners experience marriage mostly as an institution of violence and conflict.

Both men and women in male-centered cultures are familiar with relationships based on male control and dominance on the one hand and female obedience and servitude on the other. These kinds of experiences are detrimental to the growth of a healthy relationship between partners and their children, and even with *the self*. Both partners bring the negative gender experiences of their past into their marriage. For this reason, it is simply not conceivable that marriage will provide a way to escape the fate of the couple's earlier relationships. Experiences of unhealthy relationships in childhood and adolescence become the unhealthy realities of an unhealthy marriage.

Marriage is not a personal choice that men and women have the privilege to make; it is an arrangement made by the family and community, regardless of the individuals' desires and wishes. In this way, marriage is a public affair. Hence, the dichotomy of private and public spheres is quite interesting in the context of marriage. Because the commitment to marriage is a public arrangement forced on women, they have no control over their bodies, their sexuality, or the course of reproduction. By directly or indirectly forcing this arrangement on her, society leaves no choices for the woman. Marriage is not initiated for the benefit of the individual woman involved but rather in hopes of achieving objectives she has no control over. Also, because a woman's main task in her marriage is to produce sons and to serve as a sexual outlet for the husband, marriage is not exactly an affair of the private sphere; rather it is a public service. Marriage, in this respect, is the offering of a private body for the service of the public sphere and the community. Even the private, intimate domination of the husband over his wife has a public aspect. Marriage is the public, in addition to the private, subjugation of the wife to her husband. In this way, the boundaries between private and public spheres are obscured.

Dominant cultural and social values prepare men for the task of asserting their control, power, and domination, which their gender role requires. Studying gender relations in Iran, Vieille affirms that a woman in a marital relationship has no other rights than those the husband confers on her in a paternalistic way according to the habits or injunctions of custom and religion.[1] In this way, a husband exercises both physical and psychological domination over his wife. Minces implies that the husband tends to be extremely violent toward his wife by frequently venting his frustration on her.[2] The process of family socialization bestows on men the freedom to control and dominate their female relatives, permitting men to physically punish their sisters. Following marriage, it is the wife who is the recipient of male punishment. In fact, by preaching the virtue of a wife's obedience, religion and culture encourage the husband to control his wife. El-Saadawi emphasizes:

> Among the sacred duties of the wife is complete obedience to the husband. She is not allowed to differ with him, to ask questions, or even to argue certain points. The man on the other hand is not expected to obey his wife. On the contrary, it is considered unworthy of a man to do what his wife suggests or asks of him. . . . Authority is the right of men, and obedience the duty

of women. . . . Woman's status within marriage is even worse than that of the slave, for the woman is exploited both economically and sexually.[3]

The sexual deprivation the husband suffers from during adolescence leads to a subconscious resentment toward women. Abu-Odeh explains: "They frustrate him, and he feels hatred and resentment towards them for making him feel so helpless."[4] After all, his wife symbolizes the woman that was unavailable to him, or difficult for him to obtain, which has prevented him from satisfying both his sexual and emotional needs prior to marriage. For the husband, his wife represents that perpetually unavailable woman. Thus, women are blamed for being unavailable to satisfy men's sexual desires, even though it is the unchallenged cultural norms and values that are truly responsible for this.

As discussed earlier, patriarchy creates a gap and conflict between nature and social existence that can affect both men and women in their relationship with the *other*. Marital relationships inherently entail love, emotionality, and affection, which are all genuine sentiments that marriage forces men to experience. Inevitably, marriage also exposes individuals' strengths and weaknesses. Yet this experience creates a conflict for men between the masculine image this male-centered culture promotes and his feelings and emotions. Previously, the man has lived his life entirely in a world of men; marriage is a drastically new and different experience for the husband. For him, marriage is no longer this mythical, all powerful world of ethos that is portrayed in the dominant culture. Goldner et al. hint: "A husband is 'hooked in' to a woman's experience and to see the world through a woman's eyes."[5]

Living together, the husband naturally develops love for his wife and attachment to her. This creates a duality in the minds of men as they are tormented by two conflicting worlds. On the one hand, there is the simple reality of ordinary married life, where the conditions for love and friendship are present and viable. And on the other hand exists the mythical world that men have been socialized to believe in, where not only their superiority is legitimized, *but so is the inferiority of the very same persons they share married life with*. Thus, for the first time in their lives, marriage forces men to question and challenge the basic premises that dictate their world. Yet very few accept the challenge and most opt for the familiar and comfortable world of privileged masculinity. What makes the situation worse for men is that the extended family, along with society, continues to enforce this mythical world.

This widens the gap between the mythical masculine world men have come to expect and the reality of their nuptial relationships with their wives. Since male-centered culture considers attachment to women a weakness, this duality is difficult and frustrating for men to reconcile, which may cause further violence in marriage. Thus, whether a man succeeds or fails to overcome this duality is a crucial factor in the success of the marriage. According to Goldner et al.:

> Men, like women and children, often feel dependent, scared, sad and in need of protection. Since the prohibitions against such "feminized" feelings include the man's "private" sense of himself, and not only his public persona, the psychological task of denial is constant. This is why intimacy can be so dangerous. When the man's terror of not being different enough from "his" woman overtakes him, violence becomes one means of reasserting gender difference and male power. The injunction against having "unmasculine" feelings is sent to all men through the channels of the culture.[6]

It is not only men who contribute to violence in marriage, though; women also have a hand in institutionalizing conflict and violence. In Middle Eastern societies, before marriage, females live their lives bereft of respect and appreciation and lacking a sense of worth or power. When a woman marries and becomes the mistress of her house, a sense of day-to-day power rests with her for the first time in her life. It is interesting, however, the way she perceives her new position and power and how her previous experiences influence this perception. Her bitter experiences of relationships in her natal home, which were fraught with control, domination, disrespect, submissiveness, and fear, leave a deep imprint on her relationships with her husband and children.

It is difficult for a female who has lived her entire life in a segregated world to initiate and maintain a healthy, successful relationship with the male sex, even though he may be her legitimate partner. The same is true for men. Mernissi explains: "The woman who uses her subterranean silence, the woman who engulfs him in a sea of lies and in swamps of sordid manipulation, is applying the law of retaliation: an eye for an eye, a lie for a lie. It is the vicious circle of an impossible dialogue between partners mutilated by an insane patriarchy."[7]

Most of the violence that occurs between partners is reciprocal, and as we have seen, violence breeds violence. Women also participate in domestic violence, not only by accepting their role as the victim, but also by maintaining conditions favorable for violence. Rejecting the fate bestowed on her for being born on the wrong side of the gender line was not possible in her parental home. Debasement and oppression of women starts in early childhood, making the act of rejection or rebellion by the female child much more difficult to realize. A child is not strong or mature enough to even comprehend, let alone challenge or rebel against, the social system that oppresses her. As a result, girls surrender completely, whether by force or indoctrination, to the system before the age of maturity. Moreover, even the thought of rebelling against close family members is difficult for a woman to contemplate. She was born and raised in the same home as her oppressors and develops an attachment to the people who debase her. Yet, because it is her close family that causes her sufferings, the psychological effects of this oppression are pervasive and gravely damaging. It is also interesting to note that after living with the husband for some significant period of time, she will eventually develop an attachment to him that may induce her to tolerate his violence toward her.

Regardless, moving out of the house and into marriage is a woman's first real opportunity to rebel against the injustices she has suffered beginning with birth. Marriage provides the wife with a new situation, a new home, and new people to live with, which make it easier for her to show signs of her resentment. However, this rebellion is not overtly directed towards the initial causes of her misery, but rather her resentment is oriented toward her husband. She objectively rejects her husband, regardless of his manner, preferences, or subjectivity. For women, the husband symbolizes the irrational and unjust culture of honor and control. However, a wife's rejection of her husband is usually more hidden than overt, more subconscious than conscious. Through the husband, she takes revenge on all the previous injustices she has suffered at the hands of her parents, brothers, and society as a whole.

The husband, after all, represents the patriarchal society that has disrespected and degraded her. Rejecting her husband as a partner in marriage is in fact a woman's symbolic rejection of her fate and the conditions of being born female. This rebellion manifests as the rejection of the husband rather than the parents or brothers because they are her closest family and, consequently, are more difficult to reject, whereas the husband is a stranger. By exerting social control, power, and domination over his partner, the husband aggravates the situation. The subconscious feelings of animosity that women cultivate during childhood toward their brothers for being the most favored, and towards their parents for differentiating between their children, all come to the fore in marriage.

Yet the husband is in a strong position of control and domination, as he is the provider of the family and is backed and supported by a well-entrenched system of shame and honor. Religion and culture condition the wife to obey her husband and not to contest him. This religious sanctioning of the wife's obedience augments domestic violence and fertilizes the grounds for animosity and reciprocal violence within the relationship.

Mernissi perceives that in Middle Eastern society, marriage is conflict.[8] The institution of marriage represents the intersection of hierarchy, conflict, control, domination, submission, resistance, and violence. It is a story of power and accommodation. The dominant cultural and social values ensure that marriage functions only as an institution of violence and resistance in the form of violence. Prevailing social values prevent males and females from being able to love or be loved. Wife and husband meet in marriage as strangers, and because of cultural socialization, they bring with them feelings of animosity toward one another even though they are strangers. The laden animosities they have for one another taint any potential attachment between the partners as it is seen as a weakness or surrender. Mernissi remarks: "Men and women were, and still are, socialized to perceive each other as enemies."[9]

Domestic violence is an expression of dominance and control within the family structure. Understood in a broad and comprehensive sense, it is the manifestation and the intersection of male and female power. Violence reflects the relationship between the socially acknowledged and religiously sanctioned dominant power and authority of the male, and the unacknowledged, hidden power of the female. In fact, the significant disparity between these two powers is why domestic violence is so extreme and damaging. The fact that one power is culturally sanctioned and expected from society while the other power is suppressed increases the rate and intensity of violent marital unions. The destructive powers of both sexes synergistically increase in this situation. The destructiveness of the male power is equally matched by the undefeated and destructive, yet unsanctioned, female power. It is this intersection of destructive powers that creates the cycle of violent tension in family life.

Thus, marriage represents a conflict between the wife's desire to rebel, because marriage provides opportunity to do so, and the strong economic and cultural control of the husband. This conflict often poisons the relationship between partners. However, the wife's struggle is not rebellion against the cultural and patriarchal values she suffers from, but against her husband as a person and as a symbol of this culture. The wife seldom takes the other, more peaceful road, exposing the ugliness of the system that has victimized her, by trying to negotiate a different relationship with her husband. He is also a victim of the same system, and she could try to win him over to her side. Instead, the wife suffers in silence. She treats her husband as an enemy incapable of being an understanding, sensitive, and cooperative partner. The husband, on the other hand, sees this conflict as a threat to his position and an attack on his personality and, therefore, tends to be defensive. By defending himself, he misses the point of this conflict. In fact, both partners miss the true purpose of this conflict. Both partners personify and personalize an intense structural conflict. In this situation, both partners personify a conflict that is deeply rooted in the oppressive gender structure by becoming direct actors in the disaccord. They also personalize this rather deeply ingrained structural conflict, adopting it as personal conflict between them, a conflict between two different personalities. The failure of marriage to meet the high expectations of both partners contributes to the exasperation felt between them.

The fact is, unhappy wives create unhappy families. Women who increasingly lose hope of ever becoming an equal, respected, and nurtured partner increasingly become bitter and hostile in many overt and hidden ways. It is true that women resign to their fate, yet no victim accepts complete and final defeat. Instead of resisting this fate altogether, a women creates misery for everyone else around her. She reasons out that because she leads such a miserable life, why should her partner have a better one? Ortner points out: "It is no wonder that women later may resent their husbands as deeply as husbands resent their wives, not only or even necessarily because of the husbands' direct domination, but for what their husbands represent in status terms."[10] The husband is the target of his wife's hostility, not only because of his dominant, controlling role in the marriage, but also because he personifies the unjust system that oppresses and degrades women. Wives punish their husbands not always for real or actual things they do or do not do, but for a system that men are a part of yet not solely responsible for.

Moreover, living with someone is living with the true, entire nature of that person, including all of his positive and the negative aspects. The myth of the powerful, strong, and dominating man is no longer so seamless after marriage. From a woman's standpoint, living with a man reveals his true size, shattering the mythical, inflated, all-powerful image of men she has come to know. This also reinforces the doubts and questions females had in childhood as to why society regards men so highly and favorably when they too can be so weak. These reinforced doubts increase the bitterness women feel toward their marriages, making it easier for them to antagonize their husbands.

The subconscious motives that both partners accumulate prior to marriage make it difficult for an intimate, sincere, respectful, and fruitful relationship between the partners to develop. The husband interprets his wife's attitude as the rejection of him, his character, and his personality, which also leads to more hostility between them. Quite often, in fact, a wife's subconscious rejection of her husband causes her to spotlight and exaggerate every negative aspect and weakness in her husband's character and actions. She uses these faults as "conscious" justifications for her subconscious rejection of the husband. Likewise, the husband begins to do the same, creating an unhealthy atmosphere of negativity in the new family. The husband does not realize that there are deeply rooted causes for his wife's hidden resentment and perceives her to be an aggressive and hostile person. This, ultimately, induces him to be more violent. Thus, both partners enter into an overt and hidden game of physical and psychological violence. This game extends to the children as well and the whole family; the entire marriage falls victim to the violent social system of control and domination. According to Vieille:

> In fact it is not rare, especially in that period of sexual dazzlement that follows marriage, that a true amorous passion ties the couple. But how to conciliate the egalitarian and personal relationship of sentiment with the hierarchical and reified relationship of law? Their joining is impossible in principle and in fact; a greater or lesser tension always exists between them. The "official" model, weighing on the total organization of society beyond the couple, tends to crush the spontaneous model which scarcely finds any external support. At any rate, the relations of the husband and wife tend to contradict the model images of masculine culture.[11]

Thus, violence is the natural outcome of a relationship fraught with mistrust, inequality, and hostility. Violence is the natural outcome when hopes are dashed and dreams are broken. Violence is the outcome when marriage, increasingly, is the place where men and women collide with unrealistic hopes and unfulfilled expectations. Violence is the failure of marriage to significantly change the lives of young people, who in their naïveté thought marriage would be the solution to or salvation from their premarital frustrations. Violence in marriage is a reflection of marriage's failure to end a brutal system of violence and domination. Considering the centrality of marriage in Middle Eastern societies, it is only natural to expect that the failure of marriage, with its unfulfilled expectations and accumulated frustrations, influences the level and intensity of violence in society overall.

THE "VIRTUE" OF OBEDIENCE

The family is a key factor in the connection between gender relations and authoritarianism. Joseph and Slymovics argue: "Given the centrality of family, its patriarchal structure is crucial in understanding gender relationships in the Middle East."[12] The patriarchal structure of the family reflects the authority, control, power, and domination of the male over the female and the old over the young, resulting in the unchallenged obedience and submissiveness of the female and the younger generations. Karmi illustrates:

> In Arab society, the patriarchal structure has been enshrined and most effectively perpetuated through the Arab family. In its typical form, the Arab family is patriarchal and hierarchical in relation to age and sex, the old and the males having authority over the young and the females. The father holds a key position with regard to power and authority. He expects and exacts unquestioning obedience from his wife and children and may punish disobedience harshly.[13]

Other scholars also emphasize the central father figure in the patriarchal and authoritarian structure. "The father is the authoritarian figure in the family," al-Khayyat comments.[14] Ortner concurs: "Fathers are constructed as disciplined positions within a hierarchy."[15] According to Wilhelm Reich: "The patriarchal relationship of the father to the remainder of the family does reflect his political and economic position. In the figure of the father, the authoritarian state has its representative in every family, so that the family becomes its most important instrument of power."[16] He also adds: "The sons, apart from a subservient attitude toward authority, develop a strong identification with the father, which forms the basis of the emotional identification with every kind of authority."[17]

Barakat, on the other hand, emphasizes the link between religion and the authoritarian, patriarchal structure of the family. He states: "Religion stresses the holiness of a family and its ties as well as the value of obedience to parents. Hence such proverbs as *ridha al-ab min ridha ar-rabb* (a father's satisfaction is part of God's satisfaction) or *ghadhab al-ab min ghadhab ar-rabb* (father's anger is part of God's anger)."[18] "There are," Barakat continues, "striking similarities between the religious concepts of the father and that of God, indicating that God is an extension or abstraction of the father."[19] In the words of Beauvoir: "The father personifies transcendence; he is God."[20]

Thus, religion reinforces obedience within the family as a religious duty. The dominant religious and cultural values do not, however, distinguish between respect for one's parents, which is desirable, and obeying one's parents, which is harmful and unhealthy. The system of patriarchal social values is not troubled by this rather contradictory, enforced association between the two. In fact, these are mutually exclusive in the sense that respect is the negation of obedience, while obedience is the very negation of respect. Surely, obedience is not the more desirable of the two, neither is it the only way to show respect toward parents. Nevertheless, the son is socialized to show obedience to his father, which will ultimately incline him to remain obedient to the ruler. The father becomes the dictator of each family. He exercises monopoly over finances, decision-making, authority, power, and control. Vis-à-vis the powerless, submissive, and subordinate women and children, he is dominant, powerful, omnipotent, and uncompromising.

Studying women in Saudi Arabia, al-Torki stresses: "The ideology of parent-child relationships censors challenges and defiance of parents' wishes through the concept of *ghadab* [anger], which appears more effectively on women than on men."[21] Likewise, in his study of Moroccan proverbs, Westermarck observes that parents possess, for use at their disposal, a terrible method of punishing a wicked or neglectful child, namely, their curse. A parent's curse is more powerful than those of saints. This is reflected in the following two proverbs: "He who has been broken by his parents will not be repaired by the saints, and he who has been broken by the saints will be repaired by his parents" and "He who is blessed by his parents is covered by them, and he who is cursed by his parents is stripped of his clothes by them."[22]

Gender relations manifest as life's daily experience of obedience to authority and power. Authoritarianism garners the same kind of coercive, obedient relationship. Children, regardless of gender, experience

firsthand how power, authority, control, submissiveness, and obedience play out on a daily basis in their homes. As they grow up, they
discover that the public sphere is not much different from the situation in the domestic sphere that they have come to know. Their domestic experiences prepare men and women for their transition into
the new, yet subtly familiar, authoritarian public sphere, making this a
more acceptable and tolerable shift. It is, perhaps, not an exaggeration
to say that an individual in Middle Eastern society is *born in patriarchy
and dies in authoritarianism*. Barakat writes:

> The hierarchical structure of the Arab family based on sex and
> age traditionally requires the young to obey the old and adhere
> to their expectations. This hierarchy creates vertical rather than
> horizontal relationships between the young and the old. In such
> relationships downward communication often takes the form of
> orders, instructions, warnings, threats, reprehensions, shaming,
> and the like. Furthermore, while downward communication may
> be accompanied by anger and punishment, upward communica-
> tion may be accompanied by crying, self-censorship, obfuscation,
> and deception.[23]

Moreover, marriage is a violent institution aiming to ensure the
conformity, subordination, and obedience of women. Religion dele-
gates the position of family leadership to the husband. The obedience
of women is strongly reinforced by the ease of repudiating wives and
the right to polygamy, which are accorded to men only. The structure of polygamy is, in fact, a small-scale authoritarian order. Like
any absolute ruler, one man is the center of attention and is the sole
decision-maker while several women compete for the favors and lar-
gesse of the husband who is the sole master in this petite authoritarian
arrangement.

The institution of marriage is an authoritarian arrangement based
on the unidirectional obedience of the wife to her husband. Studying
the situation of women in Iraq, al-Khayyat states: "Many women take
pride in being obedient, whether as daughters or wives."[24] She also
observes that Iraqi women see the obedient woman as happier than
the more independent-minded one,[25] and that most of the women still
viewed obedience as better than a strong personality.[26] These convictions are explicitly reflected in the following opinions of Iraqi women.
"A woman with a strong personality would be very tired mentally
or generally over-stressed as a wife. I think the subordinate ones are

much more successful."[27] "Obedience is better; a strong woman can cause conflict between herself and her husband";[28] "If a woman isn't obedient she would only harm herself";[29] or "If every wife tried to understand her husband and every girl tried to understand her father and brothers, everybody would live in peace."[30] Thus, many women hold on to the conviction that obedience is the solution to marital conflict and violence.

A field study of Egyptian adolescents conducted by Mensch et al. finds similar convictions among Egyptian women. When asked whether a wife needs her husband's "permission for everything," 91.8 percent of the males responded "yes," while an astonishingly high 87.5 percent of females agreed with this statement. When asked who should be responsible for decision-making, regarding whether or not the wife works for pay outside the home, 63.8 percent of males agreed that the husband alone should make that decision, while 28 percent of females agreed. Regarding the question of who the breadwinner of the family should be, 87 percent of males and 83.7 percent of females stated that the husband should be the only breadwinner.[31] These are very high rates of affirmative female responses considering the answers to these questions significantly affect their daily lives.

Wherever there is authority and control there will be both obedience and disobedience. Mernissi explains this phenomenon: "The relationship within the Muslim family is dominated by the leadership/obedience pattern. Disobedience, or *nushuz*, in Arab heritage signifies a woman's rebellion against her husband and her refusal to obey his word."[32] As a consequence of this, the first duty expected from a wife is obedience to her husband. Similarly, in authoritarian politics, obedience to the ruler follows the very same logic. A "good" citizen is one who is obedient to the ruler. This is similar to the norm that a "good" wife is one who is obedient to her husband. Not only does obedience becomes a "virtue" in this context, but also society considers merely contemplating disobedience to be a most serious crime against the established patriarchal and authoritarian order. Studying Persian folktales, Friedl concludes: "By far the most frequent wifely misbehavior is disobedience. Eight times in the stories the events take a dramatic turn when a woman refuses to obey her husband. Good wives are often mentioned in the folktales as complaisant and cooperative."[33]

Barakat argues that much of the legitimacy of political rulers and their orders is derived from the family and its orientation of values.[34] Culturally and religiously enforced obedience is a precursor to the level and intensity of obedience in society, the basis for a thriving system of authoritarianism. Hence, obedience is a common feature of both gender relations and authoritarianism. The gender structure paves the way for the authoritarian state to dominate and control society. When half of a society is controlled and submissive at home, it is not difficult for an authoritarian regime to subdue the entire society into the same state. Neither is it difficult for an authoritarian ruler to imprison its population when half of the citizens are already imprisoned. Reich strongly emphasizes the importance of the family to the political authoritarian order:

> The family is the authoritarian state in miniature, to which the child must learn to adapt himself as a preparation for the general social adjustment required of him later. The family becomes the most important source, and the most essential institution for the preservation, support, and reproduction of the authoritarian social system. Thus, the authoritarian state gains an enormous interest in the authoritarian family: *it becomes the factory in which the state's structure and ideology are molded.*[35]

Indeed, the socialization of boys within the family leads not only to their despotic rule over the family and women, but these domestic despots strengthen the authoritarian order that dominates society. Within this authoritarian, despotic atmosphere, politics, economy, and culture are negotiated and allowed to function. The consequence of this is a more structurally violent society, and the establishment of a cycle of violence beginning with the family, transferring to society and back again.

Authoritarian and hierarchal family structures tend to familiarize and normalize violence and obedience. These aspects are crucial to the way authoritarianism functions in the lives of citizens. The political and economic world revolves around its ruler in the same way the family revolves around the man. Thus, patriarchy is conducive for the emergence and sustainability of the authoritarian state. Karmi refers to this relationship:

> There is a fundamental structure within Arab society that has a direct effect on collective and political life: the patriarchal and hierarchal family. Although it is not in itself the sole cause of the problems faced by the Arab world, its continued existence will frustrate every effort made to bring about the effective modernization of Arab society and political structures unless its nature is

addressed and its contradictions are resolved. One of the ways in which progress will be blocked is because the replication of the family structure and values at the political level will contribute powerfully to the perpetuation of dictatorial regimes, since it innately shares a set of values with them: values of hierarchy, obedience, absolute authority and patriarchal domination.[36]

Conversely, the authoritarian political structure also reinforces despotic family structures. The lack of political, economic, social, or intellectual advancement in the public sector that is due to the domination of the state strengthens conservative family norms and supports authoritarian structure in the family. However, nonauthoritarian political systems that ensure increased political participation and access to economic resources positively affect individuals' self-esteem and family relations. If ordinary men, not merely the elite, had the opportunity to advance in society, perhaps they would not feel the need to conquer their women, wives, or daughters. Therefore, when it comes to violence and obedience, patriarchal family structure and authoritarianism are mutually reinforcing. However, there are other common features of both systems that contribute to violence in society, as we shall see in the subsequent chapters.

CHAPTER 13

Gender and Authoritarian Social Contract

Our bodies are our gardens to which our wills are gardeners. We may make them idle producing nothing, or make them rich and useful by our labours.

—*William Shakespeare*, Othello

SOCIAL CONTRACT: LOYALTY AND REWARD

The social contract that governs Middle Eastern society has three interrelated dimensions. The first is the religious dimension in which God is the creator and the provider for people in exchange for their worship and obedience. The second is the sexual or gender dimension in which women are offered protection and security from birth to death in exchange for chastity and obedience. The third is the political, authoritarian dimension in which the state offers its citizens security, services, and economic and social benefits in exchange for their docility and obedience. These three interrelated dimensions of the social contract are similar in several aspects: they function through a specific social construction of reality, wastefulness, and obedience. Foucault suggests: "All modes of domination, submission, and subjugations are ultimately reduced to an effect of obedience."[1]

While people have invented the idea of God, God himself has become their creator. People have created him so that he may respond to their wishes, yet with time people have become obedient to God rather than the inverse. People devote much of their resources to worshiping, honoring, and abiding by the detailed and extensive religious rules and duties that are imposed on believers, even though it is believed that the faithful receive their reward mostly in the next life and much less in this world.

The basis of the sexual social contract is the guarantee of life security for women in exchange for their virginity, honor, and conformity. In this process, women become dependent on their fathers, husbands, brothers, or sons. In her study of Iraqi women, al-Khayyat remarks that a woman is brought up to feel insecure without a man and to be absolutely dependent.[2] Although patriarchy stipulates material security for women, which is provided by the man and considered to be a justification for gender inequality, it distorts the fact that women are capable of providing for themselves. From this perspective, if protecting women by way of providing for them is used to justify controlling women, it would make little sense to permit or encourage women to provide for themselves. Obedience would not be justified in the same way if women were able to sustain and protect themselves. Yet outside the prevailing gender system this "patriarchal insurance" is not the only way for women to achieve protection, subsistence, and security. Working and attaining financial independence is another option. However, the basis of the gender system rests on limiting women's choices to only patriarchal options, and female independence is not such an option.

The foundation for the political, authoritarian social contract is built on a trade-off of security and services from the state, in exchange for passivity and obedience from ordinary people. The state controls the country's economic and financial resources and offers part of these resources to the people in the form of economic rewards such as job security, short working hours, low or no taxes, early retirement, subsidies (mostly for cheap food and fuel), cheap credit facilities for housing, and so forth. Nonetheless, there is a huge price to pay for these economic "benefits": the tolerance of dictatorship and the absence of the rule of law, the disrespect of basic human rights, and the lack of freedom and democracy in society. However, considering the state to be the people's provider is different from the simple reality that these economic benefits provided by the state are, in fact, derived from the common wealth of the nation, which every citizen is entitled to a fair share of. In fact, the state has no wealth of its own apart from the wealth of its people. In other words, society provides for the state, not the opposite. Moreover, the state's domination over all aspects of life prevents people from seeking economic opportunities beyond the domain of the state. Therefore, more than being a provider, the state is an obstacle to people's ability to provide for themselves. Consequently, if the state encouraged other economic opportunities, thereby enabling people to provide for themselves, dictatorship and state violence would not be justified by the exchange of state benefits for people's obedience.

Thus, linking tangible benefits to people's duty to abide by the social contract is rather a particular social construction of reality. Through their imposition of the social contract on society and its people, the state, patriarchy, and religion create their own realities based on control, violence, intimidation, and submission. This is a severely detrimental social construction because it denies the existence of alternatives. It would be unnecessary for people to give their obedience in exchange for something if they themselves could acquire it, granted they were given the chance. The fact that all three dimensions of the social contract limit the choices available to people clearly reflects the violent and coercive political tendency of the social contract. Imposing this social construct on society and denying people a dignified and peaceful life is a violation of basic human rights.

The social contract is based on security, dependency, waste, and obedience, and there is no place whatsoever for disobedience in this social arrangement. Unthinkable acts that violate the social contract result in severe punishment: hell, honor killing, prison, and torture. For the state, smothering disobedience requires cutting down opportunities and advantages. Because of the state's suppression of opportunities, people's dependence on the state to provide the necessities for survival prevents ordinary people from doubting the indispensability of obedience. In fact, even though the state controls the economy and politics, and therefore material benefits, ordinary people still consider the state to be foreign and remote. When it comes to gender relations, it is even more difficult for women to challenge the sexual social contract for the simple fact that it is women's closest relatives who provide security in exchange for their obedience, including fathers, brothers, sons, or husbands. Therefore, challenging the patriarchal social contract is much more difficult than challenging the authoritarian social contract in which the state is a distant body.

Moreover, the social contract, which is founded in obedience, is strongly linked to loyalty. Loyalty is a confusing and contradictory aspect in women's lives in the Middle East. Joseph contends: "Women were structurally caught between competing loyalties. Husbands demanded loyalty from their wives. Children expected the undivided involvement of their mothers. Women often felt torn between families of origin and of procreation as they matured."[3] Men also experience conflicting loyalties between their natal families and their marital families. The husband, torn apart by his loyalty to his wife and loyalty to his mother, is a prime illustration of these troublesome, conflicting loyalties. Children are always troubled by the dichotomy of their loyalty to their mother and to their father that is caused by the complex relationship between parents. Likewise, husbands and wives are constantly distressed by the conflict of their loyalty to the natal family versus their loyalty to the marital family. Thus, the patriarchal gender structure complicates and problematizes the aspect of loyalty in men and women's lives.

Loyalty is also awkward and suspicious in authoritarian politics. Political loyalty is always demanded by the state, and it is expected to be one-dimensional, straightforward, and unhesitant. There is no room in authoritarian, patriarchal orders for naturally existing, multidimensional forms of loyalty. Even if multilayered loyalties are recognized, they are considered to be in a state of conflict. The enforced exclusiveness of loyalty is a source of contention in politics. Reducing the dynamic and complex concept of loyalty in this manner to a simple, static, and nonnegotiable social display is a violent interpretation.

Obedience in the authoritarian sense means submitting to absolute loyalty. Competing and conflicting loyalties are a constant source of contention in authoritarian politics because there is little room for reconciliation. People are either loyal to the regime or they are against it; there is no middle ground. Often loyalty to the political regime also means uncritical loyalty, because any sign of criticism would indicate either a shift or change in loyalty, or worse, betrayal. To be disloyal in the patriarchal, authoritarian sense is betrayal, which is accompanied by a strong sense of guilt if an individual is perceived to have betrayed. Thus, loyalty in the context of the authoritarian, patriarchal gender structure must be simple, static, absolute, undivided, uncritical, and unquestionable. Loyalty cannot be dynamic, shifting, or multilayered and cannot intersect with any other loyalties. Being loyal to oneself first, and then to the state, religion, and gender structure is not an option in the authoritarian and patriarchal order.

Furthermore, loyalty is also highly personalized in the authoritarian and patriarchal sense. The personalization of loyalty in authoritarian politics is visible in the requirement that an individual must be loyal to the dictator or the regime and seldom anything else. Likewise, loyalty is also personalized in gender relations in the sense that loyalty is oriented toward a specific person, such as a mother, wife, son, or father.

Yet this is not the only interpretation of loyalty; loyalty does not have to be personalized in this way. That is, instead of being loyal to a person, one can be loyal to certain issues and values. If these loyalties to political leaders, husbands, wives, brothers, fathers, and mothers were rooted in moral and social values that could be applied to relationships between various individuals, then the source of contention between conflicting, personalized loyalties would be eliminated or greatly reduced. In this case, loyalty to a specific person would not exist, no matter how important a person is. There would only be loyalty to the integrity of a personality, and loyalty could shift as necessary depending on the issues at hand.

Imposed obedience and loyalty is a key element of the structural violence that lays the foundation for the authoritarian and sexual social contracts. Because freedom of choice is not tolerated by authoritarianism, only enforced, preconceived forms of loyalty are accepted. Thus, because people cannot live their lives as free, independent individual citizens, authoritarianism generates an artificial conflict regarding loyalty. This paradoxical situation, due to the lack of freedom and democracy, is paralleled by the structure of gender relations, also based on obedience and control.

The Middle Eastern social contract is also strongly connected to the concept of legitimacy. A child born male is "legitimate" in the cultural sense. The dominant culture imposes this male legitimacy on society. But, because it precludes the other sex, this is exclusive legitimacy. In this sense, gender legitimacy is limited, narrow, and discriminatory. Yet legitimacy bestowed on a child simply for being born male is a shaky and limited form of legitimacy. Therefore, a second form of legitimacy is introduced, which is rooted in the culturally and religiously sanctioned responsibility of men to protect and provide for women. The acceptance of the male legitimacy is facilitated by the internalization of cultural values and norms that are associated with the supremacy of men through the process of socialization of women.

This facet is also paralleled in authoritarianism. Authoritarian regimes that come to power and remain in power, mostly by military takeover, lack any sense of real legitimacy. The phenomenon recently seen in the region, of holding elections under the control of the authoritarian state, makes little difference in this regard. Because the legitimacy of authoritarian regimes is questionable, the second form of legitimacy, which is the quality of implementation and performance of the authoritarian system, is even more important. The state must deliver a decent level of services and a high enough standard of living, security, economic development, and prosperity to maintain its credibility. Considering this, the serious economic crisis in the Middle East clearly exposes the failure of the authoritarian and theocratic regimes to deliver on these promises, and therefore these regimes are losing their credibility and legitimacy.

In order to compensate for this lack of legitimacy, authoritarian regimes tend to invent other sources of legitimacy. They seek external sources of legitimacy such as religion, nationalism, conflict with the *other*, and fabricated conflict with, mostly, invented enemies. A clear illustration of this is the way authoritarian and theocratic regimes manipulate the Palestinian problem or confrontation with the West in domestic politics. However, this is a shaky source of legitimacy for both the gender structure and authoritarianism.

POLITICS OF DISSIPATION

The Middle Eastern social contract is an unproductive system that leads to the wasting of society's precious human resources. The sexual social contract is extremely wasteful in that it directly excludes the use of half of society's potential resources. By deeming women incapable of supporting themselves, they become idle members of society. Discussing the dualistic view of obedience and support, Mernissi points out: "Obedience is the ideal behavior pattern that determines women's status within the family and her economic role. Obedience versus support is a duality which determines women's role as that of consumer only, while men are defined as the producers who must earn their wives' obedience."[4] What is more, a large portion of the productive half of society's energy is also wasted on policing and controlling the conformity of women.

With the onset of menopause, typically the mid-40s, women are no longer considered attractive or active sexual beings, and their productive function of reproducing sons ends. With no sexual appeal or reproductive capabilities, women are considered to be old and useless. It is also noteworthy that the authoritarian economic contract imposes early retirement on citizens, ensuring men more or less retire at the same age that women "retire." The fact that men can retire after 20–25 years of working for the state means that they can retire before reaching the age of 50 if they have started working early in life. At this age, men are also considered to be old, unproductive, and useless. In fact, both the sexual and authoritarian social contracts shorten and limit the productive life of men and women. The fact that people retire from active and productive life prematurely is a clear indication of exclusionary politics that underline the social contract.

To be sure, the social contract does recognize the energies of people but nonetheless wastes them in unproductive ways. Women's energies are considered to be useful mostly for reproducing sons, a biological reality patriarchy clearly recognizes and appreciates. In addition to the function of reproduction, female energy is oriented toward conforming to the strict moral code in society, which is ultimately an unproductive system. In addition, controlling and policing the conformity of women is considered to be the most honorable and useful investment of men's energy and creativity. In the eyes of authoritarianism, however, people offer a different sort of resource to be used at the disposal of the authoritarian regime. People can be used to engage in militarization, conflict, and wars and can be enlisted to fight the endless list of invented enemies. People's energies are wasted on antagonizing the *other*, and the *other*, in authoritarian context, is always an enemy. In this way, people actually belong to the authoritarian regime, which has the uncontested authority to determine an individual's fate as it sees best.

In this way, the dominant social contract is closely linked to the marginalization of human resources. Authoritarianism polarizes society and concentrates power, decision-making authority, and wealth into the hands of a minority, which is of course at the expense of the powerless and marginalized majority. Authoritarianism is the rule of violence and power over a weak and powerless population. Patriarchal gender relations create a similar state of powerlessness and marginalization. Women are the largest marginalized group of all in this region. Women often make up more than half of societies; however, if we include the younger generation of girls and boys in our discussion of marginalization, who are also debased by patriarchy, we can indeed talk about the majority. Paternal authoritarianism, as Bouhdiba argues, "Cannot fail to devalue childhood in the same way that it devalues femininity. The same type of barriers that separate male from female does also separate the adult from the 'little ones.' The only valid models of experience are those of the adult. It is up to children to conform to them, to approach them. Just as one can in no sense speak of the autonomy of women, so the autonomy of children is unthinkable."[5]

Because women and children are marginalized, family politics are complex and contradictory. Feeling powerless and subsidiary, a majority of the family will often form a special alliance in an effort to isolate and mitigate the authority of the husband or father. This is clearly an exercise of exclusionary politics at the domestic level. This demonstrates how exclusionary politics are not isolated to the authoritarian political regime but permeate all of society.

Avoiding authority and learning how to deal with it indirectly are lessons children learn early in their lives by observing their mother's role in family politics. The relationship of the father to his children is mostly channeled through the mother. This minimizes the contact between the children and their father, a symbol of authority. Dealing with authority indirectly is one of the fundamental principles of authoritarian politics. The absence of the rule of law, which is another decisive principle of authoritarian politics, maintains a level of remoteness between citizens and authority. This same level of remoteness is found in the structure of the family as well. Studying the relationships between mothers and daughters in Iran, Kousha observes that mothers act as mediators in the family; they are the communication channel between fathers and children.[6] Fernea also points out that it is the mother who teaches the child the art of *wasta*, of finding a mediator, like her, to deal with the supreme authority of his father or patron.[7]

Early family experiences expose children to humiliation or depreciation of the people around them. Children are socialized to accept this as normal behavior. In this way, trivialization of women in the family facilitates the degradation of people in the public authoritarian order. While marginalization normally affects minorities in societies, or several minorities or sections of the society, authoritarianism and patriarchy manage to marginalize the majority of Middle Eastern society. Thus, gender relations tend to serve the interests and the objectives of authoritarian rule by ensuring the powerlessness and marginalization of more than half of the population. Domestic relationships tend to weaken the resistance of society as a whole to the domination of the authoritarian state. While gender relations effectively marginalize women, stripping them of power, men's active role in gender domination preoccupies them and consumes their energies.

Because authoritarianism fails to effectively channel these resources for productive purposes, human potential must be curtailed and discouraged. There is no room for human initiative in an authoritarian world where the few dominate everything. Because there is no room for these resources in political, economic, and social life, these resources are not only diminished, they are confined to the domestic space, the world of women in which dominant gender ideology exhausts human energies and resources. This is the only way to compensate for the lack of space for these energies elsewhere in society.

Essentially, though, any situation in which men have all the power and control, while women are debased and submissive, will only lead to further violence and passivity. Violent and patriarchal gender structures discourage positive, productive uses of human agency. How much political power is directed toward human resources and to what purposes they are used is a reflection of the way a society respects or appreciates its own resources. The prevailing gender structure and cultural norms in Middle Eastern societies support authoritarianism by ignoring, neglecting, and denigrating the human resources available in society. When cultural values fail to understand, nurture, and develop the resources of a society, violent, unproductive, and wasteful political power is created.

In other words, authoritarianism and patriarchy unite in their disrespect, depreciation, and waste of productive human resources. Both authoritarianism and the gender structure are rigid systems that fail to stimulate, absorb, or encourage productive uses of energies and initiatives. Most people's energies dissipate through their involvement in unhealthy gender relations and their contributions to a system that dictates the lives of both men and women. Therefore, economic miseries and the lack of economic development are natural outcomes of the intersection of authoritarianism and the gender structure. By blocking access to power, authoritarianism supports the gender structure, and the gender structure ensures the human resources that are of no use or value to the political economy of authoritarianism are wasted. Gender relations provide an outlet for men's energies that might otherwise be used to challenge the authoritarian rule. One wonders what the impact would be if these energies were liberated and channeled toward reconstruction, productive creativity, and economic development.

The Middle Eastern social contract clearly reflects a culture of inaccessibility. Dominant gender relations make women inaccessible in society and parts of society inaccessible to women. Polygamy, marriage, divorce, and remarriage do not make women more accessible despite appearances. Women are inaccessible to men and men are inaccessible to women. Because of this mutual inaccessibility, love and friendship between the sexes, understanding and appreciation of the *other*, and the development of a healthy personality are all unachievable.

Authoritarianism is also nothing other than political exclusion in a world of general inaccessibility. As society is dominated by only a few, in which decisions and key positions in politics, bureaucracy, and economy are monopolized, very little remains accessible to the majority of people. Power, wealth, knowledge, truth, creativity, initiative, ambition, and even legitimate dreams are unattainable. Ordinary people access resources mainly through the state and the state sector, while women access resources mainly through their husbands.

The true wealth of the nation is not strictly monetary but comprises mostly human resources. The wealth of the nation is in reality rich, plentiful, and available, which sharply contrasts with culturally and politically constructed scarcity and restriction. This scarcity is a harsh reality imposed on society by gender relations and authoritarianism. For instance, sexuality exists and is potentially available to everyone; however, it is culturally inaccessible, illegitimate, and criminalized. Likewise, the wealth of the nation exists for the benefit of every citizen; however, authoritarianism keeps wealth politically inaccessible to the vast majority. Thus, gender relations and authoritarianism generate a culture in which potentially available resources are not necessarily accessible. Despite the attempts of the patriarchal system and authoritarian politics to bridge the gap between the potential existence and actual access, both systems in fact widen the disparity. This gap between the potentially available and the truly accessible is one of the most important illustrations of the violent nature of both the patriarchal gender system and authoritarianism. In fact, this gap is so large that this negative and violent side of reality not only replaces any initially positive potential in society but renders positive potential a remote reality or a myth.

It is interesting to note that during the social construction of gender and politics in a patriarchal and authoritarian society, a particular social construct becomes the accepted and tolerated reality at the expense of other possible social constructions. The lack of democracy and freedom of expression compels authoritarianism not to rely on logical thinking or true intentions, which remain suppressed, but on false appearances instead. However, the outward appearances become reality under authoritarian rule. As long as this social construction of reality contributes to the survival of authoritarianism, it is both accepted and encouraged by the political regime. Similarly, the dominant cultural values of the gender system viciously impose the patriarchal construct on life's realities and the experiences of young men and women. Thus, gender relations and authoritarianism complement each other in the exclusion of other possible social constructions that might prove to be more productive and beneficial to people's lives. The social construction of reality that is imposed by the dominant social contract is based on violence, control, and the marginalization of a vast majority of people. The fact that a tiny minority monopolizes the wealth and richness of the nation, while the majority of people struggle to survive, is an authoritarian departure from the reality that this wealth should be at the disposal of every citizen and available for everyone to benefit from. This deformation is also apparent in the fact that politics and decision-making are restricted to only a very select few, perhaps even one individual, while the vast majority of people are subjected to fear, silence, and repression.

Dominant cultural values that encourage the debasement and seclusion of women, gender segregation, and sexual deprivation reflect a patriarchal construction of gender roles in society. The dominant social contract that is based on politics of dissipation unproductively wastes people's energies and talents of resourcefulness. This outcome tends to interfere and complicate the sense of maturity in the men and women who perform the enforced gender roles. Not being able or allowed to fully realize their potential, men and women who lack a complete sense of maturity feed and sustain the violent authoritarian system. The immaturity that is encouraged by patriarchy contributes to the creation of a lack of responsibility toward society, which, in turn, is conducive for the functioning of authoritarianism.

Thus, one could argue that the harsh reality of gender relations induces people to accept the harsh reality of authoritarianism. The violent system of authoritarianism, thus, is an accepted reality, and it is the duty of individuals to avoid its wrath and punishment. This situation is paralleled in gender relations also. The violent patriarchal gender structure is an accepted reality in which women, the victims of this gender system, are blamed for not protecting themselves. The requirement that women must be veiled, for instance, clearly reflects a situation in which the victim is the one who is blamed and made to suffer beyond the norms of the system. Thus, blaming and punishing women, rather than preventing men from asserting their aggressive behavior, is the accepted course of action. Both authoritarianism and patriarchy further burden the victims of these violent and intolerant systems. Thus, what is unnatural becomes natural and what is natural becomes unnatural in this twisted world of patriarchy and authoritarianism.

CHAPTER 14

Gender and Authoritarian Politics

Why does the Muslim man need such a mutilated companion?
—*Fatima Mernissi*

POLITICS OF DEHUMANIZATION

A social contract based on rewards in exchange for obedience, or more precisely, protection and provision in exchange for docility and conformity, is the foundation for the process of dehumanization. A system in which the state provides benefits and protection in exchange for obedience tends to regard human beings not as individuals with personalities and creativities but rather as a mere mass of people needing to be controlled and dominated. Likewise, the provision of male protection under the condition of female servitude and submission dehumanizes women. However, men's participation in the policing of women to the strict code of honor leads to male dehumanization as well. These patriarchal processes that dehumanize both men and women significantly contribute to the authoritarian state's ability to dominate society.

Dehumanization is also linked to the deprivation of basic human rights. The gender structure is a system in which both women and men are either directly or indirectly deprived of their basic human rights to a healthy social existence. This kind of gender structure that deprives individuals of their rights and ensures women's lower social status is also convenient for the authoritarian order. This denial of basic human rights strengthens authoritarianism, as the culture of upholding human rights is absent from this system. When the natural right to satisfy one's sexual desires is formally denied by the dominant culture, it is easy for society to deny other natural rights such as access to wealth and decision-making capabilities. Essentially, the denial of individuals' rights to sexuality supports the denial of other important economic and political rights.

The deprivation of basic human rights in this way creates a dichotomy between real and natural existence and social existence that is dictated by the dominant cultural and political norms. Disrupting the harmony that is supposed to exist between these two worlds forces people to live a divided life. Society forces people to deny their natural desires and lead a life of dual realities, which causes a crisis in the integrity and sincerity of individuals. In fact, in the Freudian sense, all societies force people to deny natural desires. The question is the degree to which this denial exists in different societies. This denial exists to an extreme degree in Middle Eastern societies. However, the outcome of the denial of natural desires supports the authoritarian system. In turn, this duality of life is also reinforced through the implementation of authoritarianism. Through its repression of men, authoritarianism causes men to be tyrants at home yet docile in public. It is not uncommon to see people in the street praising their leaders while at the same time cursing them in the privacy of their homes.

Gender alienation and gender segregation create two different worlds in the authoritarian context, a world of women and a world of men, rather than encouraging healthy relationships between the sexes. Abu-Odeh explains: "Separation of sexes and spaces is so strict there is hardly any legitimized public interaction between the sexes."[1] There is a large gap between these two worlds, which makes it difficult for men and women to interact with one another in a fruitful way or to build meaningful relationships with one another. In fact, gender segregation guarantees any relationship between the sexes will inevitably become a relationship of mistrust, suspicion, and antagonism. Segregation breeds hate and animosity rather than love and understanding. Therefore, gender alienation infringes on the basic human right to a healthy and natural existence as well as a healthy and natural relationship with the *other*.

Gender alienation also distorts the experiences of childhood and adolescence, which clearly illustrates how this process breaches individuals' basic human rights, including the right to a healthy childhood. In a world of strict control, segregation, and restriction, gender relations prevent children from living childhood to its fullest. The same can be said regarding adolescence. Men and women tend to compensate for their missed childhood and lost adolescence in adulthood. Therefore, in the end, the results are adults with child-like or adolescent mentalities, and it is this immature mentality that comes to dominate public adult life in these societies. Politics in general, as well as relationships between people, are not untouched by this mentality. Fighting, selfishness, egotism, immodesty, irresponsibility, stubbornness, and constant arguing are ingrained in Middle Eastern politics and adult life. To be sure, the situation created from this mindset facilitates the authoritarian state's mission, enabling state domination. It is interesting to note, however, that although adults hold onto a child-like mentality, the ability to forgive easily that children naturally possess does not translate into this second childhood. Adult and political life lack this virtue of reconciliation.

Both gender relations and authoritarianism contribute to the cultural prevalence of restricted discourse, forbidden actions, and fear. One Iraqi woman comments: "If you want me to count the do's and don't's, the list would go on for ever. It seems that everything is *aib* [shameful act] for girls."[2] This long list of forbidden acts and restrictions is accompanied by stern punishments, including death, for violating any of them. This results in the strict regimentation of women. Men, along with the rest of society, are also regimented by participating in the enforcement of the strict moral code. Overall this process benefits authoritarianism, because the state shares the same objective of regimentation as in the gender structure.

The repression of sexuality, emotions, aspirations, and individuality that occurs in the private sphere translates into the different forms of repression forced on society by the authoritarian state. The patriarchal structure, which operates on two levels—the gender level (male versus female) and the generational level (old versus young)—tends to diminish individuality within the family. Mensch et al. explain: "In Egypt, the important task of adolescent socialization is learning how to mobilize social networks rather than how to become autonomous as a means of achieving personal goals. Young Egyptians may experience adolescence more as a time of refining interpersonal skills than as a period in which to achieve separation or autonomy."[3]

This denial of individuality provides platform for cultural violence, repression, and authoritarianism in society. Al-Khayyat argues: "Children are not taught to think for themselves, or to develop their creativity and individuality. Later on they tend to blame other people for what goes wrong in their life."[4] However, blaming others is a symptom of the developmental deficiency of individuality and a lack of individual responsibility. This deficiency causes people to blame others for their own shortcomings and failures. With this in mind, one wonders if the predominance of conspiracy theories in Middle Eastern political and intellectual life is merely a coincidence, or whether it is structurally rooted in the patriarchal structure of gender relations.

The gender and authoritarian social contracts synergistically produce ineffective and passive personalities. This, of course, is conducive for the functioning of both socially constructed gender relations and authoritarianism. Obedience in the state sector, like women's obedience in the domestic domain, leads to rigid hierarchy and bureaucratic systems that lack avenues for creativity or initiative. Obedience and docility become the rule, and the development of independent, creative, and spontaneous personalities is discouraged. Reich argues:

> The moral inhibition of the child's natural sexuality makes the child afraid, shy, fearful of authority, obedient, "good," and "docile" in the authoritarian sense of the words. It has a crippling effect on man's rebellious forces because every vital life-impulse is now burdened with severe fear; and since sex is a forbidden subject, thought in general and man's critical faculty also become inhibited. In short, morality's aim is to produce acquiescent subjects who, despite distress and humiliation, are adjusted to the authoritarian order.[5]

One could argue that the culture of inaccessibility, which had been discussed earlier, leads to social paralysis. Both women and men are inhibited and paralyzed, which has a profoundly negative effect on individuality and personality development, resulting in an entire society of paralysis. Reich contends: "A man reared under and bound by authority has no knowledge of the natural law of self-regulation, he has no confidence in himself, he declines all responsibility for his acts and decisions, and he demands direction and guidance."[6] Thus, the power, authority, control, and repression that are associated with patriarchy repress the emergence and natural development of worthy, self-assertive, and independent personalities. From the social perspective of the patriarchal gender structure, strong personalities and individuality are perceived to be threatening. Confused, dependent, weak, and worthless individuals are the product of the dominant cultural norms, which are more conducive to authoritarianism's functioning and persistence in society than to individuality and self-assertiveness.

Dehumanized and deprived of their basic human rights, these people are only able to live passive lives. Al-Khayyat points out that because a girl is often rewarded for being submissive and obedient, she will tend to develop a passive or negative personality.[7] It is true that gender relations, which are permeated with social restrictions, encourage passivity. For example, by preoccupying women with the duty of guarding their sexuality, women become conditioned to a life of passivity. For a woman, her entire premarital life, which is a crucial stage in which personality is formed, is spent defending herself against dangers and threats, which establishes the basis for passivity. Essentially, insisting that the guarding of a young girl's virginity and sexuality is the utmost priority in her life compromises other more positive and constructive perspectives in life. The same process also subjugates men to a life of passivity by linking male honor to the sexual conduct of women. However, this is a passive notion of honor that is imposed on men. Men's passivity is also related to their role in the gender structure of policing and controlling the conformity and obedience of women. The passivity that gender relations help to nurture is overall beneficial to the authoritarian system. Obviously, individuals who have been forced to live their lives in passivity cannot form a formidable resistance or opposition to the authoritarian regime.

Moreover, gender alienation tends to complicate the concept of gender equality between men and women. Tarabishi discusses: "Equality between two beings presupposes the existence of those two beings, yet if their very existence is denied, between whom is this equality to be established?"[8] There is also a relationship between gender segregation and the control over women. Instead of encouraging gender equality, sexual segregation encourages relationships of control and submission. The lack of equality, as well as the suppression of the *self*, which deforms the relationship with the *other*, leads to a dangerous perception of reality. Socializing male and female children to deny life's realities not only adds more frustration to the life of both sexes but will also make it difficult for them to deal with social realities when they reach adulthood. Instead of encouraging young people to acknowledge or confront life realistically, society avoids reality by condemning, denying, or ignoring it. The social construct of reality that leads to incorrect understanding of complex social phenomena and human development is the root of the cycle of violence and hatred that is prevalent in the Middle East. Accordingly, the social construction of the gender structure is a distortion of relationships between the sexes and overall is a serious distortion of reality.

Because the dominant culture is a culture of restriction and forbidden acts, it is necessarily a negative and violent culture. Because knowledge and curiosity are discouraged, the pleasure of discovery is also taboo. When society forces a long list of forbidden acts and restrictions on its people, the natural process of seeking knowledge and discovery is compromised. Hence, the discovery of the *self*, the *other*, and the world around is also affected. Sexual discovery, for instance, is criminalized and discouraged. When the discovery of knowledge, appreciation for reality, and interaction with reality and knowledge are discouraged, reality is distorted, and people are only allowed to venture into distorted perceptions.

Furthermore, society and culture manage to transform beautiful and natural aspects of life like the birth of a female child, love, sex, and beauty into tragedy and ugliness. Patriarchal suppression and degradation lay the foundation for these human experiences. The woman who is suppressed, degraded, and humiliated is the same woman who will share her life with her husband and raise his children. By treating women as inferior, men themselves become inferior. Repression degrades the lives of men and their children at the same time it degrades the lives of women, creating the perfect conditions for a future of misery for everyone.

Claiming that traditional culture and religion justify the harsh system of gender segregation does not improve the patriarchal construction of gender relations. Then, the question we must ask is: How is this explanation relevant to the real world and to the real needs of young people? Does there need to be such a gap between mythical and unrealistic ideals and the life realities younger generations are subjected to? The segregation of women represents an expressed degeneration of the moral system of values and beliefs because it converts what could be a healthy, positive existence into a life burdened by negativity and control. It also indicates a lag in these societies, compared with the increase of humanism, morality, and the rise of the culture of human rights within the contemporary global world. Because the gender structures of the Middle East inhibit the healthy development of men and women, all of society is negatively affected. El-Saadawi contends:

> This discrimination between men and women leads to a distortion of the personality of both, and prevents them from becoming really mature. The tendency to exaggerate a boy's feeling for his own ego and masculinity will usually end in an inferiority complex, since he will always feel that he is unable to rise up to

the image expected of him. On the other hand, a tendency to exaggerate the need for a girl to withdraw, and to shrink into an attitude of passivity, (under the guise of femininity and refinement) tends to build up in her a form of superiority complex which results from the feeling of being better than the image that has been created for her. A superiority complex creates masochistic tendencies in women, and inferiority complex breeds sadistic and aggressive tendencies in men. Both of these are compensatory mechanisms, and are the two faces of the same coin.[9]

Could these inferiority and superiority complexes be fueling violence and authoritarianism in Middle Eastern societies? The dominant gender structure is so powerful, violent, strict, and uncompromising that very few escape it. This social structure traps the majority of the population with its perverted rationale, and the majority of people diligently play their role in the cycle of domination and subordination.

POLITICS OF EXCLUSION

The culture of inaccessibility, the cultivation of individual passivity and social paralysis are closely linked to politics of exclusion. In this sense, the politics of exclusion attempt to institutionalize a mentality of passivity and inaccessibility. Exclusionary politics are reinforced by gender relations in the gender structure's segregation and seclusion of women. Dominant cultural values and norms divide social space into two separate, differentiated worlds. The first is the domestic world—the passive, marginal, alienated, and trivial world of women, children, and the home and reproduction. The second is the public world—the active, important, intellectual, political, and business-related world of men.

However, having two different, separated worlds for elite men and marginalized women and children is hardly desirable for society. This polarization of society, in terms of gender or wealth, harms national integration. Gender segregation and seclusion facilitate the creation of a female world, or subsociety, with its own subculture. Likewise, authoritarianism establishes a world of power and wealth that is above the majority of society. This process of splitting society into two different yet interrelated worlds can lead to increased social violence.

The world of men and the world of women, that is to say the world of power and the world of marginalization, are hierarchically arranged, separated worlds existing side by side and created by gender and authoritarian politics. The existence of these two different worlds affects the boundaries between private and public spaces. In the public space, this polarization contributes to the domination of a few individuals over decision-making regarding all-important aspects of society, which, in real terms, constitute the marginalization of the majority of men in this sphere. In this way, ordinary men's control over their own destinies within the public sphere is more a theory than a reality. In this sense, authoritarianism deletes the artificial demarcation between public and private spaces for the majority of men; therefore, this demarcation between public and private is valid only for those in power. Thus, by stripping power from the majority of men, authoritarianism extends elements of the world of domesticity to the public space by *genderizing*, or more precisely *feminizing* the majority of men in the dominant patriarchal sense. Patriarchy denies women formal power in society. This lack of formal power is the feminizing aspect of the social structure. In this sense, when men are denied real power in authoritarianism, in reality they join the ranks of those who lack formal power, the world of women. Likewise, because a male child is still weak and powerless, the patriarchal gender ideology considers him to have feminine qualities until he enters manhood. In this case, the world of children, including boys, is feminized.

Social space is not only gendered in this way, but it is also exclusionary. The gender structure results in political exclusion beginning with early childhood. The segregation and seclusion of girls and women is a clear illustration of exclusionary politics. Even men are subjected to exclusion as is apparent in the case of the husband's marginalization regarding the intricacies of family politics. Everyone in society is affected by this, either by being excluded or by witnessing exclusion. Exclusion becomes a routine practice in the lives of Middle Eastern families long before the authoritarian regime introduces political exclusion at the societal level. While women dominate the home, men dominate the streets, workplaces, coffee shops, and political spaces. This gender division of space is closely linked to exclusion, and exclusion is the negation and rejection of the *other's* existence. Socially constructed gender relations guarantee the absence of women with individual personalities and integrity. Authoritarianism, on the other hand, is the absence of the majority of people from positions of power and decision-making capacities.

Trespassing in between these secluded, separate worlds is unwelcome and discouraged. Men are not expected to trespass from the world of marginalization into the world of power and wealth, and, likewise, women are barred from leaving the world of the private sphere and entering into the public world. Society considers this unnatural and a problem warranting punishment. Authoritarianism's exclusionary politics ensure that male acts of trespassing into the world of power and authority, in the public space, are risky and dangerous affairs. In the same vein, requiring women to be veiled through rising, conservative Islamic fundamentalism is considered to be a solution to the problem of women trespassing into the world of men. The veil, in this respect, helps strengthen the exclusionary process that dominates gender relations. It is the negation of the *other's* presence in a world where she supposedly does not belong.

Exclusion, segregation, and the veiling of women has led to the negation of the *other* and a lack of diversity in society. It is this absence of the naturally existing *other* that also leads to the lack of recognition, appreciation, partnership, trust, and friendship between members of society regardless of sex. Ignorance of the *other* enhances hierarchy, animosity, and conflict. This is the common ground where the authoritarian order and gender relations intersect. Intolerance and the inability to compromise or reconcile are common features of the gender structure and authoritarian order. The main objective of gender relations is safeguarding the honor of women at all costs. The chief purpose of authoritarianism, on the other hand, is securing the survival of the regime. In authoritarian politics, this leads to an uncompromising rationale in which the very raison d'être of the political regime is maintaining its power and control. These objectives and the rationale that justify them encourage the suspicion of the *other*, and animosity toward it. Conversely, knowing the *other* would help emphasize similarity, equality, and respect between the *self* and the *other*, between people in general, and could at least result in less conflict, if not harmony.

Exclusionary politics are in reality politics of violence. Marginalization of the majority of the population is part of the structure of violence that dominates society. Yet exclusion of the majority of men from centers of power and wealth limits the legitimacy of the regime and aggravates the serious political and economic problems in society. Furthermore, gender exclusion and negation of the *other* contribute to the authoritarian political negation of those who are not an official part of the regime. Females and young men who are alienated and marginalized by the dominant culture find themselves marginalized by the authoritarian regime as well. Exclusion of women from politics and public spaces is an exercise in violence that wastes women's

resourcefulness and creativities that could otherwise positively contribute to political life and society as a whole. However, this by no
means implies that politics would necessarily become less violent if
women are involved. At any rate, the claim that if women were to be
involved in politics there would be less violence is difficult to quantify
or prove.

On the other hand, the exclusion of men from domesticity, from
raising and nurturing children, is not a positive experience either. One
Lebanese woman says: "There is a stark contradiction between considering women subservient to men and at the same time leaving to them
the significant role of building up the basic social unit, the family."[10]
Reflecting on this paradox, Beauvoir says: "It is outrageously paradoxical to deny woman all activity in public affairs, to shut her out of masculine careers, to assert her incapacity in all fields of efforts, and then
to entrust to her the most delicate and the most serious undertaking of
all: the molding of a human being."[11] Ironically, it is the marginalized,
secluded, and inferior woman who is entrusted with the task of rearing
the future generations of society. Expecting an "inferior" woman to
nurture the "superior" qualities in a boy is surely one of the basic contradictions of patriarchal gender politics. In reality, however, inferior
women are only able to produce inferior men. The "sacred" mission of
segregating and oppressing half of society is a self-damaging cultural
system that augments the misery of the whole society.

Nonetheless, the perceived contradiction and paradox fits very well
and makes sense within the rationales of the patriarchal system. The
patriarchal division of labor that results from economic and cultural
developments relegates women to the domestic sphere. This patriarchal trade-off is inevitable in order to make it possible for men to
be able to dominate the increasingly significant worlds of economy
and culture. Yet even the relegation of women to domesticity is conditioned by the very same patriarchal rationales. This is clearly illustrated by the fact that the family, where the role and agency of women
is dominant, functions as the incubator of patriarchy's value system.
On the other hand, raising children to internalize patriarchal values
and norms is exactly what is needed and tolerated by the authoritarian
public domain. The social contract that governs life in Middle Eastern
societies reinforces this patriarchal arrangement by imposing further
patriarchal and authoritarian trade-offs in both domestic and public
domains, as we have seen earlier.

Furthermore, gender relations result in female suffering and injustice, while the rest of the family and various members within the

private sphere develop a culture of silence, indifference, and apathy toward women's miseries. The experience of one Iraqi woman was summarized like this: "She gave birth to a girl, which was met with silence on the part of her husband."[12] Silence is an exercise in violence. When a baby girl is born there is no celebration or appreciation, only silence. When she has grown up, she is made to suffer in silence and receives no sympathy or understanding from those around her. Silence is a constant theme that surrounds a woman's life. Silence is a woman's faithful companion. The lack of understanding and support for her suffering spawns apathy in her adult character. For her, it is the only way to make sense of the neglect and lack of empathy she has experienced in childhood.

Politics, economics, and society adopt this very same culture of silence as the injustices founded in gender relations find their way into every aspect of life. As the female world tells a story of struggle and suffering, the violence imposed by authoritarian rule is the story of the suffering and silence of society as a whole. Authoritarianism thrives on this culture of silence. Authoritarian politics are supported by the gender order, which reinforces this culture of silence through its many restrictions and its religious, political, and sexual taboos.

Moreover, silence and apathy weaken society's resistance to the authoritarian regime. When the imbalance between the state and society is so great that the authoritarian state tends to swallow and control society, resistance is dependant on the activation of the *entire* civil society from all social classes. However, as we have seen, gender relations disqualify half of society from the game as women surrender their fate to the ideology of patriarchy. This weakens society to the point that it is no match for an increasingly powerful state. What makes the situation in the Middle East even worse is that these societies are further divided along ethnic and religious lines. State control and its monopoly of the economic resources of the country, particularly oil revenues, shift the balance of power even farther into the hands of the state. This gives the authoritarian state an even greater advantage

Although the state appears to be very strong, the relationship between the state and society is distorted and imbalanced. It is only because society is weak that the state appears to be so powerful. Gender relations parallel this phenomenon as men appear to be strong, superior, and dominating only because women are considered to be weak and inferior. However, the pervasiveness of control, violence, and apathy renders any attempts of resistance to these systems futile. Eventually, women become overwhelmed and resign to their fate of suppression and weakness. Likewise, people and societies surrender to the domination of authoritarian rule. Even when the extremely cruel and brutal authoritarian regime of Saddam Hussein reached its climax of wars, death, destruction, deprivation, and impoverishment, people more or less continued their surrender and acquiescence. In the same way, a woman suppressed by the gender structure is as hopeless as a citizen of an authoritarian regime. The silent suffering of people and their surrender to violence and injustice are the common grounds between patriarchal gender relations and the authoritarian order.

CHAPTER 15

Gender, Authoritarianism, and Violence

A woman is man's slave and the man is the slave of his ruler. He is the oppressor in his house and is oppressed when he leaves it.
—*Qasim Amin*

GENDER AND NORMALIZATION OF VIOLENCE

Undoubtedly, the patriarchal gender structure contributes to the spread and increasing intensity of violence in Middle Eastern society. Gender relations nationalize and popularize, or more accurately *normalize*, violence. The gender structure touts violence as an honorable national undertaking, at all levels of society. In fact, no other social system succeeds in nationalizing violence like the Middle Eastern gender structure does.

Attempts to criticize or condemn the authoritarianism state cannot garner support from within a culture in which policing one another is a routine part of daily life, and the gender system encourages everyone to play the part of policeman or policewoman. Policing women preoccupies the lives of both men and women within the domestic sphere. Reproving the authoritarian rule for creating a police state is pointless considering most of society finds it a natural and honorable mission to police, oppress, and control the weaker half of society. Watching and controlling women is a major undertaking for males within the patriarchal gender system. The authoritarian system and the patriarchal gender structure are rooted in a similar set of logic, principles, and mechanisms of implementation when it comes to policing. Both systems foster a condition of self-policing, involving everyone in society, by cultivating a culture of surveillance. The surveillance of the population at large by the secret police, *mukhabarat*, is not unusual in societies where the surveillance and policing of women is a central aspect of traditional culture and ordinary daily life.

Patriarchal gender relations generate a complex system of victimizers and victims. Victimizers and victims often change places, which results in a complex and inflexible system that spreads violence to all levels of society. A female is a victim of this system in her role as a female child, a grown woman, a wife, a sister, and a mother; however, at the very same time she is a victimizer as a wife, a mother, and mother-in-law. A male is also a victim as a child, an adult man, and a husband; however, he is a victimizer as a husband, a father, and a father-in-law. The gender structure compels every individual within society to play the dual role of victim and victimizer, to the extent that the real boundaries between these two categories are blurred. Yet in the end, Middle Eastern *gender relations victimize every one.*

The fact that everyone in society participates in violence as a victim, an abuser, or both negatively affects society. Gender relations normalize violence by infusing a cult and culture of violence into society. Violence becomes a normal, routine part of daily life. One may ask whether this conditions people to be more susceptible to violence of the authoritarian regime, or at least to be more accepting, accommodating, and tolerant of political violence and abuse and less inclined to resist it. Yet what actually makes authoritarianism tolerable is the fact that the majority of the population that is victimized by the regime feels compensated when they too become the victimizer in the gender structure. This is true for both men and women.

Thus, gender relations are a compensating mechanism for being victimized under authoritarian rule, allowing victims to play the role of abusers. While authoritarianism is the monopoly of power and violence by the elite few, gender relations allow the majority of the population to exercise violence. In other words, in a culture of violence where access to power at the state level is limited, gender relations provide an outlet for everyone to exercise power in the form of violence. In this sense, gender relations complement authoritarianism. Yet one wonders what sort of mechanism of compensation or outlet society would develop to counterbalance the excessively violent nature of authoritarianism in the absence of violent gender relations.

Regardless, the relationship between these two systems is mutually supportive, helping to maintain the integrity of both. Authoritarianism reinforces the violent structure of gender relations in various ways. Authoritarianism is an institution of violence in its most archetypal form, where the state is the main institutionalization of power in society. Rather than violence being an independent force imposed from the outside, authoritarianism is an expression of internal violence. This is the point of intersection between gender and authoritarianism—internal violence. Authoritarianism is the monopoly of power and violence that ensures the rule of a small minority over the majority of the population. Authoritarianism aims to regiment and control every aspect of political, social, and economic life in society. It is the exclusionary politics of the authoritarian regime that restricts the control and power in the public sphere to only an elite minority, denying the rest of the male population these benefits.

The state's monopoly over nearly all aspects of life diminishes the chances for ordinary citizens to develop their own productive energies and initiatives. Consequently, this breeds a sense of deep frustration, disappointment, and bitterness in society. Furthermore, the state is becoming increasingly more brutal, all-powerful, and capable of crushing resistance. Any acts of resistance to the state lose their resiliency and end up being very costly, or even futile, for those involved. When acts of public protest and venting frustrations become dangerous, the domestic sphere appears to be the only space available for men to articulate their sufferings. This is, however, at the expense of their wives and children, as it aggravates domestic violence. The consequences of the increasingly hostile authoritarian state do, in fact, aggravate the already intolerable domestic gender situation. Essentially, publicly humiliated and frustrated men make terrible fathers and husbands.

Women are the targets of guilt and suspicion from the very first day of their lives in Middle Eastern culture. Girls are continuously suspected of violating the honor of the family by engaging in different sorts of sexual and emotional relationships with members of the other sex. The patriarchal gender structure persuades society to suspect and distrust women in general. Culture supposes a female's guilt from the day she is born until she can prove otherwise. This is the cultural burden placed on women in Middle Eastern societies. It is perhaps no exaggeration to say that the very task of proving her innocence is the raison d'être for the life of a woman in these societies, aside from reproducing sons. Authoritarianism functions through this same logic of suspicion and guilt. As the raison d'être of the authoritarian rule is survival, suspecting others of plotting against the regime, whether real or imaginary, is the main preoccupation of the authoritarian ruler.

Every citizen is irrationally suspected of conspiring to take power and is condemned to false accusation and guilt. The lack of justice, democracy, and legitimacy requires authoritarianism to defend its position through animosity, hostility, and suspicion of the population.

The fact that the state watches everyone proves violence and obedience are indispensable tools of the authoritarian system. This is paralleled in religious discourse that states Allah also knows the actions of every individual. However, instilling fear and intimidation, whether done by the state or through religion, is a violent approach to managing society. This coercive approach leads to social paralysis and inhibition. It also causes a conflict between the *self* and external appearances.

Both the gender structure and the authoritarian order suppose the guilt of an individual until innocence is proven; however, this opposes a fundamental value in the culture of human rights. Even so, burdening the *other* with this task of proving their own innocence is a point of intersection between the two systems. In this way, both gender relations and authoritarianism contribute to the spread of guilt and suspicion throughout society. This enforced sense of guilt and suspicion also fosters a culture of fear.

Fear is a normal feature of family and social life in Middle Eastern society. At least half of the society is directly subjected to fear on a daily basis. The other half participates in forcing this culture of fear on women. Al-Khayyat also stresses the role that gossip plays in cultivating the culture of fear: "Since gossip mainly concerns shame and shameful behavior, fear of gossip may make parents spy on their children."[1] Reflecting on her life in Syria, Shaaban remarks:

> Indeed, the word fear is quite central to my feminist analysis; through personal experience and close observation of others I have become certain that fear is the thing that most distorts women's characters. I was often living in a state of fear—lest I was discovered bleeding, writing a poem, choosing a husband. I even lived in fear of becoming pregnant with a girl rather than a boy. Why, I ask myself, are our lives as women reduced to spells of dread, anxiety and apprehension?[2]

The fear associated with political authoritarianism is firmly rooted in religiously and culturally ritualized fear and violence that stems from the gender structure. Patriarchy nurtures fear in order to control women in the family and in society. The cult of virginity is a prime illustration of how fear operates in the control of women. A woman's fear of losing her virginity and the consequences that would follow are the main factor that controls her premarital life. Incidences of honor killing, regardless of how frequently or infrequently they occur, illustrate the use of fear as a method of deterrence and control. Parrot and Cummings emphasize: "In addition to the danger of homicide in these cultures, the threat of death creates a culture of fear among women. A man can accuse a woman of anything that would tarnish the family's honor and reputation, and in many cases the woman is given no opportunity to defend herself."[3]

Incidences of violence instill fear into the conscience of the female victim, which facilitates the control over her. Violence and fear are two interrelated aspects of the same process of female victimization. Discussing the fear-victimization nexus, Yodanis states that women's fear plays an essential role in the process of violence. It is through fear that men are able to control women's behavior.[4] She says: "Not every man must be violent toward every woman in order for violence to control women's behavior. Rather, knowing that some women are victims of horrific violence is enough to control the behavior and limit the movement of all women in society."[5] The knowledge is enough to instill fear in all women, regardless of personal experiences, Yodanis continues, If a culture of violence against women is created, a culture of fear among women will accompany it.[6]

Fear is also one of the fundamental aspects of authoritarian politics. This culture of fear is cultivated, encouraged, and exaggerated by the dictatorial regime as a means to control society. It is no wonder that one of the most widely known studies regarding authoritarianism in the Middle East is titled *Iraq: Republic of Fear*.[7]

Patriarchal gender structure anchors authoritarian values and expectations into the psyche of individuals as they internalize these values and expectations as natural facets of social existence. Thus, gender relations and authoritarianism are mutually reinforcing. Even if a direct connection between the two is difficult to establish, we can be sure that the cumulative effect of both is tremendously worse than each alone. Not only do women surrender to their grim fate under the prevailing gender structure, but people also surrender to their fate of marginalization and depreciation at the hands of the authoritarian state. The gender structure enslaves women, and authoritarianism enslaves both men and women. This common feature of the two systems defeats the interests of men as well as women. Obedience is a virtue in both the authoritarian regime and gender structure, irrespective of its repercussions. The injustice and violence found in gender relations ultimately makes its way into society as a whole, cultivating an unjust, violent culture. Thus, both authoritarianism and patriarchy are deeply rooted systems in society that share many common features: power; control; cruelty; violence; marginalization; exclusiveness; alienation; intolerance; submissiveness; obedience; and political, social, and economic inequality.

THE INFLATED MALE EGO AND THE AUTHORITARIAN STATE

Religion and culture assign special rights and privileges to men by stressing male superiority over women and children. Men grow up culturally indoctrinated to think that they are the absolute superior sex. However, there is no outlet in the public domain for exercising their power or for benefiting from this alleged superiority in authoritarian societies, because only a very few individuals dominate all aspects of social, political, and economic life. The authoritarian order fails to accommodate the exaggerated male ego in the increasingly monopolized public sphere. This inflated male ego is a potential source of violence that can burden and challenge the exclusive, elitist authoritarian rule. Therefore, in order for the authoritarian rule to neutralize the danger the inflated male ego poses to its rule over society, the male ego must either be confined to domesticity, which leads to increased domestic violence, or it is externalized against outside enemies. This latter method of dealing with the male ego exposes the logic behind the externalization of violence and the supremacy of conspiracy theory as an accepted, legitimate way of explaining events in the region. Acting in self-interest, the authoritarian state facilitates both processes.

Even though cultural values encourage males to feel superior, the authoritarian state limits the ability of men to exercise their perceived power and superiority. The fact that women are absent from the public domain, which is the result of the same cultural process of male supremacy, ironically, aggravates the situation. Comprehensive female participation in the public sphere would actually allow men to exercise their superiority over the "weaker" sex through daily contact in the public domain. However, the only avenue available for exercising masculine identity, in the form of the inflated male ego, is through gender relations. State domination leaves only the domestic realm for men to actualize their male right to dominate. While there are other *external* ways of dealing with the inflated male ego, this is the only *internal* way to contend with it.

Culture grants every man the very same sense of superiority. Yet the natural object men exercise this supremacy over, women, is absent from the public domain. What is more, the state is all powerful and monopolizes all avenues of economic, political, and social developments; this further decreases men's ability to assert their supremacy. Considering this, domesticity seems to be the only sphere in which men can exercise their acquired preeminence. Not everyone is fortunate enough to be the despotic ruler of a Middle Eastern country who is able to exercise his perceived superiority not only at home but also in public, over the entire society. For ordinary men the public domain is restricted and exclusive.

Naturally, though, men have the ability to exercise their superiority over women at home. Yet this private sphere is the women's sphere, an inferior sphere, which causes sheer frustration for ordinary men. Even though the dominant culture grants men superiority, because of authoritarian restrictions it can only be implemented against the inferior sex. While this is the only avenue men are permitted to exercise their superiority, they perceive this as a degradation of their culturally legitimate superiority because it only allows control over the weak and inferior sex in an inferior domain. This realization leads to further disappointment and resentment and, therefore, to more violence in the domestic sphere and elsewhere.

Because the family is the only site for men to display their dominance, their control over wives, daughters, and young males is a sure outcome, patriarchal control at its best. This strengthens the violent authoritarian structure of domestic life and leads to more oppression and suffering within the marriage institution. The outcome of this, the miserable failure of the family unit, in turn, enhances the authoritarian order in society, creating even more violence and misery for everyone. In order to compensate for their marginalization and passiveness in the public sphere, men have no other option than to use the domestic space to feel and act as active and violent masters. Mernissi contends: "Anger towards the society turns in towards the family and woman— object of his frustrated desires. The family offers the sexually and politically oppressed male a natural outlet for his frustrations."[8] Keddie and Beck add: "This situation may encourage men lacking wealth and power to keep control in the only area they can—that of women and children."[9] This is the only area that men feel, or actually have, control in a society where the state increasingly dominates society.

The gender structure is based on clearly demarcated spaces or roles of society: domestic space for women and public space for men exclusively. However, this does not necessarily reflect the reality of the public space. The authoritarian regime concentrates all and every aspect of power into the hands of only a very few people, thus marginalizing the majority of men. Men feel that the state is an imposition on the domain that naturally belongs to them. After all, the dominant culture leads them to believe the public space has been designed for them, a place accorded to men as a world of their own.

It seems that as far as ordinary men are concerned, this culturally granted male power and superiority is a sort of myth that lacks the support of the authoritarian reality in Middle Eastern societies. Thus, the state's monopoly over power and resources is in direct conflict with the culturally acclaimed power and status of men. Because women are confined within the boundaries of domesticity, the state monopoly of power and violence mostly affects men. However, the only practical concession the oppressive authoritarian regime offers men is the freedom to oppress their wives and sisters. Other concessions may prove to be costly to the security of the regime. Therefore, crowning men the master of their private, domestic world is in fact a compensation for their marginalization and oppression in the political and economic spheres. Considering this, it is no surprise that in Middle Eastern authoritarian regimes the discriminatory and oppressive essence of personal and family law is kept intact with very few exceptions.

Men find themselves in a difficult and a contradictory situation, being powerful and masterful in their homes yet submissive and dependent in the public arena. The effect of this frustrating situation that the macho ego of men must reconcile is an increase in violence, particularly within the domestic sphere. Being the victimizer of women and children at home is the only source of power available in the authoritarian order. It is the only right the state does not seriously restrict or contest. Yet confining the inflated male ego to domesticity is only one way authoritarianism keeps the male ego in check. Another is to invest in externalizing the male ego toward conflict with the outside world.

PRIDE AND ENEMY

Patriarchal gender structures and authoritarianism inhibit the population from productively using the human resources present in society. Inaccessibility to such resources is the result of both systems. These resources are diverted and then manifest within society in the form of a particular notion of pride—pride in the form of superiority over the *other*. This negative notion of pride is a symptom of wasting creativity by maximizing and venerating the difference, and of the hostile conflict with the *other*. This misplaced pride, however, comes at the expense of more constructive notions of pride. The violent, patriarchal gender structure complicates the relationship between concepts of the *self* and the *other*, in which the *self* is always in constant conflict with, and antagonistic toward, the *other*.

By forcing individuals' creativities to be applied in the antagonistic and hostile relationship with the *other*, the gender structure negatively affects the use of potential human resources and influences how the *other* is perceived. The *other* is routinely problematized, and is considered to be a constant source of contention within the established gender structure. The *other* is always perceived as an object of conflict, and any relationship with the *other* is laden with hostility and conflict. The resulting dichotomy of the *self* and the *other* is also reflected in the relationship between this society and the outside world. The domestic social construction of gender relations is the source of perceived hostility towards the *other* that comes to dominate the authoritarian and theocratic-style politics in the Middle East. Through this lens, a foreigner, an individual who opposes all that is domestic, is necessarily in conflict with the local.

The obsession with the external enemy, or the *other*, has its roots in the obsession with the internal *other*, women. Both forms are perceived in the same way and are constructed through the same social processes. The cult of virginity and other social arrangements that guard the honor of women vilify strange or unrelated men. Men, in this regard, are always the *other*, always outsiders, external to the extended family, always aggressive and intending to dishonor women of the family. Similarly, authoritarianism condones the suspicion of foreigners by assuming their intent to dominate and steal the wealth of the nation. The social structures of gender and authoritarianism both portray the *other* as a stranger and a foreigner, a danger threatening to take away wealth, honor, or both. This requires constant vigilance and alertness in presence of the *other*. This story is found again and again throughout the saga of patriarchal gender structures and the effects of authoritarianism in these societies.

Constant conflict with the *other*, however, is convenient for the interests and objectives of both patriarchal gender relations and authoritarianism. Productive, positive, and constructive use of the human resources accessible to society threatens the very foundations of these two violent systems. Because conflict with an enemy or with the West is a constant feature of authoritarian politics in the region, there is always an object of conflict, domination, and control present in society. Yet imagining a constant, continuous external threat is a feature found only in violent societies; it is the aspect that perpetuates and recapitulates violence in society. It is the structure of violence embedded within society that has created the perceived threat in the first place.

Unfortunately, conflict with the *other* is becoming a common and unhealthy feature of political development in the Middle East, and it has significantly affected the overall development of the region. Conflict with the *other* validates wastefulness and legitimizes the diversion of human resources in a region that has not yet decided to fully develop or seriously use its potential. One grave effect of this process is the popular culture that truly believes the world is conspiring against it. The people of the region are convinced they are engaged in permanent confrontation with the "enemy."

Furthermore, this society is as keen on making up external enemies as it is about inventing an internal enemy, or enemies. Gender relations and authoritarianism are two sides of the same coin, portraying two personifications of enemies, invented by the same process. Patriarchal and authoritarian power justifies its prerogatives as necessary responses to existential threats emanating from internalized and externalized enemies, who must be conjured up if they are not plainly perceivable. These social systems portray women, and ethnic and religious minorities, as the internal *other* within these societies. Paradoxically, the majority of people indoctrinated, socialized, and manipulated by authoritarian and theocratic regimes, who readily endorse the rhetoric of permanent conflict with an external *other*, are unaware that *they* are the internal *other*—also victims within their own societies. Thus, the champions of the battle against external enemies are the very same victims of the internal battle against the *other*, which is also antagonized by the gender and political structures. This paradox can, perhaps, account for the repression, silence, indifference, and apathy found in these societies.

The obsession with threat is a common feature in undemocratic regimes in the Middle East. The hard-line rule of Mahmoud Ahmadinejad since his election in 2005 signaled an increase in the repression of women in Iran. The Islamic regime of Iran ordered the shutting down of *Zanan*, the country's premier women's magazine under the pretext that it was "a threat to the psychological security of the society."[10] The obsession with inventing external enemies and engaging in conflict with the outside world, as in the case of Iranian nuclear power, for instance, is the inevitable result of inventing internal enemies. Perceived external threats are used as a pretext to control and silence civil society and internal "threats and enemies."

Squandering available human resources in this way results in the creation and legitimization of a particular notion of pride within society. Toleration of this kind of negativity and wastefulness requires a passive notion of pride. The dominant structure of gender relations is the source of this passive notion of pride. Linking the pride, honor, and dignity of men to the sexual behavior of women is an example of a passive construction of pride. Enforcement of gender roles, the policing of women, and controlling their conformity to inflexible moral codes also promotes a violent and negative notion of pride. In the same vein, authoritarianism also encourages passive and violent notions of pride by pursuing adventurism and engaging the population in conflict with perceived enemies.

In this respect, it is important to mention that this way of constructing pride and honor is only one option among many. Obviously, people can feel dignity and pride through constructive and positive treatment of the *other*. In this case, the gap between the *self* and the *other* is small and bridgeable. One can also derive a sense of pride by nurturing a relationship of understanding, respect, and equality with the *other*. People can also gain a sense of honor and dignity by developing the potential of the economy and society and by engaging the country in a fruitful interaction with a global and dynamic world. Yet these notions and senses of honor and pride are not valued or encouraged by the authoritarian and patriarchal gender order. Naturally, these systems are not interested in supporting avenues that could eventually lead to their own demise.

However, while these alternative, positive notions of honor and pride pose a challenge to authoritarian regimes and patriarchal structures, they are at the same time challenging for ordinary people to pursue. Passivity, control, and violence provide easy avenues for people to exercise their creativity. It is much more difficult and complex to express energies and creativeness in positive, constructive, and peaceful ways. In this regard, one could argue that honor and pride are much more complex and difficult to achieve than simply guarding women's chastity. The gender arrangement that associates male honor with the sexuality of their women is a limitation and trivialization of the notions of honor and pride.

On the other hand, men agree to this restricted notion of honor out of convenience. When the devaluation of women is sanctioned and legitimized through religion and culture, men's mission of dominance becomes a simple task. Dominant cultural values turn naturally strong and creative females into weak and submissive individuals through the process of social construction. The pride that men derive from controlling and policing fragile women is an opportunistic and cheap source of pride. This is true for the simple fact that culture and religion have already rendered women weak and submissive objects for domination. However, this is the main mission in men's lives that provides them with a sense of honor and pride. Understandably, this undertaking is a compensation for all the other missions that men fail to accomplish because of the limitations of authoritarian control.

In the same vein, one could argue that the enforced empty rhetoric of the authoritarian struggle with the external enemy prevents economic and social development. Instead, honor and dignity should be linked to more challenging, productive, and peaceful goals. In fact, Middle Eastern societies do not suffer from the lack of such avenues. A different sense of pride and dignity can be achieved, for instance, by finding ways out of misery, poverty, violence, and underdevelopment, or by linking pride to intellectual, scientific, technological, economic, and social achievements.

Nevertheless, by blocking productive achievement and development, authoritarian regimes are a major obstacle to the construction of alternative notions of pride. These regimes monopolize all channels of power and creativity and squander the wealth of the nation mostly on their security and survival. Authoritarian regimes are creative, however, in inventing internal and external enemies. They are also creative in mobilizing resources and manipulating society in order to engage in conflict with the *other*. Authoritarian regimes are supported by passive, violent, and exaggerated notions of pride. This inflated pride works in conjunction with the fiery yet ultimately empty rhetoric of authoritarian politics.

At the convenience of authoritarianism, ultimately the gender structure is the source of exaggerated pride in men that begins in early childhood. While this empty sense of pride supports external conflicts and the adventurism of authoritarianism, it negatively affects political life in the region. Inflated pride, nurtured and instilled by culturally defined gender relations, continues into adult life, affecting men's behavior, attitudes, and relationships as adults. Politics that are dominated by emotions, apathy, a sense of superiority, exaggeration, foolishness, and irresponsible attitudes are symptoms of false pride. In fact, the existence of the many dictators who impose control over all aspects of economic, political, and social life in the Middle East is a prime illustration of a false and inflated pride.

Thus, gender pride and honor are closely related to authoritarian notions of pride and honor. Authoritarian regimes use these constructions of pride to continuously mobilize citizens against the outside world that is perceived to be forever conspiring against the nation. In this sense, it is not combating enemies that gives people or authoritarian leaders pride; it is the overinflated pride that instills the myth of external enemies. False pride that is derived from engaging in mythical and futile conflicts comes at the expense of more legitimate and productive sources of pride and honor. Inflated pride creates enemies, and, in turn, these enemies fuel false pride, creating a cycle of pride and violence. This vicious cycle perpetuates misery and violence in Middle Eastern societies. However, a new concept of pride, one that respects and appreciates the *other* and one that is linked to working for the benefit and welfare of the people in this region could very well offer a way out of this vicious and futile cycle of patriarchy and authoritarianism.

CHAPTER 16

Conclusion: Toward Gender Reconciliation

> Why does patriarchy assume the guise of legality in Arab countries, whereas in the developed countries it is acknowledged that its very structure is incompatible with the aspirations of democracy?
> —*Fatima Mernissi*

Violence in the Middle East is not an external phenomenon imposed from sources outside of or above society; rather, violence is usually closer to home and is an integral part of the social structure in Middle Eastern societies. Violence dominates the daily affairs of citizens and is central to life in the region. Given these circumstances, any efforts to alleviate suffering in these societies require analysis of violence's role in creating or aggravating the problems that these societies face.

Issues surrounding gender have generally been overlooked, or dismissed as an unimportant area of concern. Gender issues have been regarded as marginal issues that are primary the concern of women only. This book's central purpose is to demonstrate that gender issues, particularly gender violence, affect not only women, but also men, children, and society at large. It is imperative to treat gender as an inherent part of the social structure and a crucial feature of the problems and obstacles facing Middle Eastern society. If gender is treated as a part of the problem, or as a part of the social crisis, then it should also be a part of the solution to this crisis. Any Middle Eastern society that aspires to be a part of the global community will require an overhaul of its gender structure, relations, and roles.

The traditional, patriarchal gender structure that is prevalent in Middle Eastern societies leaves both women and men little room for choice. The structure enforces a particular perception of gender roles and relations on society, which is based on the exercise of various forms of violence. Violence is an innate part of the gender structure in this region. What is more, the arena of gender relations is ripe for the concretization of further violence. Indeed, the gender structure outdoes the authoritarian political structure in normalizing violence in everyday life. While violence at the level of the authoritarian state is obvious and easily condemned, the dominant patriarchal gender structure succeeds in defining violence as an honorable mission in people's lives.

The high levels of obvious, open male violence precipitate reciprocal female violence, which causes the entire society to plummet into a cycle of animosity, conflict, and violence. Because short-term, radical changes to the social and gender structure are not plausible in these societies, women's resistance to male violence is also a form of violence. This can be seen as a natural consequence of male violence, as the only alternatives to this course of action are accepting or submitting completely or submitting to violence, even though complete submission and acceptance is more a myth than a reality. The entire society suffers as a result of this destructive and futile gender conflict. What would be the effect on the progress and prosperity of society if men and women's creative energies were liberated from this cycle of gender violence? What would happen if these energies were oriented toward peaceful and productive purposes?

Gender conflict is no less important, nor less destructive, than the many ethnic, religious, and political conflicts that characterize the mosaic of Middle Eastern societies. In fact, it is arguable that gender conflict feeds and foments all other conflicts in these societies. It is vital that gender conflict and the social repercussions it produces are taken seriously in this region. A society that aspires to function as a peaceful and civilized society must engage itself in finding a solution to gender conflict; it must engage in *gender reconciliation.*

Thus, gender reconciliation is the conscious process a society must undertake in order to address the violent nature of gender relations in the Middle East. I argue that commencing this process is the prerequisite for transforming Middle Eastern society into a truly peaceful and tolerant society. Gender reconciliation must become a principal part of national reconciliation within Middle Eastern societies. With very few exceptions, neither gender reconciliation nor national reconciliation appears in the agendas of these societies. I argue that serious and lasting national reconciliation is not achievable without simultaneously addressing the gender problem.

Gender relations in the Middle East are characterized by harmful, unproductive, even counterproductive, violent social relationships. The patriarchal gender structure ultimately diminishes society's potential. This cycle of violence and control must be explicitly addressed through conscious intervention aimed at interrupting this cycle by engaging in reconciliation. In this context, gender reconciliation is a process of *de-emphasizing gender violence* and gradually building a more tolerant and peaceful society.

Gender reconciliation would stipulate fundamental changes in the economic, social, and political domains, as well as serious efforts at the level of the state, the community, the family, and the individual. It would mean ending the reign of cultural, traditional, patriarchal gender norms and values over women. Instead, it would mean opting for reconciling these norms and values with human nature, human dignity, and the free will of women and men. It would take an extraordinary amount of effort to work toward a new gender contract that is based on respect, tolerance, love, and appreciation. It would be a gender contract that cherishes and encourages sexual and loving relationships between men and women. A more inclusive approach such as this, as Galtung underlines, "is an approach that is able to see self in other and other in self."[1] Mackenzie adds: "We affirm ourselves as subjects only by accepting the freedom and independence of the other. Recognition therefore requires recognition of the otherness of the other, of their difference from ourselves."[2] Tohidi also asserts: "There is a need to end the insidious stereotypes of gender by creating a single uniform sexual standard for men and women."[3] Likewise, according to Accad, it is "the need for a sexual revolution that starts at the personal level, with a transformation of attitudes toward one's mate, family, sexuality, and society and specifically, a transformation of the traditional relations of domination and subordination that permeate interpersonal relationships, particularly those of sexual and familial intimacy."[4]

Gender reconciliation would also entail the development of a social contract that values men and women as independent and free human beings and constructively interacts with their creative energies, initiatives, aspirations, and dreams. Reconciliation involves bringing laws, particularly personal and family laws, into line with modernity. It would also mean having equal access to opportunities as well as democratizing opportunity in general. Under the constraints of authoritarianism, where only a few dominate power and wealth, it seems as though there are both material and symbolic rewards for being male. This is evident because of the fact that half of society is barred from participating in the exclusive economic and political game simply for being female. Nonetheless, the narrow gains of being a male in patriarchal society are not worth excluding and downgrading the other half of the society. This is particularly true considering patriarchal authoritarian social structure is only one of many options. Limiting reality to only one inequitable option is a form of violence toward social existence itself. Surely, there are other more productive and more inclusive options that could accommodate and nurture the energies made available to society by men and women alike.

Middle Eastern society cannot successfully or seriously achieve female empowerment by raising women's status in society and ending their seclusion unless a gradual empowerment of men in all political, economic, social, and intellectual domains commences as well. This, however, will require ending the dominant authoritarian and theocratic regimes' monopolization of wealth and power. It is, however, the only way to induce men to relinquish the few "rights" and privileges they have, which provide them with the only sense of power they can garner under the grip of authoritarianism, rights and privileges that are detrimental to women, men, and society as a whole. Only then will men develop other interests and new means of legitimization and aspiration and a new way of achieving a meaningful existence. In this sense, gender reconciliation can open the way toward real and veritable economic, social, cultural, and political development in society. It can pave the way for appreciating, developing, and investing in human capital. Keddie and Beck also stress this dual sense of empowerment:

> Women's liberation will also mean men's liberation. The man who cannot choose his wife, who wants a wife not sexually knowledgeable, who prefers that she contribute little or nothing to the family income, who cannot freely talk with women outside his family and has little social contact even with his wife, and who must maintain a macho image surrounded by the requirements and taboos of masculine behavior is surely less free and has a less rich life than one with freer choices.[5]

Under the constraints of authoritarianism, gender equality and the empowerment of women appear to be in conflict with the interests of men. However, the most egalitarian societies, Rosaldo suggests, "are not those in which male and female are opposed or are even competitors, but those in which men value and participate in the domestic life of the home. Correspondingly, they are societies in which women can readily participate in important public events."[6] An egalitarian society would terminate the enforced sense of shame women suffer from that inhibits their natural desires and natural existence. In fact, a society that fails to ensure dignity, justice, equality, and development for all its members is nothing but a shameful society. A long time ago, Qasim Amin argued:

> We have neglected the nurturing of our minds to such an extent that they have become like barren soil, unfit for any growth. . . . Why should a Muslim believe that his traditions cannot be changed or replaced by new ones, and that it is his duty to preserve them forever? . . . God has made change a prerequisite for life and progress, rather than immobility and inflexibility, which are characteristic of death and backwardness.[7]

It is infuriatingly astonishing that this quotation and the message it conveys are still valid in present day Middle Eastern societies just as they were in 1899–1900 when his book was written. It is perplexing to consider how little has happened with regard to the advancement of women's status in Middle Eastern societies. I do not wish to end by saying that this however, is the matter of another story, when this is indeed *the story, the real story, of the Middle East.*

Notes

CHAPTER 1: INTRODUCTION

Epigraph source: Jeff Hearn, "Men's Violence to Known Women: Historical, Everyday and Theoretical Construction by Men," in Barbara Fawcett et al., eds., *Violence and Gender Relations: Theories and Interventions* (London: Sage, 1996), 35.

1. Thomas Friedman, "Obama on the Nile," *New York Times*, June 11, 2008, http://www.nytimes.com/2008/06/11/opinion/11friedman.html.

2. December Green, *Gender Violence in Africa: African Women's Responses* (Houndmills, UK: Macmillan, 1999), 34.

3. Johan Galtung, *Peace by Peaceful Means: Peace and Conflict. Development and Civilization* (London: Sage, 1996), 196.

4. Gada Karmi, "The Saddam Hussein Phenomenon and Male-Female Relations in the Arab World," in Haleh Afshar, ed., *Women in the Middle East: Perceptions, Realities and Struggle for Liberation* (Houndmills, UK: Macmillan, 1993), 155.

5. Fatma Müge Göcek and Shiva Balaghi, "Introduction," in Fatma Müge Göcek and Shiva Balaghi, eds., *Reconstructing Gender in the Middle East: Tradition, Identity, and Power* (New York: Columbia University Press, 1994), 14–15.

6. Nikki R. Keddie, *Women in the Middle East: Past and Present* (Princeton, NJ: Princeton University Press, 2007), 10.

7. Julie Marcus, *A World of Difference: Islam and Gender Hierarchy in Turkey* (London: Zed, 1992), 121.

8. Carla Makhlouf, *Changing Veils: Women in Modernisation in North Yemen* (London: Croom Helm, 1979), 28.

9. Ziba Mir-Hosseini, "Women, Marriage and the Law in Post-Revolutionary Iran," in Afshar, ed., *Women in the Middle East*, 59.

10. Ibid., 77.

11. Sherry Ortner, *Making Gender: The Politics and Erotics of Culture* (Boston: Beacon, 1996), 16.

12. Diane Singerman, "Where Has All the Power Gone? Women and Politics in Popular Quarters of Cairo," in Göcek and Balaghi, eds., *Reconstructing Gender in the Middle East*, 177.

13. Amal Rassam, "Women and Domestic Power in Morocco," *International Journal of Middle Eastern Studies*, 12 (1980), 180.

14. Marina Lazreg, "Feminism and Difference: The Perils of Writing as a Woman on Women in Algeria," *Feminist Studies*, 14, no. 1 (1988), 97.

15. Liz Kelly, Sheila Burton, and Linda Regan, "Beyond Victim or Survivor: Sexual Violence, Identity, and Feminist Theory and Practice," in Lisa Adkins and Vicki Merchant, eds., *Sexualizing the Social: Power and the Organization of Sexuality*, (Houndmills, UK: Macmillan, 1996), 82.

16. Michel Foucault, *The History of Sexuality*, vol. 1, (London: Penguin, 1990).

17. Mahnaz Kousha, "Ties That Bind: Mothers and Daughters in Contemporary Iran," *Critique: Critical Middle Eastern Studies*, 6, no. 1 (1997), 83.

18. Nikki Keddie and Lois Beck, "Introduction," in Lois Beck and Nikki R. Keddie, eds., *Women in the Muslim World* (New York: Harvard University Press, 1978), 19.

19. Foucault, *The History of Sexuality*.

20. Kousha, "Ties That Bind," 78.

21. Erika Friedl, "Sources of Female Power in Iran," in Mahnaz Afkhami and Erika Friedl, eds., *In the Eyes of the Storm: Women in Post-Revolutionary Iran* (London: I. B. Tauris, 1994), 151.

CHAPTER 2: VIOLENCE AGAINST WOMEN
IN THE MIDDLE EAST

Epigraph source: Jam'iyat Tadamun al-Mar'ah al-Arabiya, *Al-mar'ah al-arabiya wa al-mutaghayyirat al-alamiya* [Arab Women and International Changes]. Proceedings of the Sixth International Conference of the Association of Solidarity of Arab Women (Cairo: Merit, 2003), 223.

1. United Nations Development Fund for Women, "Facts and Figures on Violence against Women," November 2007; citing General Assembly, In Depth Study on All Forms of Violence against Women: Report of the Secretary General, 2006, http://www.unifem.org/campaigns/vaw/facts_figures.php.

2. Andrea Parrot and Nina Cummings, *Forsaken Females: The Global Brutalization of Women* (Lanham, MD: Rowman and Littlefield, 2006), 151.

3. Christina Curry, "Acting with Honour," in Shahrzad Mojab and Nahla Abdo, eds., *Violence in the Name of Honour: Theoretical and Political Challenges* (Istanbul: Bilgi University Press, 2004), 179.

4. Eva Lundgren cited in Javeria Rizvi, "Violence in the Name of Honour in Swedish Society," in Mojab and Abdo, eds., *Violence in the Name of Honour*, 221.

5. Syrian Women Observatory, "Breaking the Wall of Silence on a Taboo Issue: A Third of Lebanese Women Are Abused," December 27, 2007, http://www.nesasy.org/index2.php?option=com_content&task=view&id=5307.

6. Parrot and Cummings, *Forsaken Females*, 153.

7. "Governmental Report: One in Every Ten Women Are Battered in Algeria," *Al-Sharq al-Awsat*, February 6, 2008.

8. "Statistics Prove That Violence against Women Is a Yemeni and Global Problem," *Yemen Observer*, December 2, 2007, http://www.yobserver.com/reports/printer-10013357.html.

9. Syrian Women Observatory, "Breaking the Wall of Silence."

10. IRIN (UN Office for the Coordination of Humanitarian Affairs), "Jordan: Mere Suspicion of an Illicit Affair Often Leads to 'Honour Killings,'" November 26, 2007, http://www.irinnews.org/PrintReport.aspx?ReportId=75509.

11. Middle East Online, "Jordanian Government Moves to Limit Marital Violence," January 9, 2008, http://www.middle-east-online.com/features/?id=56679.

12. Mediterranean Women, "Violence against Women in Egypt: Is It the Responsibility of the State or the Community?" February 28, 2006, http://www.mediterraneans.org/print.php3?id_article=467.

13. Tadamun, *Al-mar'ah al-arabiya*, 223–24.

14. Ibid., 224–25.

15. Human Rights Watch, "A Threat to Society? Arbitrary Detention of Women and Girls for 'Social Rehabilitation,'" *Human Rights Watch Report*, 18, no. 2 (February 2006).

16. "Syria's First Study of Violence against Women Breaks Taboo," *New York Times*, April 10, 2006; "One-Quarter of Syrian Wives Suffer Abuse, Study Says," *International Herald Tribune*, April 12, 2006.

17. "Domestic Violence Rears Its Ugly Head in Syria," *Mail and Guardian*, April 16, 2006.

18. Syrian Women Observatory, "Domestic Violence, a Global Phenomenon That We Keep in the Dark," November 23, 2007, http://www.nesasy.org/languages/index.php/En/2007/11/23/domestic_violence_a_global_phenomenon.th.

19. "Study Reveals Domestic Abuse Is Widespread in Syria," *Christian Science Monitor*, April 25, 2006.

20. "A Study in Bahrain: 95% Admit That Women Are Abused," *Al-Sharq al-Awsat*, March 20, 2006.

21. "Beating Your Maid Is Normal in Qatar BUT Also Beating Female Family Members Is Part of Being Qatari," *Gulf Times*, January 25, 2008.

22. Palestinian Central Bureau of Statistics, "2006 Report: Domestic Violence Survey in Palestinian Territory," June 2006, http://www.unfpa.org/emergencies/symposium06/docs/daytwosessionsixualuay.ppt.

23. OMCT (World Organization Against Torture), "Violence Against Women in Turkey," 2003 report, http://www.omct.org/pdf/VAW/Publications/2003/Eng_2003_09_Turkey.pdf.

24. Colleen K. Keenan, A. el-Hadad, and S. A. Balian, "Factors Associated with Domestic Violence in Low-Income Lebanese Families," *Image: Journal of Nursing Scholarship*, 30, no. 4 (1998), 358.

25. Ibid., 359.

26. OMCT, "Violence against Women in Tunisia," 2002 report, http://www.omct.org/pdf/TunisiaEng2002.pdf.

27. "Statistics Prove," *Yemen Observer*.

28. "Tiny Voices Defy Child Marriage in Yemen," *New York Times*, June 29, 2008; "Yemen: The Child Bride Who Sought a Divorce and Dared to Dream Big," *Los Angeles Times*, June 12, 2008.

29. OMCT, "Violence against Women in Turkey."

30. "Poverty, Customs and Traditions," *Yemen Observer*, April 12, 2007, http://www.yemenobserver.net/print.php?id=305.

31. "Tiny Voices Defy," *New York Times*, June 29, 2008.

32. "Sally: A Victim of Civil Society Organizations and the Authorities in Charge," *Yemen Observer*, February 26, 2008, http://www.yobserver.com/editorials/printer-10013811.html.

33. "Poverty, Customs and Traditions," *Yemen Observer*.

34. "8-Year-Old Girl Asks for Divorce in Court," *Yemen Times*, April 10–13, 2008; "Yemen: The Child Bride Who Sought a Divorce and Dared to Dream Big," *Los Angeles Times*, June 12, 2008.

35. Mahnaz Kousha, "Ties That Bind: Mothers and Daughters in Contemporary Iran," *Critique: Critical Middle Eastern Studies*, 6, no. 1 (Fall 1997), 104–5.

36. Tadamun, *Al-mar'ah al-arabiya*, 224.

37. Syrian Women Observatory, "How to Combat Sexual Rape," January 18, 2008, http://www.nesasy.org/index2.php?option=com_content&task=view&id=5590.

38. Tadamun, *Al-mar'ah al-arabiya*, 206.

39. "Beating Your Maid," *Gulf Times*, January 25, 2008.

40. Suzanne Ruggi, "Commodifying Honor in Female Sexuality: Honor Killing in Palestine," *Middle East Report*, spring (1998), 14–15.

41. Human Rights Watch, "A Threat to Society?"

42. Linda Boxberger, "From Two States to One: Women's Lives in the Transformation of Yemen," in Herbert L. Bodman and Nayereh Tohidi, eds., *Women in Muslim Societies: Diversity within Unity* (Boulder, CO: Lynne Rienner, 1998), 119–20.

43. Parrot and Cummings, *Forsaken Females*, 154.

44. "Beating Your Maid," *Gulf Times*, January 25, 2008.

45. Parrot and Cummings, *Forsaken Females*, 42.

46. Erika Friedl, "Women in Contemporary Persian Folktales," in Lois Beck and Nikki R. Keddie, eds., *Women in the Muslim World* (New York: Harvard University Press, 1978), 646.

47. Maged Thabet Al-Kholiday, "There Must Be Violence against Women," *Yemen Times*, 15, no. 1117 (December 3, 2007–January 6, 2008), http://www.yementimes.com/print_article.shtml?i=1117&p=community&a=6.

48. WHO, *Female Genital Mutilation: An Overview* (Geneva: WHO, 1998), 10.

49. Ibid., 7–8.

50. IRIN, "Middle East: FGM Still Largely an Unknown Quantity in Arab World," March 1, 2005, http://www.irinnews.org/PrintReport.aspx?ReportId=62474.

51. WHO, *Female Genital Mutilation*, 13, 17; "Combating Female Circumcision in Egypt Faces Traditions," *Middle East Online*, October 19, 2007, http://www.middle-east-online.com/features/?id=53693.

52. IRIN, "Middle East: FGM."

53. WHO, *Female Genital Mutilation*, 14.

54. Ibid., 17–18; AFROL [African News Agency], "Gender Profiles: Sudan," 2002, http://www.afrol.com/Categories/Women/profiles/sudan_women.html.

55. IRIN, "Middle East: FGM."

56. Ibid.; "Iraq: Study Says Female Genital Mutilation Widespread in North," *The Washington Times*, January 21, 2005; "Female Circumcision Surfaces in Iraq," *The Christian Science Monitor*, August 10, 2005.

57. Middle East Online, "The Custom of Female Circumcision Continues in Yemen," June 19, 2007, http://www.middle-east-online.com/features/?id=49314.

58. UNICEF, *Female Genital Mutilation/Cutting: A Statistical Exploration* (New York: UNICEF, 2005), 4.

59. IRIN, "Middle East: FGM."

60. UNICEF, *Female Genital Mutilation*, 33.

61. Ibid., 35.

62. WHO, *Female Genital Mutilation*, 23–36, 41–42.

63. Ibid., 57.

64. Nawal el-Saadawi, *The Hidden Face of Eve: Women in the Arab World* (London: Zed, 1980), 7.

65. WHO, *Female Genital Mutilation*, 58.

66. Anika Rahman and Nahid Toubia, eds., *Female Genital Mutilation: A Guide to Laws and Policies Worldwide* (London: Zed, 2000), 3.

67. WHO, *Female Genital Mutilation*, 57.

68. El-Saadawi, *Hidden Face*, 8.

69. Ibid., 7–8.

70. Daisy Hilse Dwyer, *Images and Self-Images: Male and Female in Morocco* (New York: Columbia University Press, 1978), 94.

71. WHO, *Female Genital Mutilation*, 5.

72. Rahman and Toubia, *Female Genital Mutilation*, 3.

73. Eitb24 [Basque News and Information Channel], "Egypt Strengthens Ban on Genital Mutilation Following Girl's Death," June 28, 2007, http://www.etib24,com/imprimir-noticia/en/B24_55425/.

74. UNICEF, *Female Genital Mutilation*, 24–25.

75. Ibid., 18.

76. El-Saadawi, *Hidden Face*, 8.

77. Marie Bassili Assaad, "Female Circumcision in Egypt: Social Implications, Current Research, and Prospects for Change," *Studies in Family Planning*, 11, no. 1 (January 1980), 11.

78. Alice Walker and Pratibha Parmar, *Female Genital Mutilation and the Sexual Blinding of Women* (New York: Harcourt Brace, 1993), 274.

CHAPTER 3: CRIME AND HONOR

Epigraph source: Nadera Shalhoub-Kevorkian, "Mapping and Analyzing the Landscape of Femicide in Palestinian Society," Report by Women's Center for Legal Aid and Counseling, submitted to UNIFEM, January 2000, 49, http://www.unifem.org/attachments/stories/NaderaShalhoubKevorkian_report.pdf.

1. Andrea Parrot and Nina Cummings, *Forsaken Females: The Global Brutalization of Women* (Lanham: Rowman and Littlefield, 2006), 173.

2. "Statistics Prove that Violence against Women is a Yemeni and Global Problem," *Yemen Observer*, December 2, 2007, http://www.yobserver.com/reports/printer-10013357.html.

3. Mediterranean Women, "Rana Husseini: Created a New Beat Honor Crimes in Jordan," March 5, 2005, http://www.mediterraneas.org/print.php3?id_article=469.

4. IRIN (UN Office for the Coordination of Humanitarian Affairs), "Jordan: 'Honour' Killings Pose Serious Challenge to Rule of Law," October 2, 2007, http://www.irinnews.org/PrintReport.aspx?ReportId=74591.

5. IRIN, "Jordan: Mere Suspicion of an illicit Affair Often Leads to 'Honour Killings,'" November 26, 2007, http://www.irinnews.org/PrintReport.aspx?ReportId=75509.

6. Ibid.

7. Mediterranean Women, "Palestine: Murder of Faten Habash," May 5, 2005, http://www.mediterraneas.org/print.php3?id_article=345.

8. Suzanne Ruggi, "Commodifying Honor in Female Sexuality: Honor Killing in Palestine," *Middle East Report* spring (1998), 13.

9. Human Rights Watch, "Gaza Activists Brace for Harder Times under Hamas," July 9, 2007, http://www.whrnet.org/docs/issues-gaza-0707.html.

10. Syrian Women Observatory, "Killing Syrian Women Continues, a New 'Honor Crime' in Edleb!" January 5, 2008, http://www.nesasy.org/languages/index.php/En.

11. "Syria's First Study of Violence against Women Breaks Taboo," *New York Times*, April 10, 2006.

12. Mediterranean Women, "Beirut Hosts 'Honour Killing' Conference," May 13, 2001, http://www.mediterraneas.org/print.php3?id_article=138.

13. "One Honor Killing Is a Tragedy, Many Others Are Just Statistics," *Turkish Daily News*, April 7, 2007.

14. "'Honor' Killings Grow as Girl, 17, Stoned to Death," *Sunday Times*, November 4, 2007.

15. IRIN, "Iraq: 'Honour Killings' Persist in Kurdish North," December 6, 2007, http://www.irinnews.org/PrintReport.aspx?ReportId=75714.

16. OMCT (World Organization against Torture), "Violence against Women in Turkey," 2003 report, http://www.omct.org/pdf/VAW/Publications/2003/Eng_2003_09_Turkey.pdf.

17. "'Fall' från balkonger kan vara hedersmord ['Fall' from Balconies Could Be Honor killing]," *Metro* (Swedish version), February 28, 2008.

18. "Turkey Works to Stop 'Honor' Killings," *Los Angeles Times*, January 9, 2007.

19. Shalhoub-Kevorkian, "Mapping and Analyzing," 69.

20. OMCT, "Violence against Women in Turkey."

21. Shalhoub-Kevorkian, "Mapping and Analyzing," 51.

22. Ibid., 49.

23. Ruggi, "Commodifying Honor," 15.

24. Shalhoub-Kevorkian, "Mapping and Analyzing," 51.

25. Parrot and Cummings, *Forsaken Female*, 178.

26. OMCT, "Violence against Women in Turkey."

27. Ruggi, "Commodifying Honor," 13.

28. OMCT, "Violence against Women in Turkey."

29. The poll was conducted between January 16 and February 16, 2008, at http://www.nesasy.org.

30. IRIN, "Jordan: Honour Killings Still Tolerated," March 11, 2007, http://www.irinnews.org/PrintReport.aspx?ReportId=70634.

31. "'Honor' Killings Grow," *Sunday Times*, November 4, 2007.

32. IRIN, "Jordan: Honour Killings Still Tolerated."

33. Ibid.

34. Shalhoub-Kevorkian, "Mapping and Analyzing," 50.

35. Ibid.

36. Syrian Women Observatory, "Killing Syrian Women Continues."

37. IRIN, "Jordan: 'Honour' Killings Pose Serious Challenge."

38. Mediterranean Women,." Palestine: Murder of Faten Habash."

39. IRIN, "Jordan: Mere Suspicion."

40. Parrot and Cummings, *Forsaken Female*, 177.

41. Ibid.

42. OMCT, "Violence against Women in Turkey."

43. IRIN, "Jordan: Mere Suspicion."

44. Shalhoub-Kevorkian, "Mapping and Analyzing," 68.

45. Parrot and Cummings, *Forsaken Females*, 180.

46. Mediterranean Women, "Rana Husseini: Created."

47. Shalhoub-Kevorkian, "Mapping and Analyzing," 62.

48. Syrian Women Observatory, "The Knife of Honor Slices Zahra's Throat!" January 22, 2007, http://www.nesasy.org/languages/index.php/En/2007/01/24/the_knife_of_honor_slices_Zahra_s_throat.

49. IRIN, "Jordan: 'Honour' Killings Pose Serious Challenge."

50. Parrot and Cummings, *Forsaken Females*, 175.

51. Bouthaina Shaaban, *Both Right and Left Handed: Arab Women Talk about Their Lives* (London: The Women's Press, 1988), 3–5.

52. "'Honor' Killings Grow," *Sunday Times*, November 4, 2007.

53. Ibid.

54. Ibid.

55. Norma Khouri, *Honor Lost: Love and Death in Modern-Day Jordan* (New York: Atria, 2003).

CHAPTER 4: ISLAM, GENDER, AND VIOLENCE

Epigraph source: Wisam Mansour, "Arab Women in Nizar Kabbani's Poetry," *Comparative Studies of South Asia, Africa and the Middle East*, 25, no.2 (2005), 482.

1. Colleen K. Keenan, A. el-Hadad, and S. A. Balian, "Factors Associated with Domestic Violence in Low-Income Lebanese Families," *Image: Journal of Nursing Scholarship*, 30, no. 4 (1998), 360.

2. *The Koran*, N. J. Dawood, trans., fourth revised edition (Harmondsworth, UK: Penguin, 1974).

3. Andrea Parrot and Nina Cummings, *Forsaken Females: The Global Brutalization of Women* (Lanham, MD: Rowman and Littlefield, 2006), 202.

4. Ibid., 201.

5. Soraya al-Torki, *Women in Saudi Arabia: Ideology and Behavior among the Elite* (New York: Columbia University Press, 1986), 76–77.

6. Fatima Mernissi, *Beyond the Veil: Male-Female Dynamics in Muslim Society* (Cambridge, MA: Schekman, 1975), 61.

7. Carrie L. Yodanis, "Gender Inequality, Violence against Women, and Fear: A Cross-National Test of the Feminist Theory of Violence against Women," *Journal of Interpersonal Violence*, 19, no. 6 (2004), 671.

8. Suad Joseph, "Brother/Sister Relationships: Connectivity, Love, and Power in the Reproduction of Patriarchy in Lebanon," *American Ethnologist*, 21, no. 1 (1994), 57.

9. Erika Friedl, "Sources of Female Power in Iran," in Mahnaz Afkhami and Erika Friedl, eds., *In the Eyes of the Storm: Women in Post-Revolutionary Iran*, (London: I. B. Tauris, 1994), 156–57.

10. Yodanis, "Gender Inequality," 656.

11. "A Study in Bahrain: 95% Admit That Women Are Abused," *Al-Sharq al-Awsat*, March 20, 2006.

12. "Divorce in Ta'if Involves 6 Women, 14 Children," *Al-Sharq al-Awsat*, December 28, 2007.

13. Denis MacEoin, "Why Do Muslims Execute Innocent People? Islamist Ideology," *Middle East Quarterly*, fall 2006.

14. Human Rights Education Associates, "Campaign to Stop Death by Stoning in Iran," January 18, 2008, http://www.nesasy.org/index2.php?option=com_content&task=view&id=5589.

15. Suzanne Ruggi, "Commodifying Honor in Female Sexuality: Honor Killings in Palestine," *Middle East Report*, spring (1998), 13.

16. Human Rights Watch, "Iran: Judiciary Must Prevent Imminent Executions by Stoning," February 6, 2008, http://hrw.org/english/docs/2008/02/06/iran17989.htm.

17. Phyllis Chesler, "A Speech for the 12/14/05 Senate Hearing Organized by the American Committee for Democracy in the Middle East," December 16, 2005, http://www.frontpagemag.com/Articles/Printable.aspx?GUID=6D9C0007-A2D2-4C48-A29B-DA9FE4FB8C68.

18. IRIN (UN Office for the Coordination of Humanitarian Affairs), "Iraq: Extremists Fuel Anti-Women Violence in Basra," November 26, 2007, http://www.irinnews.org/report.aspx?ReportId=75396.

19. Ibid.

20. Ibid.

21. Ibid.

22. CORPUN (World Corporal Punishment Research), "Violence against Women Concern in the Sudan," November 26, 2002, http://www.corpun.com/sdj00211.htm.

23. AFROL [African News Agency], "Sudan Denounced for Stoning and Amputation Sentences," February 2, 2002, http://www.afrol.com/News2002/sud004_stoning.htm.

24. AFROL, "Gender Profiles: Sudan," 2002, http://www.afrol.com/Categories/Women/profiles/sudan_women.html.

25. Ibid.

26. AFROL, "UN Agency Condemns Slavery in Sudan," June 5, 2002, http://www.afrol.com/News2002/sud010_slavery_ilo.htm.

27. AFROL, "Sudanese Govt Accept Slavery," May 27, 2002, http://www.afrol.com/News2002/sud009_slavery.htm.

28. Phyllis Chesler, "Feminism's Deafening Silence," July 26, 2004, http://www.frontpagemag.com/Articles/Printable.aspx?GUID=8AFDE624-EA22-4A6E-96AB-8671B7962212.

29. Mediterranean Women, "Algeria Islamic Body Rules on 'Terror Rape,'" April 12, 1998, http://www.mediterraneas.org/print.php3?id_article=545.

30. Syrian Women Observatory, "Algerian Woman: A Second Class Citizen," January 15, 2008, http://www.nesasy.org/index2.php?option=com_con

tent&task=view&id=5557; Syrian Women Observatory, "Algerian Women: Violence Denies Them Equality," December 20, 2007, http://www.nesasy. org/index2.php?option=com_content&task=view&id=5378.

31. "Saudi Women See a Brighter Road on Rights," *Washington Post*, January 31, 2008.

32. "Brewing Support for 'Coffee' Victim," *Arab News*, February 6, 2008.

33. Phyllis Chesler, "A Speech for the 12/14/05 Senate."

34. "Stalking Yemen's Streets: Self-Appointed Morals Police," *Washington Post*, June 17, 2008.

35. Human Rights Watch, "Saudi Arabia: Rape Victim Punished for Speaking Out," November 17, 2007, http://hrw.org/english/docs/2007/11/16/saudia 17363_txt.htm; Abeer Mishkhas, "Lashing Out at the Media Over the Qatif Girl Case," November 22, 2007, http://www.arabview.com/articles.asp?article=935; Abeer Mishkhas, "Violence against Women Is Still a Problem," November, 29, 2007, http://www.arabview.com/articles.asp?article=938; "Ruling Jolts Even Saudis: 200 Lashes for Rape Victim," *New York Times*, November 16, 2007; "My Harrowing Story, by the Teenage Girl Who Was Sentenced to 200 Lashes after Being Gang Raped in Saudi Arabia," *Daily Mail*, November 30, 2007; "Double Indemnity," *The Economist*, November 22, 2007; "Rape Victim Sentenced to 200 Lashes and Six Months in Jail," *The Guardian*, November 17, 2007; "Gang-Rape Victim Vows to Fight On," *Arab News*, November 18, 2007; "'Qatif Girl' Subjected to Brutal Crime," *Arab News*, December 19, 2007.

36. Human Rights Watch, "Saudi Arabia: Halt Woman's Execution for 'Witchcraft,'" February 14, 2008, http://hrw.org/english/docs/2008/02/14/saudia18051_txt.htm.

37. Human Rights Watch, "Saudi Arabia: Officials Harrass Forcibly Divorced Couple," July 17, 2007, http://hrw.org/english/docs/2007/07/18/saudia16399_txt.htm.

38. Ibid.

39. Middle East Online, "Saudi Women Complain of Discrimination," February 13, 2008, http://www.middle-east-online.com/english/?id=24320.

40. Omaima Al-Jalahma, "As a Proud Saudi Woman, I Speak," *Arab News*, February 5, 2008.

41. "Rania Al-Baz Lashes Out at Abuse of Women," *Arab News*, April 12, 2004; "Rania's Husband Gets Six Months' Jail, 300 Lashes," *Arab News*, May 31, 2004; "Breaking the Silence," *The Guardian*, October 5, 2005; "Interview: Matthew Campbell Meets Rania al-Baz," *The Sunday Times*, October 16, 2005; "Saudi TV Host's Beating Raises Taboo Topic: Domestic Violence against Muslim Women," *The Christian Science Monitor*, May 12, 2004.

CHAPTER 5: GENDER ALIENATION

Epigraph Source: Simone de Beauvoir, *The Second Sex* (London: Jonathan Cape, 1968), 676.

1. de Beauvoir, *The Second Sex*, 301.
2. Sana al-Khayyat, *Honour and Shame: Women in Modern Iraq* (London: Saqi, 1990), 27.
3. Paul Vieille, "Iranian Women in Family Alliance and Sexual Politics," in Lois Beck and Nikki R. Keddie, eds., *Women in the Muslim World* (New York: Harvard University Press, 1978), 453.
4. Susan Schaefer Davis and Douglas Davis, *Adolescence in a Moroccan Town: Making Social Sense* (New Brunswick: Rutgers University Press, 1989), 77.
5. Gary Gregg, *The Middle East: A Cultural Psychology* (New York: Oxford University Press, 2005), 229.
6. Barbara Mensch et al., "Gender-Role Attitudes among Egyptian Adolescents," *Studies in Family Planning*, 34, no. 1 (2003), 16.
7. Ibid., 10.
8. Raphael Patai, *The Arab Mind* (New York: Hatherleigh, 2002), 29.
9. Gregg, *The Middle East*, 252.
10. Nawal el-Saadawi, *Memoirs of a Woman Doctor* (London: Saqi, 1988), 13.
11. Ibid., 48.
12. Ibid., 10.
13. Johan Galtung, *Peace by Peaceful Means: Peace and Conflict. Development and Civilization* (London: Sage, 1996), 197.
14. Ibid., 199.
15. de Beauvoir, *The Second Sex*, 334.
16. Al-Khayyat, *Honour and Shame*, 43.
17. Nawal el-Saadawi, *The Hidden Face of Eve: Women in the Arab World* (London: Saqi, 1980), 13.
18. Catriona Mackenzie, "A Certain Lack of Symmetry: Beauvoir on Autonomous Agency and Women's Embodiment," in Ruth Evans, ed., *Simone de Beauvoir's The Second Sex: New Interdisciplinary Essays* (Manchester, UK: Manchester University Press, 1998), 136.
19. Victoria Best, "Between the Harem and the Battlefield: Domestic Space in the Works of Assia Djebar," *Signs: Journal of Women in Culture and Society*, 27, no. 3 (2002), 876.
20. de Beauvoir, *The Second Sex*, 308.
21. Ibid., 400.
22. Ibid., 330.
23. Sherry Ortner, "Is Female to Male as Nature Is to Culture?" in Michelle Zimbalist Rosaldo and Louse Lamphere, eds., *Women, Culture and Society* (Stanford, CA: Stanford University Press, 1974), 73.
24. Lila abu-Lughod, *Veiled Sentiments: Honor and Poetry in a Bedouin Society* (Berkeley: University of California Press, 1988), 124f
25. Mackenzie, "A Certain Lack Symmetry," 124.
26. de Beauvoir, *The Second Sex*, 362.
27. Georges Tarabishi, *Woman against Her Sex: A Critique of Nawal el-Saadawi* (London: Saqi, 1988), 38.

28. Peggy R. Sanday, "Introduction," in Peggy R. Sanday and Ruth G. Goodenough, eds., *Beyond the Second Sex: New Directions in the Anthropology of Gender* (Philadelphia: University of Pennsylvania Press, 1990), 17.

29. Mackenzie, "A Certain Lack of Symmetry," 135–36 (emphasis added).

30. El-Khayyat, *Honour and Shame*, 162.

31. Ibid.

32. Norma Khouri, *Honor Lost: Love and Death in Modern-Day Jordan* (New York: Atria, 2003), 102.

33. de Beauvoir, *The Second Sex*, 290.

34. Davis and Davis, *Adolescence in a Moroccan Town*, 138.

35. Khouri, *Honor Lost*, 102.

36. Virginia Goldner et al., "Love and Violence: Gender Paradoxes in Volatile Attachments," *Family Process*, 29, no. 4 (December 1990), 4.

37. Mary Maynard and Jan Winn, "Women, Violence and Male Power," in Victoria Robinson and Diane Richardson, eds., *Introducing Women's Studies: Feminist Theory and Practice* (Houndmills, UK: Macmillan, second edition, 1997), 195.

38. Cited in Yvonne Y. Haddad, "Islam and Gender: Dilemmas in the Changing Arab World," in Yvonne Y. Haddad and John L. Esposito, eds., *Islam, Gender and Social Change* (New York: Oxford University Press, 1998), 11.

CHAPTER 6: GENDER AND POWER

Epigraph source: Amal Rassam, "Women and Domestic Power in Morocco," *International Journal of Middle Eastern Studies*, 12, no. 2 (1980), 178.

1. Michelle Zimbalist Rosaldo, "Women, Culture and Society: A Theoretical Overview," in Michelle Zimbalist Rosaldo and Louise Lamphere, eds., *Women, Culture and Society* (Stanford, CA: Stanford University Press, 1974), 34.

2. December Green, *Gender Violence in Africa: African Women's Responses* (Houndmills, UK: Macmillan, 1999), 152.

3. Michel Foucault, *The History of Sexuality*, vol. 1 (London: Penguin, 1990).

4. Rosaldo, "Women, Culture and Society," 21.

5. Rassam, "Women and Domestic Power," 171.

6. Arlene Elowe MacLeod, "Hegemonic Relations and Gender Resistance: The New Veiling as Accommodating Protest in Cairo," *Signs: Journal of Women in Culture and Society*, 17, no. 3 (1992), 534.

7. Erika Friedl, "Sources of Female Power in Iran," in Mahnaz Afkhami and Erika Friedl, eds., *In the Eyes of the Storm: Women in Post-Revolutionary Iran* (London: I.B. Tauris, 1994), 151.

8. Diane Singerman, "Where Has all the Power Gone? Women and Politics in Popular Quarters of Cairo," in Fatma Müge Göcek and Shiva Balaghi, eds., *Reconstructing Gender in the Middle East: Tradition, Identity, and Power* (New York: Columbia University Press, 1994), 176.

9. Ibid., 177.

10. Nadia Hijab, *Womanpower: The Arab Debate on Women at Work* (Cambridge, UK: Cambridge University Press, 1988), 138.

11. Ibid., 140.

12. Mary Caprioli, "Democracy and Human Rights versus Women's Security: A Contradiction?" *Security Dialogue*, 35, no. 4 (2004), 421.

13. Haideh Moghissi, *Feminism and Islamic Fundamentalism: The Limits of Postmodern Analysis* (London: Zed, 1999), 92.

14. Asma Afsaruddin, "Introduction: The Hermeneutics of Gendered Space and Discourse," in Asma Afsaruddin, ed., *Hermeneutics and Honor: Negotiating Female "Public" Space in Islamic/ate Societies* (Cambridge, MA: Harvard University Press, 1999), 5.

15. Cynthia Nelson, "Public and Private Politics: Women in the Middle Eastern World," *American Ethnologist*, 1, no. 3 (1974), 552.

16. See for instance, Afsaruddin, "Introduction: The Hermeneutics," 3; Dina Rizk Khoury, "Slippers at the Entrance or behind Closed Doors: Domestic and Public Space for Mosuli Women," in Madeline C. Zilfi, ed., *Women in the Ottoman Empire: Middle Eastern Women in the Early Modern Era* (Leiden: Brill, 1997); Nelson, "Public and Private Politics"; and Hammed Shahidian, *Women in Iran: Gender, Politics in the Islamic Republic* (Westport, CT: Greenwood Press, 2002), 12.

17. Khoury, "Slippers at the Entrance," 107.

18. Rassam, "Women and Domestic Power," 173.

19. Nelson, "Public and Private Politics," 559.

20. Carla Makhlouf, *Changing Veils: Women in Modernisation in North Yemen* (London: Croom Helm, 1979), 28.

21. Gada Karmi, "The Saddam Hussein Phenomenon and Male-Female Relations in the Arab World," in Haleh Afshar, ed., *Women in the Middle East: Perceptions, Realities and Struggle for Liberation* (Houndmills, UK: Macmillan, 1993), 152.

22. Rassam, "Women and Domestic Power," 173.

23. Mahnaz Kousha, "Love and Control: Relationships between Fathers and Daughters in Iran," *Critique: Critical Middle Eastern Studies*, 11, no. 1 (2002), 94.

24. M. E. Combs-Schilling, *Sacred Performances: Islam, Sexuality, and Sacrifice* (New York: Columbia University Press, 1989), 99.

25. Lila abu-Lughod, "The Romance of Resistance: Tracing Transformations of Power through Bedouin Women," in Peggy Reeves Sanday and Ruth Gallagher Goodenough, eds., *Beyond the Second Sex: New Directions in the Anthropology of Gender* (Philadelphia: University of Pennsylvania Press, 1990), 324.

26. Fatma Müge Göcek and Shiva Balaghi, "Introduction," in Göcek and Balaghi, eds., *Reconstructing Gender*, 15.

27. Nelson, "Public and Private Politics," 559.

28. Erika Friedl, "Women in Contemporary Persian Folktales," in Lois Beck and Nikki R. Keddie, eds., *Women in the Muslim World* (Cambridge, MA: Harvard University Press, 1978), 647.

29. Makhlouf, *Changing Veils*, 24.

CHAPTER 7: POWER AND PRICE

Epigraph source: Sherry Ortner, *Making Gender: The Politics and Erotics of Culture* (Boston: Beacon, 1996), 20.

1. Ortner, *Making Gender*, 19.

2. Nikki R. Keddie and Lois Beck, "Introduction," in Lois Beck and Nikki R. Keddie, eds., *Women in the Muslim World* (Cambridge, MA: Harvard University Press, 1978), 19.

3. Juliette Minces, *The House of Obedience: Women in Arab Society* (London: Zed, 1982), 44.

4. Paul Vieille, "Iranian Women in Family Alliance and Sexual Politics," in Beck and Keddie, eds., *Women in the Muslim World*, 457.

5. Soraya al-Torki, *Women in Saudi Arabia: Ideology and Behavior among the Elite* (New York: Columbia University Press, 1986), 81.

6. Simone de Beauvoir, *The Second Sex* (London: Jonathan Cape, 1968), 354.

7. Erika Friedl, "Women in Contemporary Persian Folktales," in Beck and Keddie, eds., *Women in the Muslim World*, 637.

8. Elizabeth W. Fernea, *Guest of the Sheik: An Ethnography of an Iraqi Village* (New York: Anchor, 1989), 65.

9. Suad Joseph, "Brother/Sister Relationships: Connectivity, Love, and Power in the Reproduction of Patriarchy in Lebanon," *American Ethnologist*, 21, no. 1 (1994), 56.

10. Daisy Hilse Dwyer, *Images and Self-Images: Male and Female in Morocco* (New York: Columbia University Press, 1978), 39.

11. Al-Torki, *Women in Saudi Arabia*, 99.

12. Ibid., 155–56.

13. Ortner, *Making Gender*, 18.

14. Edward Westermarck, *Wit and Wisdom in Morocco: A Study of Native Proverbs* (London: George Routledge, 1930), 66.

15. Barbara Mensch et al., "Gender-Role Attitudes among Egyptian Adolescents," *Studies in Family Planning*, 34, no. 1 (2003), 16.

16. Amal Rassam, "Women and Domestic Power in Morocco," *International Journal of Middle Eastern Studies*, 12, no. 2 (1980), 176.

17. Ibid., 172.

18. A. D. Spellberg, *Politics, Gender, and the Islamic Past: The Legacy of 'A'isha bint Abi Bakr* (New York: Columbia University Press, 1994), 63.

19. Friedl, "Women in Contemporary Persian Folktales," 633.

20. Rassam, "Women and Domestic Power," 172.

21. Ibid., 177.

22. Sana al-Khayyat, *Honour and Shame: Women in Modern Iraq* (London: Saqi, 1990), 184.

23. Michelle Zimbalist Rosaldo, "Woman, Culture and Society: A Theoretical Overview," in Michelle Zimbalist Rosaldo and Louise Lamphere, eds., *Woman, Culture and Society* (Stanford, CA: Stanford University Press, 1974), 42.

24. Erika Friedl, "Sources of Female Power in Iran," in Mahnaz Afkhami and Erika Friedl, eds., *In the Eye of the Storm: Women in Post-Revolutionary Iran* (London: I. B. Tauris, 1994), 158.

25. Arlene Elowe MacLeod, "Hegemonic Relations and Gender Resistance: The New Veiling as Accommodating Protest in Cairo," *Signs: Journal of Women in Culture and Society*, 17, no. 3 (1992), 556.

26. Friedl, "Sources of Female Power," 159.

27. Ibid., 153.

28. Cited in Valentine M. Moghadam, "Introduction and Overview," in Valentine M. Moghadam, ed., *Gender and National Identity: Women and Politics in Muslim Societies* (London: Zed, 1994), 5.

29. "Saudi Women Rise in Defense of the Veil," *The Washington Post*, June 1, 2006.

CHAPTER 8: VIOLENCE, VICTIMIZATION, AND CONFORMITY

Epigraph Source: Catriona Mackenzie, "A Certain Lack of Symmetry: Beauvoir on Autonomous Agency and Women's Embodiment," in Ruth Evans, ed., *Simone de Beauvoir's The Second Sex: New Interdisciplinary Essays*, (Manchester, UK: Manchester University Press, 1998), 135–36.

1. Johan Galtung, "Violence, Peace, and Peace Research," *Journal of Peace Research*, 6, no. 3 (1969), 168.

2. Ibid., 172.

3. Ibid.

4. Ibid., 171.

5. Ibid., 180.

6. Johan Galtung, *Peace by Peaceful Means: Peace and Conflict. Development and Civilization* (London: Sage, 1996), 199.

7. Galtung, *Peace by Peaceful Means*, 208.

8. Ibid., 200.

9. Gail Mason, *Spectacle of Violence: Homophobia, Gender, and Knowledge* (Florence: Routledge, 2001), 128.

10. Ibid., 130.

11. Virginia Goldner et al., "Love and Violence: Gender Paradoxes in Volatile Attachments," *Family Process*, no. 29 (1990), 2.

12. Mason, *Spectacle of Violence*, 123.

13. Carrie L. Yodanis, "Gender Inequality, Violence against Women, and Fear: A Cross-National Test of the Feminist Theory of Violence against Women," *Journal of Interpersonal Violence*, 19, no. 6 (2004), 657.

14. Ibid., 673.

15. Mary Maynard and Jan Winn, "Women, Violence and Male Power," in Victoria Robinson and Diane Richardson, eds., *Introducing Women's Studies: Feminist Theory and Practice* (Houndmills, UK: Macmillan, second edition, 1997), 176.

16. Mason, *Spectacle of Violence*, 128.

17. Fatima Mernissi (writing under the pseudonym Fatna Ait Sabbah), *Women in the Muslim Unconscious* (New York: Pergamon, 1984), 45.

18. Galtung, *Peace by Peaceful Means*, 47.

19. December Green, *Gender Violence in Africa: African Women's Responses* (Houndmills, UK: Macmillan, 1999), 13.

20. Galtung, *Peace by Peaceful Means*, 40.

21. Mason, *Spectacle of Violence*, 123.

22. Green, *Gender Violence*, 15.

23. Galtung, *Peace by Peaceful Means*, 42.

24. Sana al-Khayyat, *Honour and Shame: Women in Modern Iraq* (London: Saqi, 1990), 199.

25. Ibid., 23.

26. Green, *Gender Violence*, 20.

27. Ibid., 26.

28. Galtung, *Peace by Peaceful Means*, 203.

29. Simone de Beauvoir, *The Second Sex* (London: Jonathan Cape, 1968), 677.

30. Kersti A. Yllö, "Gender, Diversity, and Violence," in Donileen R. Loseke, R. J. Gelles, and M. M. Cavanaugh, eds., *Current Controversies on Family Violence* (Thousand Oaks, CA: Sage, 2005), 22.

31. Maynard and Winn, "Women, Violence," 177.

32. Liz Kelly, S. Burton, and L. Regan, "Beyond Victim or Survivor: Sexual Violence, Identity, and Feminist Theory and Practice," in Lisa Adkins and Vicki Merchant, eds., *Sexualizing the Social: Power and the Organization of Sexuality* (Houndmills, UK: Macmillan, 1996), 82.

33. Yllö, "Gender, Diversity," 20.

34. Goldner, "Love and Violence," 1.

35. Liz Kelly, "Wars against Women: Sexual Violence, Sexual Politics and the Militarised State," in Susie Jacobs, R. Jacobson, and J. Marchbank, eds., *States of Conflict: Gender, Violence and Resistance* (London: Zed, 2000), 46.

36. Fatma Müge Göcek and Shiva Balaghi, "Introduction," in Fatma Müge Göcek and Shiva Balaghi, eds., *Reconstructing Gender in the Middle East: Tradition, Identity, and Power* (New York: Columbia University Press, 1994), 14–15.

37. Haleh Afshar, "Development Studies and Women in the Middle East: The Dilemmas of Research and Development," in Haleh Afshar, ed., *Women in the Middle East: Perceptions, Realities and Struggle for Liberation* (Houndmills, UK: Macmillan, 1993), xi.

38. Arlene Elowe MacLeod, "Hegemonic Relations and Gender Resistance: The New Veiling as Accommodating Protest in Cairo," *Signs: Journal of Women in Culture and Society*, 17, no. 3 (1992), 535.

39. Kelly, "Wars against Women," 46.

40. Donileen R. Loseke, "Complexities of Family Violence," in Loseke et al., eds., *Current Controversies*, 42.

41. Stevi Jackson, "Heterosexuality as a Problem for Feminist Theory," in Adkins and Merchant, eds., *Sexualizing the Social*, 17.

42. Galtung, *Peace by Peaceful Means*, 200.

43. Julliette Minces, *The House of Obedience: Women in Arab Society* (London: Zed, 1982), 20.

44. Mernissi, *Women in the Muslim Unconscious*, 32.

45. de Beauvoir, *The Second Sex*, 351.

46. Ibid., 670.

47. Ibid., 674.

48. Mackenzie, "A Certain Lack of Symmetry," 135.

49. Deniz Kandiyoti, "Beyond Beijing: Obstacles and Prospects for the Middle East," in Mahnaz Afkhami and Erika Friedl, eds., *Muslim Women and the Politics of Participation: Implementing the Beijing Platform* (Syracuse, NY: Syracuse University Press, 1997), 10.

50. de Beauvoir, *The Second Sex*, 677.

51. MacLeod, "Hegemonic Relations," 535.

52. Sherry Ortner, "Is Female to Male as Nature Is to Culture?" in Michelle Zimbalist Rosaldo and Louise Lamphere, eds., *Women, Culture and Society* (Stanford, CA: Stanford University Press, 1974), 85.

53. Elizabeth A. Mann, "Education, Money, and the Role of Women in Maintaining Minority Identity," in Zoya Hasan, ed., *Forging Identities: Gender, Communities, and the State in India* (Boulder, CO: Westview, 1994), 134.

54. Mahnaz Kousha, "Ties That Bind: Mothers and Daughters in Contemporary Iran," *Critique: Critical Middle Eastern Studies*, 6, no. 1 (1997), 83.

55. Green, *Gender Violence*, 13.

56. Sherifa Zuhur, *Revealing Reveiling: Islamist Gender Ideology in Contemporary Egypt* (New York: State University of New York Press, 1992), 21.

57. Ibid., 28.

58. Jam'iyat Tadamun al-Mar'ah al-Arabiya, *Al-mar'ah al-arabiya wa al-mutaghayyirat al-alamiya* [Arab Women and International Changes]. Proceedings of the Sixth International Conference of the Association of Solidarity of Arab Women (Cairo: Merit, 2003), 36.

59. Al-Khayyat, *Honour and Shame Iraq*, 71.

60. Ibid., 188.

61. Ibid., 9.

62. Soraya al-Torki, *Women in Saudi Arabia: Ideology and Behavior among the Elite* (New York: Columbia University Press, 1986), 136.

63. Safia K. Mohsen, "New Images, Old Reflections: Working Middle-Class Women in Egypt," in Elizabeth Warnock Fernea, ed., *Women and the Family in the Middle East: New Voices of Change* (Austin: University of Texas Press, 1985), 70.

64. Ayesha Jalal, "The Convenience of Subservience: Women and the State of Pakistan," in Deniz Kandiyoti, ed., *Women, Islam and the State* (Houndmills, UK: Macmillan, 1991), 78.

65. Ibid., 79.

66. Zuhur, *Revealing Reveiling*, 28.

67. Mackenzie, "A Certain Lack of Symmetry," 138.

68. Jalal, "The Convenience of Subservience," 78–79.

CHAPTER 9: GENDER, RESISTANCE, AND SUBVERSION

Epigraph source: Azar Nafisi, "Imagination as Subversion: Narrative as a Tool of Civic Awareness," in Mahnaz Afkhami and Erika Friedl, eds., *Muslim Women and the Politics of Participation: Implementing the Beijing Platform* (Syracuse, NY: Syracuse University Press, 1997), 59.

1. Michel Foucault, *The History of Sexuality*, vol. 1 (London: Penguin, 1990), 95.

2. Lila abu-Lughod, "The Romance of Resistance: Tracing Transformations of Power through Bedouin Women," in Peggy Reeves Sanday and Ruth Gallagher Goodenough, *Beyond the Second Sex: New Directions in the Anthropology of Gender* (Philadelphia: University of Pennsylvania Press, 1990), 314–15.

3. Erika Friedl, "Sources of Female Power in Iran," in Mahnaz Afkhami and Erika Friedl, eds., *In the Eyes of the Storm: Women in Post-Revolutionary Iran* (London: I. B. Tauris, 1994), 152.

4. Ibid., 155.

5. Gail Mason, *Spectacle of Violence: Homophobia, Gender, and Knowledge* (Florence: Routledge, 2001), 129.

6. Ibid., 130.

7. Friedl, "Sources of Female," 154.

8. Sherry Ortner, *Making Gender: The Politics and Erotics of Culture* (Boston: Beacon, 1996), 57.

9. December Green, *Gender Violence in Africa: African Women's Responses* (Houndmills, UK: Macmillan, 1999), 12.

10. Ortner, *Making Gender*, 15.

11. Gada Karmi, "The Saddam Hussein Phenomenon and Male-Female Relations in the Arab World," in Haleh Afshar, ed., *Women in the Middle East: Perceptions, Realities and Struggle for Liberation* (Houndmills, UK: Macmillan, 1993), 154.

12. Green, *Gender Violence*, 12.

13. Janet Afary and Kevin B. Anderson, *Foucault and the Iranian Revolution: Gender and the Seductions of Islamism* (Chicago: The University of Chicago Press, 2005), 27.

14. Sana al-Khayyat, *Honour and Shame: Women in Modern Iraq* (London: Saqi, 1990), 23.

15. Khawla abu-Baker, "Marital Problems among Arab Families," *Arab Studies Quarterly*, 25, no. 4 (2003), 65.

16. Ibid., 66.

17. Abu-Lughod, "The Romance of Resistance," 314.

18. Ibid., 313.

19. Edward Westermarck, *Wit and Wisdom in Morocco: A Study of Native Proverbs* (London: George Routledge, 1930), 66.

20. Erika Friedl, "Women in Contemporary Persian Folktales," in Lois Beck and Nikki R. Keddie, eds., *Women in the Muslim World* (New York: Harvard University Press, 1978), 640.

21. Amal Treacher and Halla Shukrallah, "The Realm of the Possible: Middle Eastern Women in Political and Social Spaces," *Feminist Review*, 69 (2001), 160.

22. Fatima Mernissi (writing under the pseudonym of Fatna Ait Sabbah), *Women in the Muslim Unconscious* (New York: Pergamon, 1984), 35.

23. Ibid., 44.

24. Nafisi, "Imagination as Subversion," 68.

25. Julliette Minces, *The House of Obedience: Women in Arab Society* (London: Zed, 1982), 43.

26. Nikki R. Keddie and Lois Beck, "Introduction," in Beck and Keddie, eds., *Women in the Muslim World*, 19.

27. Fatima Mernissi, "Virginity and Patriarchy," *Women's Studies International Forum*, 5, no. 2 (1982), 188.

28. Friedl, "Sources of Female," 156.

29. Abu-Lughod, "The Romance of Resistance," 323.

30. Nawal el-Saadawi, *Memoirs of a Woman Doctor* (London: Saqi, 1988), 11.

31. Carla Makhlouf, *Changing Veils: Women in Modernisation in North Yemen* (London: Croom Helm, 1979), 96.

32. Ibid., 45.

33. Abu-Lughod, "The Romance of Resistance," 320.

34. Daisy Hilse Dwyer, *Images and Self-Images: Male and Female in Morocco* (New York: Columbia University Press, 1978), 153.

35. Minces, *The House*, 36.

36. Suad Joseph, "Brother/Sister Relationships: Connectivity, Love, and Power in the Reproduction of Patriarchy in Lebanon," *American Ethnologist*, 21, no. 1 (1994), 62.

37. Dwyer, *Images and Self-Images*, 164.

CHAPTER 10: STATUS AND VICTIMIZATION

Epigraph source: Abdel Wahab Bouhdiba, *Sexuality in Islam* (London: Saqi, 1998), 215.

1. Edward Westermarck, *Wit and Wisdom in Morocco: A Study of Native Proverbs* (London: George Routledge, 1930), 89.

2. Raphael Patai, *The Arab Mind* (New York: Hatherleigh, 2002), 31.

3. Paul Vieille, "Iranian Women in Family Alliance and Sexual Politics," in Lois Beck and Nikki R. Keddie, eds., *Women in the Muslim World* (New York: Harvard University Press, 1978), 457.

4. Westermarck, *Wit and Wisdom*, 89.

5. Bouhdiba, *Sexuality in Islam*, 214.

6. Ibid., 217.

7. Daisy Hilse Dwyer, *Images and Self-Image: Male and Female in Morocco* (New York: Columbia University Press, 1978), 115.

8. Bouhdiba, *Sexuality in Islam*, 220–21.

9. Mahnaz Kousha, "Ties That Bind: Mothers and Daughters in Contemporary Iran," *Critique: Critical Middle Eastern Studies*, 6, no. 1 (1997), 66.

10. Ibid., 68.

11. Amal Rassam, "Women and Domestic Power in Morocco," *International Journal of Middle Eastern Studies*, 12, no. 2 (1980), 174–75.

12. Kousha, "Ties That Bind," 70.

13. Vieille, "Iranian Women," 457.

14. Susan Schaefer Davis and Douglas Davis, *Adolescence in a Moroccan Town: Making Social Sense* (New Brunswick, NJ: Rutgers University Press, 1989), 76.

15. Simone de Beauvoir, *The Second Sex* (London: Jonathan Cape, 1968), 502.

16. Davis and Davis, *Adolescence*, 77.

17. Sana al-Khayyat, *Honour and Shame: Women in Modern Iraq* (London: Saqi, 1990), 162.

18. Westermarck, *Wit and Wisdom*, 89.

19. Homa Hoodfar, "Child Care and Child Health in Low-Income Neighbourhoods of Cairo," in Elizabeth Warnock Fernea, ed., *Children in the Muslim Middle East* (Austin: University of Texas Press, 1995), 160.

20. Al-Khayyat, *Honour and Shame*, 40–41.

21. Ibid., 43.

22. Bouthaina Shaaban, *Both Right and Left Handed: Arab Women Talk about Their Lives* (London: The Women's Press, 1988), 70.

23. Al-Khayyat, *Honour and Shame*, 42.

CHAPTER 11: PATRIARCHY AND AGENCY

Epigraph Source: Edward Westermarck, *Wit and Wisdom in Morocco: A Study of Native Proverbs* (London: George Routledge, 1930), 68.

1. Fatima Mernissi, *Beyond the Veil: Male-Female Dynamics in Muslim Society* (Cambridge, MA: Schekman, 1975).

2. Sherifa Zuhur, *Revealing Reveiling: Islamist Gender Ideology in Contemporary Egypt* (New York: State University of New York Press, 1992), 28.

3. Soheir A. Mohsen, "Sex Differences and Folk Illness in an Egyptian Village," in Lois Beck and Nikki R. Keddie, eds., *Women in the Muslim World* (New York: Harvard University Press, 1978), 607–8.

4. Amal Rassam, "Women and Domestic Power in Morocco," *International Journal of Middle Eastern Studies*, 12, no. 2 (1980), 175.

5. Mübeccel Kiray, "The New Role of Mothers: Changing Intra-Familial Relationships in a Small town in Turkey," in J. G. Peristiany, ed., *Mediterranean Family Structures* (Cambridge, UK: Cambridge University Press, 1976), 266.

6. Nikki R. Keddie and Lois Beck, "Introduction," in Beck and Keddie, eds., *Women in the Muslim World*, 24–25.

7. Deniz Kandiyoti, "Islam and Patriarchy: A Comparative Perspective," in Nikki R. Keddie and Beth Baron, eds., *Women in Middle Eastern History: Shifting Boundaries in Sex and Gender* (New Haven, CT: Yale University Press, 1991), 32.

8. Daisy Hilse Dwyer, *Images and Self-Images: Male and Female in Morocco* (New York: Columbia University Press, 1978), 4.

9. Kandiyoti, "Islam and Patriarchy," 32–33.

10. Rassam, "Women and Domestic Power," 176–77.

11. Erika Friedl, "Sources of Female Power in Iran," in Mahnaz Afkhami and Erika Friedl, eds., *In the Eyes of the Storm: Women in Post-Revolutionary Iran* (London: I. B. Tauris, 1994), 156.

12. Rassam, "Women and Domestic Power," 175.

13. Westermarck, *Wit and Wisdom*, 79.

14. Rassam, "Women and Domestic Power," 175.

15. Colleen K. Keenan, A. el-Hadad, and S. A. Balian, "Factors Associated with Domestic Violence in Low-Income Lebanese Families," *Image: Journal of Nursing Scholarship*, 30, no. 4 (1998), 359.

16. Kandiyoti, "Islam and Patriarchy," 33.

17. Gary Gregg, *The Middle East: A Cultural Psychology* (New York: Oxford University Press, 2005), 341.

18. Rassam, "Women and Domestic Power," 175.

19. Westermarck, *Wit and Wisdom*, 67.

20. Ibid., 68.

21. Ibid.

22. Erika Friedl, "Women in Contemporary Persian Folktales," in Beck and Keddie, eds., *Women in the Muslim World*, 641.

23. Ibid., 634.

24. Sheila K. Webster, "Women, Sex, and Marriage in Moroccan Proverbs," *International Journal of Middle East Studies*, 14 (1982), 181.

25. Keenan et al., "Factors Associated," 359.

26. Ibid., 358–59.

CHAPTER 12: AUTHORITARIAN FAMILY STRUCTURE

Epigraph source: Edward Westermarck, *Wit and Wisdom in Morocco: A Study of Native Proverbs* (London: George Routledge, 1930), 77.

1. Paul Vieille, "Iranian Women in Family Alliance and Sexual Politics," in Lois Beck and Nikki R. Keddie, eds., *Women in the Muslim World* (New York: Harvard University Press, 1978), 459.

2. Juliette Minces, *The House of Obedience: Women in Arab Society* (London: Zed, 1982), 43.

3. Nawal el-Saadawi, *The Hidden Face of Eve: Women in the Arab World* (London: Saqi, 1980), 141–42.

4. Lama abu-Odeh, "Crimes of Honour and the Construction of Gender in Arab Societies," in Mai Yamani, ed., *Feminism and Islam: Legal and Literary Perspective* (London: Ithaca, 1996), 182.

5. Goldner et al., "Love and Violence: Gender Paradoxes in Volatile Attachments," *Family Process*, 29, no. 4 (1990), 6.

6. Ibid., 5–6.

7. Fatima Mernissi, "Virginity and Patriarchy," *Women's Studies International Forum*, 5, no. 2 (1982), 185.

8. Fatima Mernissi, *Beyond the Veil: Male-Female Dynamics in Muslim Society* (Cambridge, MA: Schekman, 1975), 59.

9. Ibid., xvi.

10. Sherry Ortner, *Making Gender: The Politics and Erotics of Culture* (Boston: Beacon, 1996), 57.

11. Vieille, "Iranian Women," 471.

12. Suad Joseph and Susan Slymovics, "Introduction," in Joseph Suad and Susan Slymovics, eds., *Women and Power in the Middle East* (Philadelphia: University of Pennsylvania Press, 2001), 8.

13. Gada Karmi, "Women, Islam, Patriarchalism," in Yamani, ed., *Feminism and Islam*, 82.

14. Sana al-Khayyat, *Honour and Shame: Women in Modern Iraq* (London: Saqi, 1990), 45.

15. Ortner, *Making Gender*, 45.

16. Wilhelm Reich, *The Mass Psychology of Fascism* (New York: Farrar, Straus and Giroux, 1970), 53.

17. Ibid., 54.

18. Halim Barakat, *The Arab World: Society, Culture and the State* (Berkeley: University of California Press, 1993), 116.

19. Ibid.

20. Simone de Beauvoir, *The Second Sex* (London: Jonathan Cape, 1968), 291.

21. Soraya al-Torki, *Women in Saudi Arabia: Ideology and Behavior among the Elite* (New York: Columbia University Press, 1986), 146.

22. Westermarck, *Wit and Wisdom*, 95.

23. Barakat, *The Arab World*, 106.

24. Al-Khayyat, *Honour and Shame*, 34.

25. Ibid., 164.
26. Ibid., 165.
27. Ibid., 164.
28. Ibid., 166.
29. Ibid.
30. Ibid., 181.
31. Barbara Mensch et al., "Gender-Role Attitudes among Egyptian Adolescents," *Studies in Family Planning*, 34, no. 1 (2003), 14.
32. Fatima Mernissi, "Democracy as Moral Disintegration: The Contradiction between Religious Belief and Citizenship as a Manifestation of the Ahistoricity of the Arab Identity," in Nahid Toubia, ed., *Women of the Arab World: The Coming Challenge* (London: Zed, 1988), 39.
33. Erika Friedl, "Women in Contemporary Persian Folktales," in Beck and Keddie, eds., *Women in the Muslim World*, 640.
34. Barakat, *The Arab World*, 116.
35. Reich, *The Mass Psychology*, 30 (emphasis in original).
36. Karmi, "Women, Islam," 155.

CHAPTER 13: GENDER AND AUTHORITARIAN SOCIAL CONTRACT

1. Michel Foucault, *The History of Sexuality*, vol. 1 (London: Penguin, 1990), 85.
2. Sana al-Khayyat, *Honour and Shame: Women in Modern Iraq* (London: Saqi, 1990), 112.
3. Suad Joseph, "Brother/Sister Relationships: Connectivity, Love, and Power in the Reproduction of Patriarchy in Lebanon," *American Ethnologist*, 21, no. 1 (1994), 57.
4. Fatima Mernissi, "Democracy as Moral Disintegration: The Contradiction between Religious Belief and Citizenship as a Manifestation of the Ahistoricity of the Arab Identity," in Nahid Toubia, ed., *Women of the Arab World: The Coming Challenge* (London: Zed, 1988), 39.
5. Abdel Wahab Bouhdiba, *Sexuality in Islam* (London: Saqi, 1998), 219.
6. Mahnaz Kousha, "Ties That Bind: Mothers and Daughters in Contemporary Iran," *Critique: Critical Middle Eastern Studies*, 6, no. 1 (1997), 70.
7. Robert Fernea, "Gender, Sexuality and Patriarchy in Modern Egypt," *Critique: Critical Middle Eastern Studies*, 12, no. 2 (2003), 147.

CHAPTER 14: GENDER AND AUTHORITARIAN POLITICS

Epigraph source: Fatima Mernissi, *Women and Islam: An Historical and Theological Enquiry* (Oxford: Basil Blackwell, 1991), 194.
1. Lama abu-Odeh, "Crimes of Honour and the Construction of Gender in Arab Societies," in Mai Yamani, ed., *Feminism and Islam: Legal and Literary Perspective* (London: Ithaca, 1996), 170.

2. Sana al-Khayyat, *Honour and Shame: Women in Modern Iraq* (London: Saqi, 1990), 33.

3. Barbara S. Mensch et al., "Gender-Role Attitudes among Egyptian Adolescents," *Studies in Family Planning*, 34, no. 1 (2003), 10.

4. Al-Khayyat, *Honour and Shame*, 54.

5. Wilhelm Reich, *The Mass Psychology of Fascism* (New York: Farrar, Straus and Giroux, 1970), 30.

6. Ibid., 111.

7. Al-Khayyat, *Honour and Shame*, 43.

8. Georges Tarabishi, *Woman against Her Sex: A Critique of Nawal el-Saadawi* (London: Saqi, 1988), 43.

9. Nawal el-Saadawi, *The Hidden Face of Eve: Women in the Arab World* (London: Zed, 1980), 81.

10. Bouthaina Shaaban, *Both Right and Left Handed: Arab Women Talk about Their Lives* (London: The Women's Press, 1988), 127.

11. Simone de Beauvoir, *The Second Sex* (London: Jonathan Cape, 1968), 501.

12. Al-Khayyat, *Honour and Shame*, 131.

CHAPTER 15: GENDER, AUTHORITARIANISM, AND VIOLENCE

Epigraph source: Qasim Amin, *The Liberation of Women. The New Women* (Cairo: The American University in Cairo Press, 2000) [1899] [1900], 121.

1. Sana al-Khayyat, *Honour and Shame: Women in Modern Iraq* (London: Saqi, 1990), 23.

2. Bouthaina Shaaban, *Both Right and Left Handed: Arab Women Talk about Their Lives* (London: The Women's Press, 1988), 15.

3. Andrea Parrot and Nina Cummings, *Forsaken Females: The Global Brutalization of Women* (Lanham, MD: Rowman and Littlefield, 2006), 176.

4. Carrie Yodanis, "Gender Inequality, Violence against Women, and Fear: A Cross-National Test of the Feminist Theory of Violence against Women," *Journal of Interpersonal Violence*, 19, no. 6 (2004), 657.

5. Ibid., 658.

6. Ibid., 671–72.

7. Kanan Makiya, *Republic of Fear* (Berkeley: University of California Press, 1998).

8. Fatima Mernissi, *Women's Rebellion and Islamic Memory* (London: Zed, 1996), 75.

9. Nikki R. Keddie and Lois Beck, "Introduction," in Lois Beck and Nikki R. Keddie, eds., *Women in the Muslim World* (Cambridge, MA: Harvard University Press, 1978), 28.

10. "Shutting Down Zanan," editorial, *New York Times*, February 7, 2008.

CHAPTER 16: CONCLUSION

Epigraph source: Fatima Mernissi, "Democracy as Moral Disintegration: The Contradiction between Religious Belief and Citizenship as a Manifestation of the Ahistoricity of the Arab Identity," in Nahid Toubia, ed., *Women of the Arab World: The Coming Challenge* (London: Zed, 1988), 37.

1. Johan Galtung, *Peace by Peaceful Means: Peace and Conflict. Development and Civilization* (London: Sage, 1996), 46.

2. Catriona Mackenzie, "A Certain Lack of Symmetry: Beauvoir on Autonomous Agency and Women's Embodiment," in Ruth Evans, ed., *Simone de Beauvoir's The Second Sex: New Interdisciplinary Essay*, (Manchester, UK: Manchester University Press, 1998), 132.

3. Nayereh Tohidi, "Modernity, Islamization, and Women in Iran," in Valentine M. Moghadam, ed., *Gender and National Identity: Women and Politics in Muslim Societies* (London: zed, 1994), 110.

4. Evelyne Accad, *Sexuality and War: Literary Masks of the Middle East* (New York: New York University Press, 1990), 12.

5. Nikki R. Keddie and Lois Beck, "Introduction," in Lois Beck and Nikki R. Keddie, eds., *Women in the Muslim World* (Cambridge, MA: Harvard University Press, 1978), 20.

6. Michelle Zimbalist Rosaldo, "Women, Culture and Society: A Theoretical Overview," in Michelle Zimbalist Rosaldo and Louise Lamphere, eds., *Women, Culture and Society* (Stanford, CA: Stanford University Press, 1974), 41.

7. Qasim Amin, *The Liberation of Women. The New Women* (Cairo: The American University in Cairo Press, 2000) [1899], [1900], 4–5.

Selected Bibliography

Abu-Baker, Khwla. "Marital Problems among Arab Families." *Arab Studies Quarterly*, 25, no. 4 (2003).

Abu-Lughod, Lila. *Remaking Women: Feminism and Modernity in the Middle East*. Princeton, NJ: Princeton University Press, 1998.

———. "The Romance of Resistance: Tracing Transformations of Power through Bedouin Women." In Peggy Reeves Sanday and Ruth Gallagher Goodenough, eds., *Beyond the Second Sex: New Directions in the Anthropology of Gender*. Philadelphia: University of Pennsylvania Press, 1990.

———. *Veiled Sentiments: Honor and Poetry in a Bedouin Society*. Berkeley: University of California Press, 1988.

Abu-Odeh, Lama. "Crimes of Honour and the Construction of Gender in Arab Societies." In Mai Yamani, ed., *Feminism and Islam: Legal and Literary Perspectives*. London: Ithaca, 1996.

Accad, Evelyne. *Sexuality and War: Literary Masks of the Middle East*. New York: New York University Press, 1990.

Afary, Janet, and Kevin B. Anderson. *Foucault and the Iranian Revolution: Gender and the Seductions of Islamism*. Chicago: University of Chicago Press, 2005.

Afkhami, Mahnaz, and Erika Friedl. "Introduction." In Mahnaz Afkhami and Erika Friedl, eds., *Muslim Women and the Politics of Participation: Implementing the Beijing Platform*. Syracuse, NY: Syracuse University Press, 1997.

Afsaruddin, Asma. "Introduction: The Hermeneutics of Gendered Space and Discourse." In Asma Afsaruddin, ed., *Hermeneutics and Honor: Negotiating Female "Public" Space in Islamic/ate Societies*. Cambridge, MA: Harvard University Press, 1999.

Afshar, Haleh. "Development Studies and Women in the Middle East: The Dilemmas of Research and Development." In Haleh Afshar, ed., *Women in the Middle East: Perceptions, Realities and Struggle for Liberation.* Houndmills, UK: Macmillan. 1993.

Ahmed, Leila. *Women and Gender in Islam: Historical Roots of a Modern Debate.* New Haven, CT: Yale University Press, 1992.

Amin, Qasim. *The Liberation of Women. The New Women.* Cairo: The American University in Cairo Press, 2000. [1899] [1900].

As'ad, Abu-Khalil. "Toward the Study of Women and Politics in the Arab World: The Debate and the Reality." *Feminist Issues,* 13, no. 1 (1993),

Assaad, Marie Bassili. "Female Circumcision in Egypt: Social Implications, Current Research, and Prospects for Change." *Studies in Family Planning,* 11, no. 1 (1980).

Azzam, Maha. "Gender and the Politics of Religion in the Middle East." In Mai Yamani, ed., *Feminism and Islam: Legal and Literary Perspectives.* London: Ithaca, 1996.

Barakat, Halim. *The Arab World: Society, Culture, and the State.* Berkeley: University of California Press, 1993.

Beauvoir, Simone de. *The Second Sex.* London: Jonathan Cape, 1968 [1949].

Best, Victoria. "Between the Harem and the Battlefield: Domestic Space in the Work of Assia Djebar." *Signs: Journal of Women in Culture and Society,* 27, no. 3 (2002).

Bouhdiba, Abdel Wahab. *Sexuality in Islam.* London: Saqi, 1998.

Boxberger, Linda. "From Two States to One: Women's Lives in the Transformation of Yemen." In Herbert L. Bodman and Nayereh Tohidi, eds., *Women in Muslim Societies: Diversity within Unity.* Boulder, CO: Lynne Rienner, 1998.

Caprioli, Mary. "Democracy and Human Rights versus Women's Security: A Contradiction?" *Security Dialogue,* 35, no. 4 (2004).

Combs-Schilling, M. E. *Sacred Performances: Islam, Sexuality, and Sacrifice.* New York: Columbia University Press, 1989.

Connell, R. W. *Gender and Power: Society, the Person and Sexual Politics.* Stanford, CA: Stanford University Press, 1987.

———. "The State, Gender, and Sexual Politics: Theory and Appraisal." *Theory and Society,* 19 (1990).

Davis, Susan Schaefer, and Douglas A. Davis. *Adolescence in a Moroccan Town: Making Social Sense.* New Brunswick, NJ: Rutgers University Press, 1989.

Dobash, R. Emerson, and Russell P. Dobash. "Violent Men and Violent Contexts." In Emerson R. Dobash and Russell P. Dobash, eds., *Rethinking Violence against Women.* Thousand Oaks, CA: Sage, 1998.

Donno, Daniela, and Bruce Russett. "Islam, Authoritarianism, and Female Empowerment: What Are the Linkages?" *World Politics,* 56 (2004).

Dunne, Bruce. "Power and Sexuality in the Middle East." *Middle East Report* (Spring 1998).

Dwyer, Daisy Hilse. *Images and Self-Images: Male and Female in Morocco.* New York: Columbia University Press, 1978.

Esposito, John L. "Women in Islam and Muslim Societies." In Yvonne Yazbeck Haddad and John L. Esposito, eds., *Islam, Gender and Social Change.* New York: Oxford University Press, 1998.

Ferdows, F. Adele. "Women and the Islamic Revolution," *International Journal of Middle Eastern Studies,* 15 (1983).

Fernea, Elizabeth W. "Childhood in the Muslim Middle East." In Elizabeth W. Fernea, ed., *Children in the Muslim Middle East.* Austin: University of Texas Press, 1995.

———. *Guest of the Sheik: An Ethnography of an Iraqi Village.* New York: Anchor, 1989 [1965].

Fernea, Robert. "Gender, Sexuality and Patriarchy in Modern Egypt." *Critique: Critical Middle Eastern Studies,* 12, no. 2 (2003).

Fluehr-Lobban, Carolyn. "Toward a Theory of Arab-Muslim Women as Activists in Secular and Religious Movements." *Arab Studies Quarterly,* 15, no. 2 (1993).

Foucault, Michel. *The History of Sexuality.* Vol. 1. London: Penguin, 1990.

Friedl, Erika. "Sources of Female Power in Iran." In Mahnaz Afkhami and Erika Friedl, eds., *In the Eyes of the Storm: Women in Post-Revolutionary Iran.* London: I. B. Tauris, 1994.

———. "Women in Contemporary Persian Folktales." In Lois Beck and Nikki R. Keddie, eds., *Women in the Muslim World.* Cambridge, MA: Harvard University Press, 1978.

Galtung, Johan. *Peace by Peaceful Means: Peace and Conflict. Development and Civilization.* London: Sage, 1996.

———. "Violence, Peace, and Peace Research." *Journal of Peace Research,* 6, no. 3 (1969).

Ghoussoub, Mai. "Feminism—or the Eternal Masculine—in the Arab World." *New Left Review,* 161 (1987).

Ghoussoub, Mai, and Emma Sinclair-Webb, eds. *Imagined Masculinities: Male Identity and Culture in the Modern Middle East.* London: Saqi, 2000.

Göcek, Fatma Müge, and Shiva Balaghi. "Introduction." In Fatma Müge Göcek and Shiva Balaghi, eds., *Reconstructing Gender in the Middle East: Tradition, Identity, and Power.* New York: Columbia University Press, 1994.

Goldner, Virginia, Peggy Penn, Marcia Sheinberg, and Gillian Walker. "Love and Violence: Gender Paradoxes in Volatile Attachments." *Family Process,* 29, no. 4 (1990).

Göle, Nilufer. *The Forbidden Modern: Civilization and Veiling.* Ann Arbor: University of Michigan Press, 1996.

Green, December. *Gender Violence in Africa: African Women's Responses.* Houndmills, UK: Macmillan, 1999.

Gregg, S. Gary. *The Middle East: A Cultural Psychology.* New York: Oxford University Press, 2005.

Haddad, Yazbeck Yvonne. "Islam and Gender: Dilemmas in the Changing Arab World." In Yvonne Yazbeck Haddad and John L. Esposito, eds., *Islam, Gender and Social Change.* New York: Oxford University Press, 1998.

Haeri, Shahla. *Law of Desire: Temporary Marriage in Iran.* London: I. B. Tauris, 1989.

Hamadeh, Najla. "Islamic Family Legislation: The Authoritarian Discourse of Silence." In Mai Yamani, ed., *Feminism and Islam: Legal and Literary Perspectives.* London: Ithaca, 1996.

Hasan, Zoya, ed. *Forging Identities: Gender, Communities, and the State in India.* Boulder, CO: Westview, 1994.

Hearn, Jeff. "Men's Violence to Known Women: Historical, Everyday and Theoretical Construction by Men." In Barbara Fawcett, ed., *Violence and Gender Relations: Theories and Interventions.* London: Sage, 1996.

Hijab, Nadia. *Womanpower: The Arab Debate on Women at Work.* Cambridge, UK: Cambridge University Press, 1988.

Hoffman-Ladd, J. Valerie. "Polemics on the Modesty and Segregation of Women in Contemporary Egypt." *International Journal of Middle Eastern Studies,* 19 (1987).

Hoodfar, Homa. "Child Care and Child Health in Low-Income Neighbourhoods of Cairo." In Elizabeth Warnock Fernea, ed., *Children in the Muslim Middle East.* Austin: University of Texas Press, 1995.

Jackson, Stevi. "Heterosexuality as a Problem for Feminist Theory." In Lisa Adkins and Vicki Merchant, eds., *Sexualizing the Social: Power and the Organization of Sexuality.* Houndmills, UK: Macmillan, 1996.

Jalal, Ayesha. "The Convenience of Subservience: Women and the State of Pakistan." in Deniz Kandiyoti, ed., *Women, Islam and the State.* Houndmills, UK: Macmillan, 1991.

Jam'iyat, Tadamun al-Mar'ah al-Arabiya. *Al-mar'ah al-arabiya wa al-Mutaghiyrat al-alalamiya* [Arab Women and International Changes]. Proceedings of the Sixth International Conference of the Association of Solidarity of Arab Women. Cairo: Merit, 2003.

Joseph, Suad. "Brother/Sister Relationships: Connectivity, Love, and Power in the Reproduction of Patriarchy in Lebanon." *American Ethnologist,* 21, no. 1 (1994).

Joseph, Suad, and Susan Slyomovics. "Introduction." In Suad Joseph and Susan Slyomovics, eds., *Women and Power in the Middle East.* Philadelphia: University of Pennsylvania Press, 2001.

Kandiyoti, Deniz. "Beyond Beijing: Obstacles and Prospects for the Middle East." In Mahnaz Afkhami and Erika Friedl, eds., *Muslim Women and the Politics of Participation: Implementing the Beijing Platform.* Syracuse, NY: Syracuse University Press, 1997.

———. "Introduction." In Deniz Kandiyoti, ed., *Women, Islam and the State.* Houndmills, UK: Macmillan, 1991.

———. "Islam and Patriarchy: A Comparative Perspective." In Nikki R. Keddie and Beth Baron, eds., *Women in Middle Eastern History: Shifting Boundaries in Sex and Gender.* New Haven, CT: Yale University Press, 1991.

Karmi, Ghada. "The Saddam Hussein Phenomenon and Male-Female Relations in The Arab World." In Haleh Afshar, ed., *Women in the Middle East: Perceptions, Realities and Struggle for Liberation.* Houndmills, UK: MacMillan, 1993.

———. "Women, Islam and Patriarchalism." In Mai Yamani, ed., *Feminism and Islam: Legal and Literary Perspectives.* London: Ithaca, 1996.

Keddie, Nikki R. "Introduction: Deciphering Middle Eastern Woman's History." In Nikki R. Keddie and Beth Baron, eds., *Women in Middle Eastern History: Shifting Boundaries in Sex and Gender.* New Haven, CT: Yale University Press, 1991.

———. *Women in the Middle East: Past and Present.* Princeton, NJ: Princeton University Press, 2007.

Keddie, Nikki R., and Lois Beck. "Introduction." In Lois Beck and Nikki R. Keddie, eds., *Women in the Muslim World.* Cambridge, MA: Harvard University Press, 1978.

Keenan, K. Colleen, Ayman el-Hadad, and Sossy A. Balian. "Factors Associated with Domestic Violence in Low-Income Lebanese Families." *Image: Journal of Nursing Scholarship*, 30, no. 4 (1998).

Kelly, Liz. "Wars against Women: Sexual Violence, Sexual Politics and the Militarised State." In Susie Jacobs, Ruth Jacobson, and Jennifer Marchbank, eds., *States of Conflict: Gender, Violence and Resistance.* London: Zed, 2000.

Kelly, Liz, Sheila Burton, and Linda Regan. "Beyond Victim or Survivor: Sexual Violence, Identity, and Feminist Theory and Practice." In Lisa Adkins and Vicki Merchant, eds., *Sexualizing the Social: Power and the Organization of Sexuality.* Houndmills, UK: Macmillan, 1996.

Khayyat, Sana el. *Honour and Shame: Women in Modern Iraq.* London: Saqi, 1990.

Khouri, Norma. *Honor Lost: Love and Death in Modern-Day Jordan.* New York: Atria, 2003.

Khoury, Dina Rizk. "Slippers at the Entrance or behind Closed Doors: Domestic and Public Space for Mosuli Women." In Madeline C. Zilfi, ed., *Women in the Ottoman Empire: Middle Eastern Women in the Early Modern Era.* Leiden: Brill, 1997.

Kiray, Mübeccel. "The New Role of Mothers: Changing Intra-Familial Relationships in a Small Town in Turkey." In J. G. Peristiany, ed., *Mediterranean Family Structures.* Cambridge, UK: Cambridge University Press, 1976.

Kousha, Mahnaz. "Love and Control: Relationships between Fathers and Daughters in Iran." *Critique: Critical Middle Eastern Studies*, 11, no. 1 (2002).

———. "Ties That Bind: Mothers and Daughters in Contemporary Iran." *Critique: Critical Middle Eastern Studies*, 6, no. 11 (1997).

Lazreg, Marina. "Feminism and Difference: The Perils of Writing as a Woman on Women in Algeria." *Feminist Studies*, 14, no. 1 (1988).

Loseke, R. Donileen. "Complexities of Family Violence." In Donileen R. Loseke, Richard J. Gelles, and Mary M. Cavanaugh, eds., *Current Controversies on Family Violence*. Thousand Oaks, CA: Sage, 2005.

MacEoin, Denis. "Why Do Muslims Execute Innocent People? Islamist Ideology." *Middle East Quarterly*, fall (2006).

Mackenzie, Catriona. "A Certain Lack of Symmetry: Beauvoir on Autonomous Agency and Women's Embodiment." In Ruth Evans, ed., *Simone de Beauvoir's The Second Sex: New Interdisciplinary Essays*. Manchester, UK: Manchester University Press, 1998.

MacLeod, Elowe Arlene. "Hegemonic Relations and Gender Resistance: The New Veiling as Accommodating Protest in Cairo." *Signs: Journal of Women in Culture and Society*, 17, no. 3 (1992).

Makhlouf, Carla. *Changing Veils: Women and Modernisation in North Yemen*. London: Croom Helm, 1979.

Malti-Douglas, Fedwa. *Men, Women and God(s): Nawal El Saadawi and Arab Feminist Poetics*. Berkeley: University of California Press, 1995.

———. *Women's Body, Women's Word: Gender and Discourse in Arab-Islamic Writing*. Princeton, NJ: Princeton University Press, 1991.

Mann, Elizabeth A. "Education, Money, and the Role of Women in Maintaining Minority Identity." In Zoya Hasan, ed., *Forging Identities: Gender, Communities, and the State in India*. Boulder, CO: Westview, 1994.

Marcus, Julie. *A World of Difference: Islam and Gender Hierarchy in Turkey*. London: Zed, 1992.

Mason, Gail. *Spectacle of Violence: Homophobia, Gender, and Knowledge*. Florence: Routledge, 2001.

Maynard, Mary, and Jan Winn. "Women, Violence and Male Power." In Victoria Robinson and Diane Richardson, eds., *Introducing Women's Studies: Feminist Theory and Practice* (2nd edition). Houndmills: Macmillan, 1997.

McIntosh, Mary. "Feminist Debates on Prostitution." In Lisa Adkins and Vicki Merchant, eds., *Sexualizing the Social: Power and the Organization of Sexuality*. Houndmills, UK: Macmillan, 1996.

Mensch, S. Barbara, Barbara L. Ibrahim, Susan M. Lee, and Omaima el-Gibaly. "Gender-Role Attitudes among Egyptian Adolescents." *Studies in Family Planning*, 34, no. 1 (2003).

Mernissi, Fatima. *Beyond the Veil: Male-Female Dynamics in Muslim Society*. Cambridge, MA: Schekman, 1975.

———. "Democracy as Moral Disintegration: The Contradiction between Religious Beliefs and Citizenship as a Manifestation of the Ahistoricity of the Arab Identity." In Nahid Toubia, ed., *Women of the Arab World: The Coming Challenge*. London: Zed, 1988.

———. "Virginity and Patriarchy." *Women's Studies International Forum*, 5, no. 2 (1982).

———. *Women and Islam: An Historical and Theological Enquiry*. Oxford: Basil Blackwell, 1991.

———. *Women in the Muslim Unconscious*. New York: Pergamon, 1984 (published under pseudonym Fatna Ait Sabbah).

———. *Women's Rebellion and Islamic Memory*. London: Zed, 1996.

Minces, Juliette. *The House of Obedience: Women in Arab Society*. London: Zed, 1982.

Mir-Hosseini, Ziba. "Women, Marriage and the Law in Post-Revolutionary Iran." In Haleh Afshar, ed., *Women in the Middle East: Perceptions, Realities and Struggle for Liberation*. Houndmills, UK: Macmillan, 1993.

Moghadam, Valentine M. "Introduction and Overview: Gender Dynamics of Nationalism, Revolution and Islamization." In Valentine M. Moghadam, ed., *Gender and National Identity: Women and Politics in Muslim Societies*. London: Zed, 1994.

Moghissi, Haideh. *Feminism and Islamic Fundamentalism: The Limits of Postmodern Analysis*. London: Zed, 1999.

Mohsen, Safia K. "New Images, Old Reflections: Working Middle-Class Women in Egypt." In Elizabeth Warnock Fernea, ed., *Women and the Family in the Middle East: New Voices of Change*. Austin: University of Texas Press, 1985.

Mojab, Shahrzad, and Nahla Abdo, eds. *Violence in the Name of Honour: Theoretical and Political Challenges*. Istanbul: Bilagi University Press, 2004.

Morsy, Soheir A. "Sex Differences and Folk Illness in an Egyptian Village." In Lois Beck and Nikki R. Keddie, eds., *Women in the Muslim World*. Cambridge, MA: Harvard University Press, 1978.

Nafisi, Azar. "Imagination as Subversion: Narrative as a Tool of Civic Awareness." In Mahnaz Afkhami and Erika Friedl, eds., *Muslim Women and the Politics of Participation: Implementing the Beijing Platform*. Syracuse, NY: Syracuse University Press, 1997.

Nelson, Cynthia. "Public and Private Politics: Women in the Middle Eastern World." *American Ethnologist*, 1, no. 3 (1974).

Ortner, Sherry. "Is Female to Male as Nature Is to Culture?" In Michelle Zimbalist Rosaldo and Louise Lamphere, eds., *Woman, Culture and Society*. Stanford, CA: Stanford University Press, 1974.

———. *Making Gender: The Politics and Erotics of Culture*. Boston: Beacon, 1996.

Osten-Sacken-von, Thomas der, and Thomas Uwer. "Is Female Genital Mutilation an Islamic Problem?" *Middle East Quarterly*, winter (2007).

Parrot, Andrea, and Nina Cummings. *Forsaken Females: The Global Brutalization of Women.* Lanham, MD: Rowan and Littlefield, 2006.

Patai, Raphael. *The Arab Mind.* New York: Hatherleigh, 2002.

Rahman, Anika, and Nahid Toubia, eds. *Female Genital Mutilation: A Guide to Laws and Policies Worldwide.* London: Zed, 2000.

Rassam, Amal. "Women and Domestic Power in Morocco." *International Journal of Middle Eastern Studies,* 12, no. 2 (1980).

Reich, Wilhelm. *The Mass Psychology of Fascism.* New York: Farrar, Straus and Giroux, 1970.

Richardson, Diane. "Sexuality and Feminism." In Victoria Robinson and Diane Richardson, eds., *Introducing Women's Studies: Feminist Theory and Practice* (2nd edition). Houndmills, UK: Macmillan, 1997.

Rosaldo, Michelle Zimbalist. "Woman, Culture and Society: A Theoretical Overview." In Michelle Zimbalist Rosaldo and Louise Lamphere, eds., *Woman, Culture and Society.* Stanford, CA: Stanford University Press, 1974.

Ruggi, Suzanne. "Commodifying Honor in Female Sexuality: Honor Killings in Palestine." *Middle East Report* (Spring 1998).

Saadawi, Nawal el. *The Hidden Face of Eve: Women in the Arab World.* London: Zed, 1980.

———. *Memoirs of a Woman Doctor.* London: Saqi, 1988.

———. *The Nawal El Saadawi Reader.* London: Zed, 1997.

———. "Woman and Islam." *Women's Studies International Forum,* 5, no. 2 (1982).

Sanday, Peggy Reeves. "Introduction." In Peggy Reeves Sanday and Ruth Gallagher Goodenough, eds., *Beyond the Second Sex: New Directions in the Anthropology of Gender.* Philadelphia: University of Pennsylvania Press, 1990.

Shaaban, Bouthaina. *Both Right and Left Handed: Arab Women Talk about Their Lives.* London: The Women's Press, 1988.

Shahidian, Hammed. *Women in Iran: Gender Politics in the Islamic Republic.* Westport, CT: Greenwood Press, 2002.

Shalhoub-Kevorkian, Nadera. "Mapping and Analyzing the Landscape of Femicide in Palestinian Society." Report by Women's Center for Legal Aid and Counseling submitted to UNIFEM. January 2000, http://www.unifem.org/attachments/stories/NaderaShalhoubKevorkian_report.pdf.

Sharabi, Hisham. *Neopatriarchy: A Theory of Distorted Change in Arab Society.* New York: Oxford University Press, 1988.

Singerman, Diane. "Where Has All the Power Gone? Women and Politics in Popular Quarters of Cairo." In Fatma Müge Göcek and Shiva Balaghi, eds., *Reconstructing Gender in the Middle East: Tradition, Identity, and Power.* New York: Columbia University Press, 1994.

Solh, Camillia Fawzi el, and Judy Mabro. "Introduction: Islam and Muslim Women." In Camillia Fawzi El-Solh and Judy Mabro, eds., *Muslim Women's Choices: Religious Belief and Social Reality.* Providence, RI: Berg, 1994.

Spellberg D. A. "Political Action and Public Example: 'A'isha and the Battle of the Camel." In Nikki R. Keddie and Beth Baron, eds., *Women in Middle Eastern History: Shifting Boundaries in Sex and Gender.* New Haven, CT: Yale University Press, 1991.

———. *Politics, Gender, and the Islamic Past: The Legacy of 'A'isha bint Abi Bakr.* New York: Colombia University Press, 1994.

Tarabishi, Georges. *Woman against Her Sex: A Critique of Nawal el-Saadawi.* London: Saqi, 1988.

Tillion, Germaine. *The Republic of Cousins: Women's Oppression in Mediterranean Society.* London: Saqi, 1983.

Tohidi, Nayereh. "Modernity, Islamization, and Women in Iran." In Valentine M. Moghadam, ed., *Gender and National Identity: Women and Politics in Muslim Societies.* London: Zed, 1994.

Torki, Soraya al. *Women in Saudi Arabia: Ideology and Behavior among the Elite.* New York: Columbia University Press, 1986.

Treacher, Amal, and Halla Shukrallah. "The Realm of the Possible: Middle Eastern Women in Political and Social Spaces." *Feminist Review,* 69 (2001).

UNICEF. *Female Genital Mutilation/Cutting: A Statistical Exploration.* New York: UNICEF, 2005.

UNICEF/Innocenti Research Centre. *Changing a Harmful Social Convention: Female Genital Mutilation/Cutting.* Florence: UNICEF/Innocenti Research Centre, 2005.

Vieille, Paul. "Iranian Women in Family Alliance and Sexual Politics." In Lois Beck and Nikki R. Keddie, eds., *Women in the Muslim World.* Cambridge, MA: Harvard University Press, 1978.

Walker, Alice, and Pratibha Parmar. *Female Genital Mutilation and the Sexual Blinding of Women.* New York: Harcourt Brace, 1993.

Walther, Wiebke. *Woman in Islam.* Montclair, NJ: Abner Schram, 1981.

Webster, Sheila K. "Women, Sex, and Marriage in Moroccan Proverbs," *International Journal of Middle East Studies,* 14 (1982).

Westermarck, Edward. *Wit and Wisdom in Morocco: A Study of Native Proverbs.* London: George Routledge, 1930.

World Health Organization (WHO). *Female Genital Mutilation: An Overview.* Geneva: WHO, 1998.

Yllö, Kersti A. "Gender, Diversity, and Violence." In Donileen R. Loseke, Richard J. Gelles and Mary M. Cavanaugh, eds., *Current Controversies on Family Violence.* Thousand Oaks, CA: Sage, 2005.

Yodanis, Carrie L. "Gender Inequality, Violence against Women, and Fear: A Cross-National Test of the Feminist Theory of Violence Against Women." *Journal of Interpersonal Violence,* 19, no. 6 (2004).

Zakaria, Fouad. "The Standpoint of Contemporary Muslim Fundamentalists."
    In Nahid Toubia, ed., *Women of the Arab World: The Coming Challenge.*
    London: Zed, 1988.
Zeid, Abou. "Honour and Shame among the Bedouins of Egypt." in J. G.
    Peristiany, ed., *Honour and Shame: The Values of Mediterranean Society.*
    Chicago: The University of Chicago Press, 1966.
Zuhur, Sherifa. *Revealing Reveiling: Islamist Gender Ideology in Contemporary
    Egypt.* New York: State University of New York Press, 1992.

Index

in low-income families, 27, 54;
honor killing, 41; violence
against women, 25
Legitimacy, 176, 183–84, 199, 206
Libya: General People's Congress,
25; honor, 30; rape, 30; social
rehabilitation facilities, 30; violence
against women, 25
Loseke, Donileen, 115
Love, 140–41, 157–58, 170, 187, 192,
196
Loyalty, 157, 158–59, 179, 181–83

Mackenzie, Catriona, 74, 76, 77, 109,
117, 120, 219
MacLeod, Arlene, 87, 106, 115, 117
Maklouf, Carla, 7, 90, 95, 129
Male circumcision, 35
Male control, 12–13, 54, 76, 78, 85,
110, 113
Male ego, 10, 208–10
Male guardianship, 24, 30, 67
Mann, Elizabeth, 117
Marcus, Julie, 7
Marital relationship, 97–99, 102,
125–26, 139, 140
Marriage, 7–8, 101, 103, 165–73, 175,
187; age difference between spouses,
28; arranged, 102–3; child, 60; early,
24, 28; forced, 24, 28; Islam, 56–57;
temporary, 64
Masculinity, 10, 12, 15, 35, 43, 80, 113,
130, 167, 208
Mason, Gail, 110–11, 112, 122
Maynard, Mary, and J. Winn, 80, 111,
113
Mensch, Barbara, et al., 71, 103, 176,
193
Menopause, 184
Menstruation, 71
Mernissi, Fatima, 56, 111, 116, 128,
149, 168, 170, 176, 184, 191, 209,
217
Middle East: crisis, 1–2, 4, 58–59, 184
Minces, Juliette, 99, 116, 128, 130, 166
Mir-Hosseini, Ziba, 7
Moghissi, Haideh, 88–89
Mohsen, Safia, 119, 150

Morocco, 35, 140; female power, 87;
Islamists and women, 60; proverbs,
101, 102, 127, 135, 136, 145, 149,
156, 160, 161, 165, 174; unequal
treatment of boys and girls, 70;
women in, 79, 129, 138, 153
Mother, 12; children relations, 99,
135–41; daughter relationship, 36–
37, 117, 118, 143–48; dependency of,
142–43, 145–46; motherhood, 141,
152
Mother-in-law, 93–94, 103, 106, 108,
116, 117, 140, 142, 149–62; son,
bride and, 156–59
Muhammad, Prophet, 2, 28, 55
Mussolini, Benito, 118

Nafisi, Azar, 121, 128
Nelson, Cynthia, 89, 90, 94
Norway: domestic violence, 23

Obedience, 24, 55, 104, 111, 157, 166,
170, 173–78, 179, 180, 181, 182, 184,
194, 207
Oman: female genital mutilation, 33
OMCT. *See* World Organization
against Torture
One Thousand and One Nights, 93, 105,
123, 127
Oppression, of women, 8–9, 16, 75, 76,
77, 80
Orientalism: view of women, 6
Ortner, Sherry, 10, 75, 97, 101, 117,
124, 171, 173
Other, the, 69, 70, 72, 73, 77–81, 167,
184, 185, 187, 192, 195, 196, 198,
199, 206, 211, 212, 213

Pakistan: domestic violence, 24; honor
killing, 39
Palestine: honor killing, 39, 40–41,
42, 43, 44, 45, 46, 47, 48; manhood
(*rujuleh*), 43; proverbs, 39; rape,
30; violence against women, 26–27;
women in, 125
Palestinian problem, 184
Parrot, Andrea, and N. Cummings, 23,
24, 31, 43, 55, 207

Shakespeare, William, 179
Shalhoub-Kevorkian, Nadera, 42, 43, 45, 47
Silence, culture of, 26, 37, 68, 168, 171, 189, 201, 212
Singerman, Diane, 11, 87–88
Slavery, 63
Social contract, 96, 179–84, 194, 200
Socialization, 12, 57, 103, 166, 167, 170, 177, 183, 193
Spellberg, D., 104
State, the, 2, 8, 31, 59, 60, 63, 85, 88, 90, 92, 95–96, 178, 179, 180–81, 201
Status, of women, 103–4, 108, 117, 136, 142, 143, 149, 150, 151
Subordination, 55, 75–76, 80, 99, 108, 113, 118, 123, 124, 154, 175, 197
Subversion, 12, 13, 15, 118, 119, 126–32
Sudan: female genital mutilation, 32–33, 36; Islamists and women, 59, 62–64; janjaweed militia, 64; rape, 63–64; slavery, 59, 63, 64
Surveillance, culture of, 204
Suspicion, 27, 192, 199, 205–6, 211
Sweden: honor killing, 42, 50; intimate violence, 23
Syria: General Union of Women, 26, 41; honor killing, 41, 44, 46, 48, 49; violence against women, 26; women in, 50, 146

Tarabishi, Georges, 76, 195
Terrorism, 1
Tohidi, Nayereh, 219
Torki, Soraya el, 55, 99–100, 101, 119, 174
Treacher, Amal, and H. Shukrallah, 128
Tunisia, violence against women, 27
Turkey: consent of women in marriage, 28; early marriage, 28; female genital mutilation, 33; honor killing, 41, 42, 44, 47; polygamy, 28; violence against women, 27; virginity testing, 42–43; women in, 151

United Arab Emirate (UAE), female genital mutilation, 33

United Nations Assistance Mission for Iraq (UNAMI), 41
United Nations Children's Fund (UNICEF), 32, 33, 36
United Nations Development Fund for Women (UNIFEM), 23, 24, 26

Veil (*hijab*), 7, 62, 63, 65–66, 189, 199
Victimization, 10, 15, 16, 31, 108, 114–16, 146, 150–51, 152–56, 204, 207; agency, 114–15
Vieille, Paul, 70, 99, 136, 140, 166, 172
Violence, 2, 4, 24, 109, 110, 113, 189, 197, 199, 217; condoning, 31–32, 111; consequences of reporting, 27–28; conspiracy theories, 3–4; cultural, 4, 60, 110, 147; cycle of, 9, 13, 107, 114, 153, 155, 177, 195, 219; definition of, 13–14, 23, 109–10; externalization of, 3, 5, 208; gender differences, 14–15; internalization of, 5; male, 9, 10, 14, 23–32; modalities of, 24; normalization of, 112, 203–8, 218; overlooking, 2–3, 5, 217; power nexus, 109–14; structural, 2, 3, 5, 14, 55, 109–10, 111, 114, 183; wife battering, 24, 31, 111, 113. *See also* Female violence; Sexual violence
Virginity, 28, 41, 117, 136, 180, 195, 206–7, 211; forced testing, 42–43; menstruation, 71; obedient wife, 28

Walker, Alice, 37
Webster, Sheila, 161
Westermarck, Edward, 160, 174
Women: control of, 59, 75, 80, 85–86, 99, 117, 119, 207; degradation of, 69, 76, 80, 196, 214; inferiority of, 54, 69, 85, 95, 127, 156, 157, 159, 200, 209; marginalization, 86; participation in labor market, 107; participation in parliament, 107; perpetrator of violence, 6, 9, 36, 115, 162; powerful, 8–9; relations between, 93–94; victim, 6, 9, 13, 14, 114, 115; weaknesses, 85
World Corporal Punishment Research, 62

About the Author

DAVID GHANIM is Senior Lecturer and Researcher in Middle Eastern Studies, School of Global Studies, University of Gothenburg,
Sweden. He taught previously at the Université du Tizi-Ouzou, Algeria, and conducted research at the School of Oriental and African
Studies, University of London. A native of Iraq, he holds his doctorate
from the Corvinus University of Budapest.

www.ingramcontent.com/pod-product-compliance
Lightning Source LLC
Chambersburg PA
CBHW071847270326
41929CB00013B/2134